The Chicano
Experience

For the majority of Americans, the image of the Mexican-American has been that of a picturesque and childlike figure, charming but shiftless, laughing but lazy, colorful but unwashed.

Even as similar stereotypes about Black Americans have lost favor, this distorted picture of the *Chicano* has not been seriously challenged until the last few years.

Now, as the *Chicano* voice is being heard in the economic, political, and cultural life of our nation, a new *Chicano* awareness is growing among both the *Chicanos* themselves and their Anglo neighbors.

The stories in this collection trace that growth. But even more important, they offer an unrivaled portrayal of the Chicano *experience, with its pain, its promise, its beauty, and its integrity. They perform the highest mission of literature—to open up the mind and let the truth come in.*

THE CHICANO:
From Caricature
to Self-Portrait

Edited and with an Introduction
by EDWARD SIMMEN

A MENTOR BOOK from
NEW AMERICAN LIBRARY
TIMES MIRROR
New York and Scarborough, Ontario
The New English Library Limited, London

Acknowledgments

The poem in the story "La Pérdida" by Gertrude Atherton was translated especially for this edition by Félix D. Almaráz, and is used by permission of the translator. Copyright © 1971 by Félix D. Almaráz.

"Señor Payroll" by William E. Barrett. Reprinted by permission of Harold Ober Associates Incorporated and *Southwest Review*. Copyright 1943 by *Southwest Review*.

"El Patrón" by James K. Bowman. From *New Campus Writing No. 2*, edited by Nolan Miller. Copyright © 1957 by Bantam Books, Inc.

"The Wonderful Ice Cream Suit" by Ray Bradbury. Copyright 1958 by Ray Bradbury. Reprinted by permission of Harold Matson Company, Inc.

"Mr. Iscariot" by Richard G. Brown. Reprinted from *The Literary Review* (Summer, 1963, Volume 6, Number 4), published by Fairleigh Dickinson University, Rutherford, New Jersey.

"Sánchez" by Richard Dokey. Reprinted by permission of *Southwest Review* and the author. Copyright © 1967 by *Southwest Review*.

"Un Hijo del Sol" by Genaro González. Reprinted by permission of the author. Copyright © 1971 by Genaro González.

"Sánchez and the Víbora" by Robert Granat. From *The Texas Quarterly*, Volume Seven, Number Three, Autumn 1964. Reprinted by permission of *The Texas Quarterly* and the author.

MENTOR TRADEMARK REG. U.S. PAT. OFF. AND FOREIGN COUNTRIES
REGISTERED TRADEMARK—MARCA REGISTRADA
HECHO EN CHICAGO, U.S.A.

SIGNET, SIGNET CLASSICS, SIGNETTE, MENTOR AND PLUME BOOKS
are published *in the United States* by
The New American Library, Inc.,
1301 Avenue of the Americas, New York, New York 10019,
in Canada by The New American Library of Canada Limited,
81 Mack Avenue, Scarborough, 704, Ontario,
in the United Kingdom by The New English Library Limited,
Barnard's Inn, Holborn, London, E.C. 1, England

FIRST PRINTING, MARCH, 1971

3 4 5 6 7 8 9 10 11

For My Parents

Contents

Preface

The primary intention of compiling *The Chicano* was to present for the first time in one volume the most representative short fiction written about Mexican-Americans in order that readers might have available a developing portrait of this minority group as it has been depicted from the mid-nineteenth century to the present by American short story writers—both Anglo- and Mexican-American. In addition, the stories were selected to reflect the significant trends or styles or movements that have occurred in American fiction during the last one hundred years.

Locating appropriate material, I must admit, was more frustrating than difficult. Since this book is the first published collection of short stories dealing entirely with Mexican-Americans, there were few works available to assist me. I discovered the most successful way of finding stories was simply by reading endless numbers of tables-of-contents, examining numerous issues of quarterlies and magazines, and finally by shaking the memories of editors, colleagues, and students for the names of authors and titles. Of course, I am indebted to *The Short Story Index*, an indispensable preliminary guide, and to the annual listings in *Best American Short Stories* and the *O. Henry Prize Stories*. But the single work that offered me the greatest initial stimulus and most information was Cecil Robinson's *With the Ears of Strangers* (The University of Arizona Press, 1963), a comprehensive and well-documented study of the Mexican-American in literature.

I am also deeply indebted to several persons who answered questions, offered suggestions, and clarified points or who simply provided me with a more profound understanding of Mexicans, Spanish-Americans, Latin-Americans, Mexican-Americans, and finally Chicanos. These individuals were especially helpful in assisting me with the origin and meaning of the word that is the title of this book: *Chicano*. Dictionaries were of no help; the word does not appear in even the most recently published. It doesn't even appear in print until the late 1940s. Therefore, it became a question of accepting or rejecting those theories that seem most etymologically reasonable.

Regarding the origin of *Chicano*, two particular theories prevail; each is convincing. According to Philip Ortego, a recognized authority on these matters and one of the contributors to this anthology, suggesting that one theory "ascribes the word to Nahuatl origin, suggesting that the Indians pronounced *Mexicano* as "Me-shi-ca-noh." In time evidently the first syllable was dropped and the soft "shi" was replaced with the hard "ch" and the word as we know it became commonly used in speech in the *barrio*, a predominantly Spanish-speaking community. It was, then, merely a term of ethnic identification not meant in any way to demean. More recently, however, *Chicano* has been used by Mexican-Americans in an insulting or pejorative sense referring to another Mexican-American of a "lower" class.

Another theory asserts that the word was conventionally formed by suffixing *ano* to *chico* (a young boy), exactly as one would form, for example, the word *Mexicano*. Thus, the word was used in the *barrio* for emphasis to place in a special category an individual so called. A Chicano, then, would have been any Mexican-American who acted as a "young boy." Perhaps, in this sense, *Chicano* is related to *chicazo*, meaning a poorly educated young man who aimlessly, as a vagabond, roams the streets.

Another problem arose with regard to meaning. Today, who is a Chicano? Certainly, the word is no longer used exclusively in speech by Mexican-Americans as an uncomplimentary term of address. Currently, it is used by the various media to describe the more radical and youthful Mexican-Americans whose controversial actions and statements often make the headlines. But the individual so labeled, more often than not, is dissatisfied with this definition. Rather, for the sake of unity among his people, he would have the term apply to *all* Americans of Mexican descent—no matter what profession, education, social position, or even political persuasion. However, this is not the case. For, while it will be readily agreed that all Chicanos are Mexican-Americans, it will not be agreed that *all* Mexican-Americans are Chicanos. In particular, the more conservative, generally older Mexican-American strongly resents being called a Chicano. He finds a social stigma still attached to the word and continues to consider it a term of disapprobation and not, as the younger liberal does, a term of unification.

At the moment, neither definition seems "accurate" or "correct." Presently, the word *Chicano*, in print or in speech, has less to do with social position or ethnic origin than it does with political attitude. Today, the noun *Chicano* should be defined: "A dissatisfied American of Mexican descent whose ideas regarding his position in the social and economic order are, in general, considered to be liberal or radical and whose statements and actions are often extreme and sometimes violent."

It was, then, with this definition in mind that I assembled the stories included in this anthology and wrote the introduction to it. It will be noticed that I have taken the liberty of using Mexican-American and *Chicano* interchangeably wherever I considered it appropriate and not misleading. For if I am certain of anything regarding this collection, it is that the vast majority of the stories have one characteristic in common: They essentially concern that "new" American—the outspoken and active young Mexican-American who has *always* sought to identify himself with *La Causa* or "The Movement." He may be called a "greaser" or a "dirty Mexican" or a "Latin." But whether written by Jack London in 1911 or William Saroyan in 1934 or Philip Ortego in 1968, each story has the same protagonist who will be easily recognized—in 1970 terms—as a Chicano.

Among those persons I have to thank for guiding me to my conclusions regarding Chicanos and *chicanismo* are Homer Peña, Philip Ortego, Félix Almaráz, Ricardo Arocha Morton, Leonel Solis, Yolanda Silva de Hinojosa, Corina Rodríguez, Edwardo Cantu, Antonio Baldéras, Richard Codina, Armando Alonzo, Joe Rodríguez, Fidel Dávila, and especially Genaro González.

It seems also appropriate for me to thank the Board of Regents, the administration, and the Faculty Research Grant Committee of Pan American College of Texas, who actually knew nothing of what I was doing but who provided me with the opportunity to conduct the necessary research. However, it is essential that I extend my sincere thanks to Helen Snider, my critical typist, and to

Penny Paradise and *"Las Gallinas Rápidas"*—especially María Glendelia Salinas—who typed and retyped letters, notes, and portions of the manuscript again and again.

I likewise am indebted to several interested individuals who have continued to encourage and aid me: Carl Grantz, chairman of the English Department of Pan American College; Nick Bradshaw, my research assistant at the University of Texas at Austin; Clyde Miller, a scholar and writer who pointed me in so many right directions and made the going easier; Jorge Moreno (alias, "George Natrass"), a young man who for two years has given me a very special inspiration and stability; and, finally, Ted von Ende, my friend and colleague, who has patiently tolerated more grinding from me than ever the gods intended he should.

Last, I would like to acknowledge two other individuals who are more than friends: Jim W. Corder, who deliberately pushed me onto this upward path, and Father Michael Allen, who keeps me on it—complaining but continuing. No two individuals, with the exception of my parents, have ever gotten me into so much "hot water." And still neither of them is considerate enough to answer for me one simple question: "¿ Cuál es el punto?"

—Edward Simmen
Pan American College
Edinburg, Texas

Introduction

That lazy *bandido* sleeping beneath the big sombrero in the shade of the adobe hut has suddenly awakened. And he is doing more than curling his pencil-moustache, brandishing his Pancho Villa *pistolas,* and stealing corn "cheeps" or searching through the "jello" pages. The TV commercial "cheelee bean" caricature of the Mexican-American, a shadow of the Leo Carrillo "See Señor" movie dupe, is quickly giving way to another image.

Tired of being the "new nigger," tired of being the new minority target, the real Mexican-American is standing up and speaking—speaking sense. Tired of being exploited by management, ignored by labor, and quickly forgotten by "promising" politicians, the real Mexican-American is standing up and demanding—demanding attention, recognition.

Certainly the age of self-analysis and self-discovery has finally caught up with him. Following the blacks into the headlines of many daily newspapers, weekly magazines, and nightly news programs, the Mexican-American is making himself heard and in many ways already making his presence felt. He seems to be increasingly more and more interested not only in discovering who he is, but also in having others realize that he exists in the melting pot of American society as more than just spicy seasoning.

To assist him, universities and colleges, especially those in the southwestern and western sections of the United States where this minority is the majority, have responded by offering a variety of courses and degree plans specifically designed to permit the Mexican-American and his concerned fellow Anglo students to examine his oftentimes forgotten cultural heritage as well as his dubious role in the "alien" Anglo society.

Primarily designed to enlighten not only the Mexican-

15

American but also the Anglo who lives with him and who generally teaches him in the public schools, the courses, in most cases, are offered in the areas of history, sociology, philosophy, art, and folklore.

One area of study, surprisingly enough, is consistently excluded from these ethnic programs: the study of the Mexican-American as he appears in American literature. It is reasonable to admit that any program eliminating literature would be incomplete. Yet that the Mexican-American studies programs have ignored literature is certainly understandable; it seems that it is the literature that has ignored the Mexican-American. Especially with regard to the short story, there is so little appropriate fiction *readily* available that a study of such would seem, at first glance, to be not only unrewarding and unprofitable but impossible.

There are, to be sure, several reasons why there is not a great wealth of literature about the Mexican-American. First, the Mexican-American has never, until recently, written about himself.[1] In addition, the Anglo writer, *with a few significant exceptions*, has never been keenly interested in using the Mexican-American as a realistic subject. Generally, as in the early Spanish-California romance and the later pulp magazine western, the Mexican-American has been portrayed by the Anglo writer in distorted caricature.

However difficult though material may be to locate, research has proved that enough good short stories have been written by or about this minority to publish an anthology that would present a representative and realistic portrait of the Mexican-American and his 150-year struggle within a predominantly Anglo culture.

In deciding which short stories would be appropriate for such an anthology, one question was prominent: Would it be valid to include stories by Mexican or American authors that have settings, characters, and conflicts that are Mexican rather than Mexican-American? After considerable consultation with interested Mexican-American educators and students of all ages, social backgrounds, and

---

[1] Admittedly, the Mexican-American has been sincerely interested in his cultural heritage. Since the turn of the century, he has contributed to the regional publications designed to record the tales and traditions of the early life of the Mexican in the Southwest and West. However, this literature is not considered to be part of the genre of the short story; rather, it is generally placed in the category of folklore.

political persuasions, I decided to exclude *any* short fiction that did not centrally concern the Mexican-American or the Mexican citizen living and working in the United States. After all, it is difficult to deny the fact that the contemporary Mexican-American, while he may have firm cultural roots in Mexico, is actually only a distant cousin to the *Mexicano* living in present-day Mexico—a distance that is rapidly increasing with each new generation, with each new educational opportunity offered to and taken by the Mexican-American, and certainly with each mile the Mexican-American moves north from the border. It is also pertinent to note that according to the 1960 census, 85 percent of the Mexican-Americans living in the United States were born here and that more and more are moving out of the rural agricultural areas into the urban areas where the Mexican-Americans are becoming skilled workers in offices or factories. Most Mexican-Americans are the first to admit that the conflicts experienced by the *Mexicano* are far different from his. The Mexican-American's struggles are primarily with a social system that has—consciously or unconsciously—always stifled his social mobility and discouraged his educational advancement and has always tended to insist that if he—the Mexican-American—is to be "accepted," he must "Anglocize" his life by forgetting his cultural traditions of family, language, and sometimes his Roman Catholic religion.

Simply stated, then, the short stories collected here present the Mexican-American residing in the United States as he has been characterized in the American short story, first in the popular magazines, such as *McClure's Monthly* and the *Saturday Evening Post,* and later in the quarterlies published by the university presses, such as *The Texas Quarterly* and the *Southwest Review,* and finally in the "ethnic" magazines, for example, *El Grito* and *Con Safos.* One fact is certain: Whether the writer is Mexican-American or Anglo, his view of the Mexican-American has been, if anything, certainly diverse. Sometimes it is tragic; sometimes, comic. Occasionally the Mexican-American is "victorious," but more often than not, he is defeated. Often he is mistreated; always, however, he is misunderstood. In addition, in each story, one conflict is obvious—the Mexican-American is presented as an individual caught in a social order that demands he meet that society on its own terms—or suffer.

The stories selected for study cover the time from the mid-nineteenth century to the present and have been divided into three general periods: I. *From the Beginnings to 1930: Early Caricatures;* II. *Through the Depression to 1940: Realistic Profiles;* III. *From World War II to the Present: Portraits and Self-Portraits of the Awakening Minority.*

From the Beginnings to 1930 includes George Emery's "The Water-Witch," Gertrude Atherton's "La Pérdida" and "The Vengeance of Padre Arroyo," Bret Harte's "The Devotion of Enríquez," Hamlin Garland's "Delmar of Pima," and Jack London's "The Mexican."

Period I begins with a brief sketch written by an unknown writer George Emery and published in 1869 in the California regional magazine, the *Overland Monthly.* Actually, this story, entitled "The Water-Witch," is simply a curious Anglo's observation of a "ragged, dirty Mexican" who possessed the mystical powers to detect the presence of water for a well. The next stories offered are a pair by the California regionalist, Gertrude Atherton: "The Vengeance of Padre Arroyo" and "La Pérdida." Collected and published in 1894 under the title *Before the Gringo Came,* these stories represent the sentimental fiction written about the Spanish-American in California in the tradition of Helen Hunt Jackson's classic romance *Ramona,* published in 1884.

Bret Harte, the local colorist, is the third author. His story, "The Devotion of Enríquez," published in the November 1895 issue of *The Century Magazine,* is written in the same popular romantic vein. But this story is interesting, however, in that it deals with a still current problem: the intercultural marriage. Here the Mexican is presented as an elegant Spanish Don and the American woman as a sophisticated, politely educated American visitor from Boston. With surprising ease and comic undertones, "love conquers all" too quickly and unexpectedly. The fact that he speaks decidedly broken (but quaint) English and she speaks *no* Spanish presents no immediate problem. Perhaps even more surprising is the fact that the couple seem capable of working out their religious differences even though he is a devout Roman Catholic and she is the niece of the newly arrived Congregational minister.

Together, in the dark of night, they elope to become, as the Don explains, "combined missionaries to the heathen."

Published in 1902 in *McClure's Magazine*, Hamlin Garland's "Delmar of Pima" is the first American fiction to explore a dominant theme repeated in several of the stories in this collection: the lower-class Mexican-American majority's attempt to confront and overcome the social dominance and political injustice of the local Anglo minority. In this case, the "Greaser"—as it was popular to call the "lower-class" Mexican-American at that time[2]—is victorious. However, the victory is only political; prejudice, division, and distrust remain as an accepted part of the "way of life" in a community composed of "opposites." It is pertinent to note that victory is gained by the Mexican-Americans only through the efforts of one fearless leader—who just happens to be half-Anglo and half-Mexican.

Perhaps the best of the stories in Part I is Jack London's "The Mexican," published in the *Saturday Evening Post* in 1911. As is common in much of London's work, the hero is a young Nietzschean superman. In this story he is a Mexican prizefighter who has been living and working in California in order to make enough money to support the revolution in Mexico against the dictator Díaz, a revolution that was unpopular with both the Taft *and* Wilson administrations and American business. To earn enough money to buy guns for the revolution, he must defeat a fighter of superior reputation and ability. However, London makes it quite obvious that the fighter has another more imposing adversary: the furious mob of Anglo capitalists who scream to see the Mexican destroyed. Romantic though the ending may be, the story does have a theme relevant to the fiction that is to appear later: the Mexican-American who risks self-destruction for his *causa*.

Each of these stories in the early period has one primary characteristic in common with the others: The Mexican-American always comes in conflict with a powerful Anglo social order or "way of life" and thought. And

---

[2] It is, perhaps, necessary to explain that there were essentially two classes of Mexican-Americans in these early days of western development: the *ricos*, or the landed class of Spanish origin, and the *pobres*, the laboring mestizo. The *pobre* was inevitably called "the greaser." It is in this sense, for example, that Mark Twain uses "greaser" in *Life on the Mississippi*. Additional comments on the use of this word may be found in Cecil Robinson's *With the Ears of Strangers* and Carey McWilliams' *North from Mexico*.

always, the Mexican, who is never considered a part of that social order, is in some way victorious. Justice, poetic though it may appear to today's reader, ultimately prevails.

Until the 1930s the Mexican-American—who was never very popular with fiction writers—virtually disappears from the American short story. The reasons for this abrupt disappearance are not at all obvious. Perhaps it is the result of the political estrangement between the United States and Mexico caused by the anti-American revolutionary element that toppled the "dictatorial" Díaz regime in 1911. It must be recalled that one of the revolutionaries' primary intentions was to eliminate the exploitation of Mexico by foreigners—primarily American industrialists. For this reason, the Mexicans who defeated the "friendly dictator" were definitely unpopular in the United States. It seems reasonable to conjecture that the Anglo writer and reader associated the Mexican-American with Mexico and reacted adversely (similar to the way Americans reacted to the Japanese-Americans during World War II): Since the Mexican was unpopular, so was the Mexican-American—hence, the Mexican-American was not considered a fit subject for popular fiction until the 1930s, which are covered by the next section.

Through the Depression to 1940 offers William Saroyan's "With a Hey Nonny Nonny," Paul Horgan's "The Surgeon and the Nun," and John Steinbeck's "Flight."

The first selection in this section is William Saroyan's shockingly prophetic and perceptive short story "With a Hey Nonny Nonny," published originally in *Direction* in 1934. Saroyan repeats the theme used by Garland: the Mexican-American's search for a leader to promote and direct his cause in order to gain a just place in the Anglo social and economic structure. Here, in addition, we discover the Chicano who is hopelessly caught in the inhuman and meaningless Machine Culture of the Anglo, characterized by the scintillating but senseless song whose refrain Saroyan uses not only for his title but throughout the story as a disturbing, almost nightmarish reminder of the Chicano's dilemma: of striving to find his place in a highly stratified society that will not permit him to attain his own individual identity. But in this story, unlike Garland's, the conflicts erupt into physical violence that leads to a tragic but believable conclusion.

The themes in Paul Horgan's story also have been seen before. In "The Surgeon and the Nun," published in *Harper's Bazaar* in 1936, he presents the illiterate and superstitious Mexican laborers—this time, wetbacks—who are misunderstood and mistreated by their Anglo overseer. Yet Horgan, who has written extensively about the Southwest, approaches his characters with a sincere objectivity. He presents the same Mexican laborers as incapable of understanding—because of a well-cultivated mistrust—the compassion of the Anglo doctor and nun. From a more realistic viewpoint, we see the Mexicans caught between cruelty and kindness—aware of the one and consequently mistrusting the other.

The best known of these stories is John Steinbeck's "Flight," first published in 1938 in a collection of his short stories entitled *Long Valley* and since then frequently anthologized. Steinbeck depicts the home of the rural Chicano family, with all of their natural and cultural simplicity, embroiled in tragedy. The conflicts of this story, however, are basic and universal. Steinbeck deals realistically with the timeless coming-of-age theme: expectation, confrontation, disappointment, and final defeat.

From World War II to the Present (the Anglo View) includes William E. Barrett's "Señor Payroll," Sylvan Karchmer's "A Fistful of Alamo Heroes," James K. Bowman's "El Patrón," Richard Dokey's "Sánchez," Richard Brown's "Mr. Iscariot," Ray Bradbury's "The Wonderful Ice Cream Suit," George Seale's "Dilemma, Mi Amigo," and Robert Granat's "To Endure" and "Sánchez and the Víbora."

The stories in the second section of this anthology are significant in the development of the Mexican-American's role in the American short story, since they establish the basic themes that appear in this, the third group. Essential to most of the stories is the ever-present conflict—the absence of communication between the Mexican-American and the Anglo. It is the central theme in James K. Bowman's "El Patrón," published in 1957 in *New Campus Writing*. The tragedy in his story is dependent upon a common characteristic that Octavio Paz has noted in all Mexicans and Mexican-Americans: the tendency of the Mexican to obey silently without ever revealing his personal attitudes until he explodes into action. In Bowman's story, the wetback's hate for his Anglo *patrón* is hidden until, in a single, violent act, he makes his hatred felt. The story might well make the reader judge the wetback as heartless unless he realizes that the action is simply the ultimate reaction to the oppression he has experienced on the ranch. The reader can, with this understanding, realize why the Mexican grins and rides away leaving his *patrón* to his fate.

The lack of communication theme appears also in George Seale's "Dilemma, Mi Amigo," published in *The Texas Quarterly* in 1967. Here the Mexican woman is separated from her new Mexican-American husband and deported to Mexico after an unsympathetic Anglo police force arrest and jail her for unintentionally breaking, first, a city ordinance (selling homemade candy without a permit) and, finally, a federal law (entering the United States illegally). Another aspect of the theme of the differences between the cultures is skillfully depicted in Richard Dokey's sympathetic story, "Sánchez," published in the *Southwest Review* in 1967. This time, however, the very relevant and contemporary conflict exists *within* the Mexican-American family itself as a conflict between generations. The Mexican-American father, who has given to his son all his love and all that he has loved, is forced to watch his son unconsciously reject the Mexican heritage and value system and replace it with the stainless-steel, red-convertible goals of the "American Way of Life." Richard Brown, in "Mr. Iscariot" (*The Literary Review*, 1963), also confronts a problem disturbing many of today's Chicanos: the *vendido,* that Mexican-American who "sells out" and exploits his own people in order to "make it" in the Anglo world. Brown's approach is not only perceptive and accurate, but his artistry is both compelling and appropriately complicated.

Robert Granat's "To Endure" appeared first in the *New Mexico Quarterly* and then was reprinted in *Prize Stories 1960: The O. Henry Awards*. It is certainly one of this anthology's most outstanding studies of the Chicano child as simply a human being whose secure and innocent world is quickly invaded and disrupted by death. Sylvan Karchmer's "A Fistful of Alamo Heroes," which first appeared in *The University of Kansas City Review* in 1950, is likewise revealing in that it presents two main characters— an Anglo and a Chicano—who come to realize the injustices that society has consciously or unconsciously brought upon the Mexican-American. Both men are offered the opportunity to speak and act. One elects to speak and is consequently destroyed by the blind establishment; the other chooses to remain silent and join the ranks of the Anglo society—and lives.

Several of the other stories in this third section are unique in their comic seriousness: Ray Bradbury's "The Wonderful Ice Cream Suit" (1958), William Barrett's "Señor Payroll" (1943), and Robert Granat's second story in this collection, "Sánchez and the Víbora: A New Mexican Tale" (1964). While themes peculiar to the Mexican-American dilemma and conflict are apparent in these stories, such themes are less essential to the enjoyment or appreciation of the stories. Certainly political protest or social injustices were not the primary stimulants for these three writers. In their stories, the reader meets no caricatures—only vivid characterizations and situations that become delightful and perceptive studies of human beings engaged in the sometimes serious, often pathetic, but never solemn comedy of living.

From World War II to the Present (the Mexican-American View) includes Mario Suárez' "Señor Garza," Américo Parédes' "The Hammon and the Beans," Amado Muro's "Cecilia Rosas," Philip D. Ortego's "The Coming of Zamora," Nick C. Vaca's "The Week in the Life of Manuel Hernández," and Genaro González, "Un Hijo del Sol."

These last stories were written by six Mexican-American writers and published during the last twenty years. The first sketch, entitled "Señor Garza," is by Mario Suárez and appeared with several others in the *Arizona Quarterly* in 1947. This work represents one Mexican-American's view of the variety of the inhabitants living in any *barrio* in the Southwest.

Américo Parédes, the well-known Texas folklorist and scholar, is the writer of the next story, the poignant "The Hammon and the Beans," which first appeared in 1963 in *The Texas Observer*. A study in ironies, the story contains the elements of both comedy and tragedy. It would seem to be the story of Chonita, the child who dies of malnutrition (even though the death certificate says pneumonia). But ultimately, it is the study of the narrator, a sensitive boy who is caught between being a Mexican and being an American.

Amado Muro, the next writer, seems to have written

more good short fiction than any other young Mexican-
American; yet he is not, in his own words, "a professional
writer" and does not "make a living that way. . . ."[3] On
the contrary, Muro is typical of the young Mexican-
American fictionist; he works for a railroad in El Paso
and writes in his spare time. His story "Cecilia Rosas,"
published in the *New Mexico Quarterly* in 1964, studies
the prevailing problem of the *vendida*. However, Muro
approaches the conflict with a crisp sense of humor; his
story has comic rather than tragic overtones.

The following two stories are the result of the long-
overdue formation of a publishing house devoted to the
Mexican-American artist, poet, essayist, and short fiction
author: Quinto Sol Publications. "The Coming of
Zamora," published in *El Grito* in 1968, marks the appearance of a promising Mexican-American writer, Philip
D. Ortego. Ortego offers a different view of the continuing
Mexican-American problem seen first by Garland and
then Saroyan: the search for a leader. His story pictures a
depressed and old Mexican-American left waiting patiently but optimistically in the dusty New Mexican street for
someone to arrive and lead *la gente* out of oppression.
The next story, first published in *El Espejo* (1969), an
anthology of Mexican-American creative work, is Nick C.
Vaca's "The Week in the Life of Manuel Hernández." It
is a well-controlled study of an individual—not an image—
who is torn between external and internal conflict. The
central character spends his young life searching for
meaning in a world that offers him neither meaning nor
understanding. He finds no escape from the swirling funnel that is life for a man who has lost his past and
identity.

At this point a brief word should be said about the
small number of stories discussed here that were written
by Mexican-Americans. It would seem that the most accurate, most rewarding way to understand the Mexican-
American through literature would be to read works by
those individuals who have written from personal experience. Unfortunately, as the bibliography appended to this
introduction will attest, until recently there were *no* Mexican-American writers. To explain why this is true is
difficult, but the matter may be resolved by examining the
three divisions of the Mexican-American social structure.

At the top is the well-educated and wealthy, landed

[3] Amado Muro, in a personal letter to the editor, May 17, 1970.

minority—ancestors of the *patrones* who controlled the
entire Southwest when the area was still part of Mexico.
This segment, though small in number to be sure, has
either become completely "Anglocized" or it has remained
as close as it could to the Mexican-Spanish image. This
level of society has generally attempted, at the expense of
the social and educational improvement of the masses, to
retain a vast lower class composed of *obreros* or common
workers who spend their days laboring in the fields to earn
enough money to keep themselves alive, even if it be alive
in an un-air-conditioned, "hand-me-down" world. Of
course, the Anglo, who invaded and conquered the West
and the Southwest, must accept most of the guilt of
exploiting this working class of Mexican-Americans; it is
he, with his plantations, orchards, or ranches, who has
gained materially primarily on the manual work of the
uneducated, underpaid *obrero*. At any rate, neither the
upper-class Mexican-American nor the lower-class laborer
has produced literature: The former is not inclined; the
latter is not equipped.

Then there is the growing middle class—those individuals who are educated for the white collar professions in
law, medicine, pharmacy, or business. Unfortunately, these
Mexican-Americans are not educated to read in a leisurely
fashion, much less to write creatively. As is so often the
case, these people—since they are prevented from becoming part of the upper class and do not choose to associate
with the lower class—become what is disaffectionately
called *vendidos*, those individuals who turn their backs on
their cultural heritage and try to enter (always with limited success) the Anglo society or those individuals who
use their own people for personal gain. These *vendidos* are
not, to be sure, interested in preserving or revealing in
literature the Mexican-American way of life.

In the past, then, no Mexican-American has been
equipped or inclined to contribute to American literature.
However, as the last six stories that I have mentioned
indicate, this is a condition that is rapidly changing: All of
them were written within the last two decades by Mexican-Americans. However, it must be admitted, as Stan
Steiner points out in his current study entitled *La Raza*, no
Mexican-American has yet written anything "that 'tells it
like it is' with the veracity of W. E. B. DuBois' *Souls of
Black Folk*, Richard Wright's *Native Son*, James Baldwin's
The Fire Next Time, Claude Brown's *Manchild in the*

Promised Land, or Eldridge Cleaver's *Soul on Ice*."[4] Nevertheless, what the Mexican-Americans have published indicates a beginning. And with the increase of opportunity to receive what is still considered a liberal and not a technical or professional education, more Mexican-Americans will write. More important, these young men and women, who are directly involved in and are close enough to the Mexican-American heritage to remember it, seem definitely concerned enough to relate it. Certainly, somewhere a powerful, creative voice of the Mexican-American is preparing to speak.

One such writer is Genaro González, a former migrant worker from McAllen, Texas, who is currently a student at Pomona College in Pasadena, California. His story "Un Hijo del Sol" ends this anthology and represents what can be written by the Mexican-American who can be simultaneously an active Chicano and a productive creative artist. His story possesses what any reader could expect from any short story: the accuracy to make it realistic and interesting, the force to make it effective, and the subtlety and structural complexity to make it art.

More such stories by Gonzáles and other Mexican-American writers will come.

—E. S.

[4] *La Raza: the Mexican Americans* (Harper & Row: New York, 1970), pp. 404–405.

Selected Bibliography of Short Fiction

Atherton, Gertrude. "The Vengeance of Padre Arroyo" and "La Pérdida," *The Splendid Idle Forties* (original title: *Before the Gringo Came*, 1894). The Macmillan Company: New York, 1902.

Barrett, William E. "Señor Payroll," *Southwest Review*, XXVIII (Autumn, 1943), 17–20.

Bowman, James K. "El Patrón," *New Campus Writing*, No. 2, ed. Nolan Miller. Putnam, 1957, 50–56.

Bradbury, Ray. "The Wonderful Ice Cream Suit," "I see You Never," and "En la Noche," *Twice Twenty-Two*. Doubleday & Company: Garden City, New York, 1966.

Brown, Richard G. "Mr. Iscariot," *The Literary Review*, VI (Summer, 1963), 441–451.

Chávez, Fray Angélico. "The Fiddler and the Angelito," *Southwest Review*, XXXII (Summer, 1947), 242–244.

Dokey, Richard. "Sánchez," *Southwest Review*, XLII (Autumn, 1967), 354–367.

Edelstein, Arthur. "That Time of Year," *Twenty Years of Stanford Short Stories*, ed. Wallace Stegner and Richard Scowcroft. Stanford University Press: Palo Alto, California, 1966.

Emery, George. "The Water-Witch," *Overland Monthly*, III (1869), 94–96.

Garland, Hamlin. "Delmar of Pima," *McClure's Magazine*, XVIII (February, 1902), 340–348.

Granat, Robert. "Sánchez and the Víbora: A New Mexican Tale," *The Texas Quarterly*, VII (Autumn, 1964), 128–138.

————. "To Endure," *The New Mexico Quarterly*, XXVIII (No. 1, 1958), 46–53.

Griffith, Beatrice W. "In the Flow of Time," *Best American Short Stories of 1949*, ed. Martha Foley. Houghton-Mifflin: Boston, 1949.

Gusewelle, C. W. "Robert Meléndez: Retrospect," *The Texas Quarterly*, XI (Summer, 1968), 155–167.

Harris, Larry. "Mex," *The Fantastic Universe Omnibus*, ed. Hans Stefan Santesson. Prentice-Hall: Englewood Cliffs, New Jersey, 1960.

Harte, Bret. "The Devotion of Enríquez," *Stories of The Early West*. Platt and Munk: New York, 1964.

Hawkes, John. "The Honeymoon Hideaway (Circa 1944)," *The Texas Quarterly,* VI (Summer, 1963), 20–32.

Hemingway, Ernest. "The Gambler, the Nun, and the Radio," *The Short Stories of Ernest Hemingway.* Charles Scribner's Sons: New York (n.d.).

Horgan, Paul. "The Surgeon and the Nun" and "To the Mountains," *Figures in the Landscape*. Harper and Brothers: New York, 1940.

Karchmer, Sylvan. "A Fistful of Alamo Heroes," *Twenty-One Texas Short Stories*, ed. William Peery. The University of Texas Press: Austin, Texas, 1954.

Kerouac, Jack. "The Mexican Girl," *The Paris Review*, XI (Winter, 1955), 9–32.

Kornbluth, C. M. "Gómez," *The Explorers*. Ballantine Books, Inc.: New York, 1954.

London, Jack. "The Mexican," *Best Short Stories of Jack London.* The Sundial Press: Garden City, New York, 1945.

Marriott, Alice. "El Zopilote," *Southwest Review,* XXXII (Summer, 1947), 284–290.

McGinnis, John. "The Tomato Can," *Southwest Review,* XVI (Summer, 1931), 507–516.

Muro, Amado. "Cecilia Rosas," *New Mexico Quarterly,* XXXIV (Winter, 1964), 353–364.

————. "Mala Torres," *Arizona Quarterly* (Summer, 1968).

Orr, Ellen. "Home for Consuela," *New Voices: American Fiction Today,* ed. Don M. Wolfe. Hendricks House, 1955.

Ortego, Philip D. "The Coming of Zamora: a Story," *El Grito,* I (Spring, 1968), 12–17.

Parédes, Américo. "The Hammon and the Beans," *Southwest Writers Anthology,* ed. Martin Shockley. Steck-Vaughan Company: Austin, Texas, 1967.

Rhodes, Eugene Manlove. "Paso por Aquí," *Best Novels and Short Stories.* Houghton-Mifflin Company: New York, 1949.

Ramano-V, Octavio I. "A Rosary for Doña Marina," *El Espejo.* Quinto Sol Publications: Berkeley, California, 1969.

Rosen, Roy. "Music for the Night," *Southwest Review,* XXXVIII (Spring, 1953), 102–114.

Saroyan, William. "With a Hey Nonny Nonny," *Inhale and Exhale.* Random House: New York, 1936.

————. "My Uncle and the Mexicans," *Little Children.* Harcourt, Brace & Company: New York, 1937.

Seale, George. "Dilemma, Mi Amigo," *The Texas Quarterly*, IX (Spring, 1966), 111–124.

Steinbeck, John. "Flight," *Long Valley*. Viking Press: New York, 1938.

Stevens, Helen. "The Black Shawl," *Southwest Review*, XXXII (Summer, 1947), 295–300.

Stevenson, Philip. "The Shepherd," *Southwest Review*, XVI (October, 1930), 65–74.

Suárez, Mario. "Cuco Goes to a Party," "Loco-Chu," "Kid Zopilote," "El Hoyo," and "Señor Garza," *Arizona Quarterly* (Summer, 1947), 112–137.

Trejo, Arnulfo D. "Maestro," *Arizona Quarterly* (Winter, 1960), 352–356.

Vaca, Nick C. "The Week in the Life of Manuel Hernández," *El Espejo*, Quinto Sol Publications: Berkeley, California, 1969.

————. "Martín," *El Grito*, I (Fall, 1967), 25–31.

I.
FROM THE BEGINNINGS
TO 1930:

Early Caricatures

The Water-Witch

GEORGE EMERY

There was no doubt but the weather was warm.

I lay on my back under a twisted oak, dividing my time between watching the wreaths of smoke, as they lazily curled from my pipe, and following the mad cotillion which the frolicsome flies were dancing in the sunshine. The Colonel, more meditative than myself, was turning in his lips a spear of withered grass, and dreamily gazing across the horizon, into the soft mellow vacancy that breathed around and above the landscape.

There was a problem to solve.

We had come, the Colonel and I, from the far East, leaving behind us the scenes of greenbacks and female suffrage, to make for ourselves a home in the sunny clime of Los Angeles. The land of the fruitful vineyards and the rustling olive trees, where the orange perfumes the leafy groves with the fragrance of Nature's bridal flowers, and the whole earth seems to smile—this was our chosen home.

In her great work of world-building, Nature must have had her resting-places, wherein to recruit her exhausted energies and prepare for further labors of usefulness and adornment. And on these it was her chief care to shower all the bounty of her generous hand, to deck the sward with myriads of glittering flowers, her own jewels flashing heavenward, to plan huge interweaving hedges of the leafy oak, and make rustic bowers amid their twining branches. Here, in the days when her snowy mantle draped the boundaries of less-favored climes, she enjoyed a season of repose, while her little myrmidons were busily grinding away at the immense supplies of chlorophyll to satisfy the orders of the coming year. To cheer the tiny laborers, the well-trained bands of crickets and cicadæ were wont to discourse their inspiring music, varying the intervals of toiling with their shrill, blithe notes. And when the labors of the day were over, the twittering swallow and the full-throated lark hushed them to rest. Shut in by mountains, the Dame had leisure to exert her utmost taste, and has left to mortals the relics of her industry and power. Such are the valleys of California. And in none is her hand more marked than in the charming valley of San Gabriel, ten miles from the thriving city of Los Angeles.

But here in the south there is now lacking an important element—water. The old courses are dried up and in deep concealment lies the liquid which, for purposes of cultivation at least, is indispensable to success. The thirsty earth will not bless the husbandman unless the tears of heaven, or the schemes of art, give water to the soil. It is all well enough to believe the old maxim: *seges respondet votis;* only try it once and learn.

We had found a delightful location for our home, with a view unsurpassed in loveliness, stretching away down a sloping valley, bounded by snow-capped peaks that received the matin touches of the "rosy-fingered dawn," and by rolling hills that drifted out of sight, like mammoth earth-waves suddenly congealed. But it was a melancholy truth that there was no water.

Here was our problem. We might by hard labor and constant watching seduce a rill from the distant cañons to wander to us, but this supply would be precarious and necessarily limited. Old settlers—the advice-giving miasma of every new country, of whom it can always be said that what they do *not* know will fill a large volume—declared that no surface water could be found at a less depth than a hundred feet. There was no wind for a wind-mill. Water, however, we must have, and that at once.

"Well, Colonel," said I, when the gallant flies had escorted their buzzing partners to seats on the boughs above me.

"Well, Judge," was the laconic reply.

Be it known that no one can have any social standing or consideration in California without some euphonious title. And as my companion had once assisted in letting off some fireworks and could dissect a Henry rifle, he was fully competent to aspire to military honors; while, as I had a dim remembrance of once brushing the dust from a volume of Blackstone, the mantle of the judiciary fell to me. Such is fame.

"This place suits me capitally, but we cannot do without water."

"An undeniable proposition, I guess, old fellow."

"Well?" I repeated, inquiringly.

"Yes; it is just that *well* that we want."

"I think we better try for one, at all events," said I, scorning the base attempt.

"We can do no less, but where shall it be?"

Just then came along one of our prospective neighbors, a man of good intellect, but whose general appearance was that of a parsnip gone to seed; a wiry, straggly, shiftless old fellow, who might have been the Darwinian link between a mummy and an oyster, retaining all the power of suction of the latter. Old S———— was called a hard drinker, but he seemed to drink as easily as a man could.

"Waal, what are yer going to do for water?" was this phenomenon's question, as he shambled up to our shade.

"We were just saying that we should try to get a well here, and were considering what was the most favorable spot," said the Colonel.

"Why don't you send for the water-witch?"

"The what?" was the double ejaculation.

"The water-witch, who lives down here about a mile. I'll go and fetch the critter"; and he departed straightway, leaving no sign.

Shade of Fenimore Cooper! What was to come? If the supernatural could not aid us, we were certainly in bad fortune. A water-witch! Some ethereal creature, doubtless, that with airy facility would point with gladness to the hidden stream. Some prescient sibyl that could look into the bowels of the earth and detect the wished-for torrent. My mind reverted to old Virgil, who has depicted so vividly the oracular priestess, sitting on a three-legged stool over a vent of gas, and imparting to leaves the aëriform despatches. But this I had always considered a creation of the poet's brain when he was excited with high old Falernian, or a Massic punch. Still, California is a most wonderful country, and it argues simplicity to be astonished at anything. So I refilled my pipe and awaited the issue.

"We are hardly in condition to receive this divinity, Judge; we have no ambrosia, and the nectar is just out; we must send for another case."

"*Persicos odi, puer apparatus,* or in vulgar Saxon, Style be hanged!"

We watched our friend as he began to disappear, and saw him approach a low, adobe house. A nice abode, truly, for a prophetess! But true divinity is simple. It was not long before we could see two figures advancing, one of which we recognized; the other—

P. Virgil, I am penitent! May the ashes of my ancestors be sold for dentifrice if I intended to thus wrong thee in my thought!

A ragged, dirty Mexican, whose matted hair was a model of a cactus-fence, whose tattered blanket served to make more evident his nakedness, an unmistakable, unredeemed "greaser." With his eyes glistening like New Almadén dew-drops, an emaciated cigarette between his lips, and a transparent dog at his heels, he advanced to where we stood in silent amazement, and uttered the brief "*buenas tardes*" of politeness.

"Are you a water-witch?" we at last were enabled to inquire.

"*Sí, señor.*"

The Colonel and I looked at him, at each other, and back to him again.

"Yaas!" began our loquacious friend, "he can show you where to dig."

"Let him do it then."

Without much ado, with no preliminary incantations, this sun-burned sage drew forth from his blanket his sub-soiled hands, and they contained a forked stick, about three feet long.

"Mythology, after all," I whispered; "this must be the golden bough from the Italian grove."

Grasping the forked ends of his wand firmly in his fists, and holding the point upwards, in measured pace our witch strode onward. Across the plain, down the hollows, over the hillocks, we followed him, watching the look of knowing determination that gleamed on his countenance. At last he stopped, and verily the twig was bowing downward in slow sweeps. A peculiar motion had seized it, like the feeble exertions of a decayed pump. But move it did.

"Don't you move it yourself, *hombre?*"

"No."

"I don't believe it!"

He followed the course of a supposed stream for some time and finally stopped, saying that we could find water there, and that we need not dig deeper than thirty-five feet at the utmost. An exulting glance rested upon us as he communicated the teachings of his mind.

"How do you know all this?"

"My stick, he tell me."

"Will it tell any one else?"

"Quién sabe?" with the aboriginal shrug.

I took the magic wand with fear and trembling, and grasped it firmly, standing over the designated water. Quiet as a stone. The Colonel next tried his fortune, with no better success.

"Ugh! you no *sabe!*" was the comforting grunt from Mr. Water-Witch.

"He has never missed a single well," remarked our friend, as the mystic being turned to go, after we had satisfied his reasonable demand, which was limited to *"aguardiente,"* and he too turned homeward, leaving us to our cogitations.

"What do you think of this, Judge?"

"My private impression is that it is a confounded humbug."

"But there may be something in it. His wand is made of willow, which has a known affinity for water, and there may exist some local attraction of whose force we are ignorant."

"He probably has a great dread of water, at any rate."

"I have read of some German who has been around Europe in this way, and has never failed in his predictions."

"He must be some relative of 'Planchette.' "

"The least we can do," said the Colonel, as we cinched up our saddles preparatory to riding city-ward, "is to dig, and we may as well dig where he said as anywhere."

We did dig, and found water at thirty-one feet.

I am still an unbeliever.

La Pérdida

GERTRUDE ATHERTON

On her fourteenth birthday they had married her to an
old man, and at sixteen she had met and loved a fire-
hearted young vaquero. The old husband had twisted his
skinny fingers around her arm and dragged her before the
Alcalde, who had ordered her beautiful black braids cut
close to her neck, and sentenced her to sweep the streets.
Carlos, the tempter of that childish unhappy heart, was
flung into prison. Such were law and justice in California
before the Americans came.

The haughty elegant women of Monterey drew their
mantillas more closely about their shocked faces as they
passed La Pérdida sweeping the dirt into little heaps. The
soft-eyed girls, lovely in their white or flowered gowns,
peered curiously through the gratings of their homes at
the "lost one," whose sin they did not understand, but
whose sad face and sorry plight appealed to their youthful
sympathies. The caballeros, dashing up and down the
street, and dazzling in bright silken jackets, gold-
embroidered, lace-trimmed, the sun reflected in the silver
of their saddles, shot bold admiring glances from beneath
their sombreros. No one spoke to her, and she asked no
one for sympathy.

She slept alone in a little hut on the outskirts of the
town. With the dawn she rose, put on her coarse smock
and black skirt, made herself a tortilla, then went forth
and swept the streets. The children mocked her sometimes,
and she looked at them in wonder. Why should she be

mocked or punished? She felt no repentance; neither the Alcalde nor her husband had convinced her of her sin's enormity; she felt only bitter resentment that it should have been so brief. Her husband, a blear-eyed crippled old man, loathsome to all the youth and imagination in her, had beaten her and made her work. A man, young, strong, and good to look upon, had come and kissed her with passionate tenderness. Love had meant to her the glorification of a wretched sordid life; a green spot and a patch of blue sky in the desert. If punishment followed upon such happiness, must not the Catholic religion be all wrong in its teachings? Must not purgatory follow heaven, instead of heaven purgatory?

She watched the graceful girls of the wealthy class flit to and fro on the long corridors of the houses, or sweep the strings of the guitar behind their gratings as the caballeros passed. Watchful old women were always near them, their ears alert for every word. La Pérdida thanked God that she had had no dueña.

One night, on her way home, she passed the long low prison where her lover was confined. The large crystal moon flooded the red-tiled roof projecting over the deep windows and the shallow cells. The light sweet music of a guitar floated through iron bars, and a warm voice sang:—

> *Adiós, adiós, de ti al ausentarme,*
> *Para ir en poz de mi fatal estrella,*
> *Yo llevo grabada tu imagen bella,*
> *Aquí en mi palpitante corazón.*
>
> *Pero aunque lejos de tu lado me halle*
> *No olvides, no, que por tu amor deliro*
> *Enviáme siquiera un suspiro,*
> *Que dé consuelo, a mi alma en su dolor.*
>
> *Y de tu pecho la emoción sentida*
> *Llegue hasta herir mi lacerado oido,*
> *Y arranque de mi pecho dolorido*
> *Un eco que repita, adiós ! adiós ! ***

*Farewell, farewell, from you I absent myself,
  To follow my fated star [my destiny],
  Engraved is your beautiful image,
  Here in my palpitating heart.

  Although far from your side I'll find myself
  Do not forget, no, that through your wandering love
  Send at least a sigh,
  A consolation, to my aching soul.

La Pérdida's blood leaped through her body. Her aimless hands struck the spiked surface of a cactus-bush but she never knew it. When the song finished, she crept to the grating and looked in.

"Carlos!" she whispered.

A man who lay on the straw at the back of the cell sprang to his feet and came forward.

"My little one!" he said. "I knew that song would bring thee. I begged them for a guitar, then to be put into a front cell." He forced his hands through the bars and gave her life again with his strong warm clasp.

"Come out," she said.

"Ay! they have me fast. But when they do let me out, *niña*, I will take thee in my arms; and whosoever tries to tear thee away again will have a dagger in his heart. *Dios de mi vida*! I could tear their flesh from their bones for the shame and the pain they have given thee, thou poor little innocent girl!"

"But thou lovest me, Carlos?"

"There is not an hour I am not mad for thee, not a corner of my heart that does not ache for thee! Ay, little one, never mind; life is long, and we are young."

She pressed nearer and laid his hand on her heart.

"Ay!" she said, "life is long."

"Holy Mary!" he cried. "The hills are on fire!"

A shout went up in the town. A flame, midway on the curving hills, leaped to the sky, narrow as a ribbon, then swept out like a fan. The moon grew dark behind a rolling pillar of smoke. The upcurved arms of the pines were burnt into a wall of liquid shifting red. The caballeros sprang to their horses, and driving the Indians before them, fled to the hills to save the town. The indolent women of Monterey mingled their screams with the shrill cries of the populace and the hoarse shouts of their men. The prison sentries stood to their posts for a few moments; then the panic claimed them, and they threw down their guns and ran with the rest to the hills.

Carlos gave a cry of derision and triumph. "My little one, our hour has come! Run and find the keys."

And from your breast the sensitive emotion
Arrived to pierce my unfortunate ear,
And I tore from my aching heart
An echo which repeated, "Farewell!" "Farewell!"
—translated by Félix D. Almaráz

The big bunch of keys had been flung hastily into a corner. A moment later Carlos held the shaking form of the girl in his powerful arms. Slender and delicate as she was, she made no protest against the fierceness of that embrace.

"But come," he said. "We have only this hour for escape. When we are safe in the mountains— Come!"

He lifted her in his arms and ran down the crooked street to a corral where an hidalgo kept his finest horses. Carlos had been the vaquero of the band. The iron bars of the great doors were down—only one horse was in the corral; the others had carried the hidalgo and his friends to the fire. The brute neighed with delight as Carlos flung saddle and *aquera* into place, then, with La Pérdida in his arms, sprang upon its back. The vaquero dug his spurs into the shining flanks, the mustang reared, shook his small head and silver mane, and bounded through the doors.

A lean, bent, and wiry thing darted from the shadows and hung upon the horse's neck. It was the husband of La Pérdida, and his little brown face looked like an old walnut.

"Take me with thee!" he cried. "I will give thee the old man's blessing," and, clinging like a crab to the neck of the galloping mustang, he drove a knife toward the heart of La Pérdida. The blade turned upon itself as lightning sometimes does, and went through stringy tissues instead of fresh young blood.

Carlos plucked the limp body from the neck of the horse and flung it upon a cactus-bush, where it sprawled and stiffened among the spikes and the blood-red flowers. But the mustang never paused; and as the fires died on the hills, the mountains opened their great arms and sheltered the happiness of two wayward hearts.

The Vengeance of Padre Arroyo

GERTRUDE ATHERTON

I

Pilar, from her little window just above the high wall surrounding the big adobe house set apart for the women neophytes of the Mission of Santa Inés, watched, morning and evening, for Andreo, as he came and went from the rancheria. The old women kept the girls busy, spinning, weaving, sewing; but age nods and youth is crafty. The tall young Indian who was renowned as the best huntsman of all the neophytes, and who supplied Padre Arroyo's table with deer and quail, never failed to keep his ardent eyes fixed upon the grating so long as it lay within the line of his vision. One day he went to Padre Arroyo and told him that Pilar was the prettiest girl behind the wall—the prettiest girl in all the Californias—and that she should be his wife. But the kind stern old padre shook his head.

"You are both too young. Wait another year, my son, and if thou art still in the same mind, thou shalt have her."

Andreo dared to make no protest, but he asked permission to prepare a home for his bride. The padre gave it willingly, and the young Indian began to make the big adobes, the bright red tiles. At the end of a month he had built him a cabin among the willows of the rancheria, a little apart from the others: he was in love, and association with his fellows was distasteful. When the cabin was builded his impatience slipped from its curb, and once more he besought the priest to allow him to marry.

42

Padre Arroyo was sunning himself on the corridor of the mission, shivering in his heavy brown robes, for the day was cold.

"Orion," he said sternly—he called all his neophytes after the celebrities of earlier days, regardless of the names given them at the font—"have I not told thee thou must wait a year? Do not be impatient, my son. She will keep. Women are like apples: when they are too young, they set the teeth on edge; when ripe and mellow, they please every sense; when they wither and turn brown, it is time to fall from the tree into a hole. Now go and shoot a deer for Sunday: the good padres from San Luís Obispo and Santa Bárbara are coming to dine with me."

Andreo, dejected, left the padre. As he passed Pilar's window and saw a pair of wistful black eyes behind the grating, his heart took fire. No one was within sight. By a series of signs he made his lady understand that he would place a note beneath a certain adobe in the wall.

Pilar, as she went to and fro under the fruit trees in the garden, or sat on the long corridor weaving baskets, watched that adobe with fascinated eyes. She knew that Andreo was tunneling it, and one day a tiny hole proclaimed that his work was accomplished. But how to get the note? The old women's eyes were very sharp when the girls were in front of the gratings. Then the civilizing development of Christianity upon the heathen intellect triumphantly asserted itself. Pilar, too, conceived a brilliant scheme. That night the padre, who encouraged any evidence of industry, no matter how eccentric, gave her a little garden of her own—a patch where she could raise sweet peas and Castillian roses.

"That is well, that is well, my Nausicaa," he said, stroking her smoky braids. "Go cut the slips and plant them where thou wilt. I will send thee a package of sweet pea seeds."

Pilar spent every spare hour bending over her "patch"; and the hole, at first no bigger than a pin's point, was larger at each setting of the sun behind the mountain. The old women, scolding on the corridor, called to her not to forget vespers.

On the third evening, kneeling on the damp ground, she drew from the little tunnel in the adobe a thin slip of wood covered with the labour of sleepless nights. She hid it in her smock—that first of California's love-letters— then ran with shaking knees and prostrated herself before the altar. That night the moon streamed through her grating, and she deciphered the fact that Andreo had loosened eight adobes above her garden, and would await her every midnight.

Pilar sat up in bed and glanced about the room with terrified delight. It took her but a moment to decide the question; love had kept her awake too many nights. The neophytes were asleep; as they turned now and again, their narrow beds of hide, suspended from the ceiling, swung too gently to awaken them. The old women snored loudly. Pilar slipped from her bed and looked through the grating. Andreo was there, the dignity and repose of primeval man in his bearing. She waved her hand and pointed downward to the wall; then, throwing on the long coarse gray smock that was her only garment, crept from the room and down the stair. The door was protected against hostile tribes by a heavy iron bar, but Pilar's small hands were hard and strong, and in a moment she stood over the adobes which had crushed her roses and sweet peas.

As she crawled through the opening, Andreo took her hand bashfully, for they never had spoken. "Come," he said; "we must be far away before dawn."

They stole past the long mission, crossing themselves as they glanced askance at the ghostly row of pillars; past the guard-house, where the sentries slept at their post; past the rancheria; then, springing upon a waiting mustang, dashed down the valley. Pilar had never been on a horse before, and she clung in terror to Andreo, who bestrode the unsaddled beast as easily as a cloud rides the wind. His arm held her closely, fear vanished, and she enjoyed the novel sensation. Glancing over Andreo's shoulder she watched the mass of brown and white buildings, the winding rivers, fade into the mountain. Then they began to ascend an almost perpendicular steep. The horse followed a narrow trail; the crowding trees and shrubs clutched the blankets and smocks of the riders; after a time trail and scene grew white: the snow lay on the heights.

"Where do we go?" she asked.

"To Zaca Lake, on the very top of the mountain, miles above us. No one has ever been there but myself. Often I have shot deer and birds beside it. They never will find us there."

The red sun rose over the mountains of the east. The

crystal moon sank in the west. Andreo sprang from the
weary mustang and carried Pilar to the lake.

A sheet of water, round as a whirlpool but calm and
silver, lay amidst the sweeping willows and pine-forested
peaks. The snow glittered beneath the trees, but a canoe
was on the lake, a hut on the marge.

II

Padre Arroyo tramped up and down the corridor, smit-
ing his hands together. The Indians bowed lower than
usual, as they passed, and hastened their steps. The soldiers scoured the country for the bold violators of mission
law. No one asked Padre Arroyo what he would do with
the sinners, but all knew that punishment would be sharp
and summary: the men hoped that Andreo's mustang had
carried him beyond its reach; the girls, horrified as they
were, wept and prayed in secret for Pilar.

A week later, in the early morning, Padre Arroyo sat
on the corridor. The mission stood on a plateau overlooking a long valley forked and sparkled by the broad river.
The valley was planted thick with olive trees, and their
silver leaves glittered in the rising sun. The mountain
peaks about and beyond were white with snow, but the
great red poppies blossomed at their feet. The padre,
exiled from the luxury and society of his dear Spain, never
tired of the prospect: he loved his mission children, but he
loved Nature more.

Suddenly he leaned forward on his staff and lifted the
heavy brown hood of his habit from his ear. Down the
road winding from the eastern mountains came the echo
of galloping footfalls. He rose expectantly and waddled
out upon the plaza, shading his eyes with his hand. A
half-dozen soldiers, riding closely about a horse bestridden
by a stalwart young Indian supporting a woman, were
rapidly approaching the mission. The padre returned to his
seat and awaited their coming.

The soldiers escorted the culprits to the corridor; two
held the horse while they descended, then led it away, and
Andreo and Pilar were alone with the priest. The bride-
groom placed his arm about the bride and looked defiantly
at Padre Arroyo, but Pilar drew her long hair about her
face and locked her hands together.

Padre Arroyo folded his arms and regarded them with
lowered brows, a sneer on his mouth.

"I have new names for you both," he said, in his thickest voice. "Antony, I hope thou hast enjoyed thy honeymoon. Cleopatra, I hope thy little toes did not get frost-bitten. You both look as if food had been scarce. And your garments have gone in good part to clothe the brambles, I infer. It is too bad you could not wait a year and love in your cabin at the rancheria, by a good fire, and with plenty of frijoles and tortillas in your stomachs." He dropped his sarcastic tone, and, rising to his feet, extended his right arm with a gesture of malediction. "Do you comprehend the enormity of your sin?" he shouted. "Have you not learned on your knees that the fires of hell are the rewards of unlawful love? Do you not know that even the year of sackcloth and ashes I shall impose here on earth will not save you from those flames a million times hotter than the mountain fire; than the roaring pits in which evil Indians torture one another? A hundred years of their scorching breath, of roasting flesh, for a week of love! Oh, God of my soul!"

Andreo looked somewhat staggered, but unrepentant. Pilar burst into loud sobs of terror.

The padre stared long and gloomily at the flags of the corridor. Then he raised his head and looked sadly at his lost sheep.

"My children," he said solemnly, "my heart is wrung for you. You have broken the laws of God and of the Holy Catholic Church, and the punishments thereof are awful. Can I do anything for you, excepting to pray? You shall have my prayers, my children. But that is not enough; I cannot—ay! I cannot endure the thought that you shall be damned. Perhaps"—again he stared meditatively at the stones, then, after an impressive silence, raised his eyes. "Heaven vouchsafes me an idea, my children. I will make your punishment here so bitter that Almighty God in His mercy will give you but a few years of purgatory after death. Come with me."

He turned and led the way slowly to the rear of the mission buildings. Andreo shuddered for the first time, and tightened his arm about Pilar's shaking body. He knew that they were to be locked in the dungeons. Pilar, almost fainting, shrank back as they reached the narrow spiral stair which led downward to the cells. "Ay! I shall die, my Andreo!" she cried. "Ay! my father, have mercy!"

"I cannot, my children," said the padre, sadly. "It is for the salvation of your souls."

"Mother of God! When shall I see thee again, my Pilar?" whispered Andreo. "But, ay! the memory of that week on the mountain will keep us both alive."

Padre Arroyo descended the stair and awaited them at its foot. Separating them, and taking each by the hand, he pushed Andreo ahead and dragged Pilar down the narrow passage. At its end he took a great bunch of keys from his pocket, and raising both hands commanded them to kneel. He said a long prayer in a loud monotonous voice which echoed and reëchoed down the dark hall and made Pilar shriek with terror. Then he fairly hurled the marriage ceremony at them, and made the couple repeat after him the responses. When it was over, "Arise," he said.

The poor things stumbled to their feet, and Andreo caught Pilar in a last embrace.

"Now bear your incarceration with fortitude, my children; and if you do not beat the air with your groans, I will let you out in a week. Do not hate your old father, for love alone makes him severe, but pray, pray, pray."

And then he locked them both in the same cell.

The Devotion of Enríquez

BRET HARTE

In the chronicle which dealt with the exploits of Chu Chu, a California mustang, I gave some space to the accomplishments of Enríquez Saltello who assisted me in training her, and who was also brother to Consuelo Saltello, the young lady to whom I had freely given both the mustang and my youthful affections. I consider it a proof of the superiority of masculine friendship that neither the subsequent desertion of the mustang nor the young lady ever made the slightest difference to Enríquez or me in our exalted amity. To a wondering doubt as to what I ever could possibly have seen in his sister to admire he joined a tolerant skepticism of the whole sex. This he was wont to express in that marvelous combination of Spanish precision and California slang for which he was justly famous.

"As to thees women and their little game," he would say, "believe me, my friend, your old oncle 'Enry is not in it. No, he will ever take a back seat when lofe is around. For why? Regard me here! If she is a horse you shall say, 'She will buck-jump,' 'She will ess-shy,' 'She will not arrive,' or 'She will arrive too quick.' But if it is thees women where are you? For when you shall say, 'She will ess-shy,' look you, she will walk straight; or she will remain tranquil when you think she buck-jump; or else she will arrive and, look you, you will not. You shall get left. It is ever so. My father and the brother of my father has both make court to my mother when she was but a señorita. My

48

father think she have lofe his brother more. So he say to
her, 'It is enofe; tranquilize yourself. I will go. I will efface
myself. Adiós! Shake hands! Ta-ta! So long! See you
again in the fall.' And what make my mother? Regard
me! She marry my father—on the instant! Of thees wom-
en, believe me, Pancho, you shall know nothing. Not even
if they shall make you the son of your father or his
nephew."

I have recalled this characteristic speech to show the
general tendency of Enríquez's convictions at the opening
of this little story. It is only fair to say, however, that his
usual attitude toward the sex he so cheerfully maligned
exhibited little apprehension or caution in dealing with
them. Among the frivolous and light-minded intermixture
of his race he moved with great freedom and popularity.
He danced well; when we went to fandangos together his
agility and the audacity of his figures always procured him
the prettiest partners—his professed sentiments, I presume, shielding him from subsequent jealousies, heartburn-
ings or envy. I have a vivid recollection of him in the
mysteries of the *semicuacua*, a somewhat corybantic
dance which left much to the invention of the performers
and very little to the imagination of the spectator. In one
of the figures a gaudy handkerchief, waved more or less
gracefully by dancer and danseuse before the dazzled eyes
of each other, acted as love's signal and was used to
express alternate admiration and indifference, shyness and
audacity, fear and transport, coyness and coquetry, as the
dance proceeded. I need not say that Enríquez's pantomimic illustration of these emotions was peculiarly extravagant, but it was always performed and accepted with a
gravity that was an essential feature of the dance. At such
times sighs would escape him which were supposed to
portray the incipient stages of passion; snorts of jealousy
burst from him at the suggestion of a rival; he was over-
taken by a sort of St. Vitus's dance that expressed his timidity in making the first advances of affection; the scorn of
his ladylove struck him with something like a dumb ague,
and a single gesture of invitation from her produced
marked delirium. All this was very like Enríquez, but on
the particular occasion to which I refer, I think no one
was prepared to see him begin the figure with the waving
of *four* handkerchiefs! Yet this he did, pirouetting, caper-
ing, brandishing his silken signals like a ballerina's scarf in
the languishment or fire of passion until, in a final figure

where the conquered and submitting fair one usually sinks into the arms of her partner, need it be said that the ingenious Enríquez was found in the center of the floor supporting four of the dancers! Yet he was by no means unduly excited either by the plaudits of the crowd or by his evident success with the fair.

"Ah, believe me it is nothing," he said quietly, rolling a fresh cigarette as he leaned against the doorway. "Possibly I shall have to offer the chocolate or the wine to thees girls, or make to them a promenade in the moonlight on the veranda. It is ever so. Unless, my friend," he said suddenly turning toward me in an excess of chivalrous self-abnegation, "unless you shall yourself take my place. Behold, I gif them to you! I vamos! I vanish! I make track! I skedaddle!"

I think he would have carried his extravagance to the point of summoning his four gypsy witches of partners and committing them to my care, if the crowd had not at that moment parted before the remaining dancers and left one of the onlookers, a tall slender girl, calmly surveying them through gold-rimmed eyeglasses in complete critical absorption. I stared in amazement and consternation, for I recognized in the fair stranger Miss Urania Mannersley, the Congregational minister's niece!

Everybody knew Rainie Mannersley throughout the length and breadth of the Encinal. She was at once the envy and the goad of the daughters of those southwestern and eastern immigrants who had settled in the valley. She was correct, she was critical, she was faultless and observant. She was proper yet independent; she was highly educated; she was suspected of knowing Latin and Greek; she even spelled correctly! She could wither the plainest field nosegay in the hands of other girls by giving the flowers their botanical names. She never said, "Ain't you?" but "Aren't you?" She looked upon "Did I which?" as an incomplete and imperfect form of "What did I do?" She quoted from Browning and Tennyson and was believed to have read them. She was from Boston. What could she possibly be doing at a free-and-easy fandango?

Even if these facts were not already familiar to everyone there, her outward appearance would have attracted attention. Contrasted with the gorgeous red, black and yellow skirts of the dancers, her plain tightly fitting gown and hat, all of one delicate gray, were sufficiently notable in themselves even had they not seemed, like the girl

herself, a kind of quiet protest to the glaring flounces
before her. Her small straight waist and flat back brought
into greater relief the corsetless, waistless, swaying figures
of the Mexican girls, and her long, slim well-booted feet
peeping from the stiff white edges of her short skirt, made
their broad low-quartered slippers, held on by the big toe,
appear more preposterous than ever. Suddenly she seemed
to realize that she was standing there alone, but showed
no fear or embarrassment. She drew back a little, glancing
carelessly behind her as if missing some previous companion, and then her eyes fell upon mine. She smiled an easy
recognition; then a moment later her glance rested more
curiously upon Enríquez, who was still by my side. I
disengaged myself and instantly joined her, particularly as
I noticed that a few of the other bystanders were beginning
to stare at her with little reserve.

"Isn't it the most extraordinary thing you ever saw?"
she said quietly. Then, presently noticing the look of
embarrassment on my face she went on, more by way of
conversation than of explanation: "I just left uncle making
a call on a parishioner next door, and was going home
with Jocasta" (a peon servant of her uncle's) "when I
heard the music, and dropped in. I don't know what has
become of her," she added, glancing around the room
again. "She seemed perfectly wild when she saw that
creature over there bounding about with his handkerchiefs. You were speaking to him just now. Do tell me—is
he real?"

"I should think there was little doubt of that," I said
with a vague laugh.

"You know what I mean," she said simply. "Is he quite
sane? Does he do that because he likes it, or is he paid for
it?"

This was too much. I pointed out somewhat hurriedly
that he was a scion of one of the oldest Castilian families,
that the performance was a national gypsy dance which he
had joined in as a patriot and a patron, and that he was
my dearest friend. At the same time I was conscious that I
wished she hadn't seen his last performance.

"You don't mean to say that all that he did was in the
dance?" she said. "I don't believe it. It was only like
him." As I hesitated over this palpable truth she went on,
"I do wish he'd do it again. Don't you think you could
make him?"

"Perhaps he might if *you* asked him," I said a little maliciously.

"Of course I shouldn't do that," she returned quietly. "All the same, I do believe he is really going to do it—or something else. Do look!"

I looked and to my horror saw that Enríquez, possibly incited by the delicate gold eyeglasses of Miss Mannersley, had divested himself of his coat and was winding the four handkerchiefs tied together picturesquely around his waist, preparatory to some new performance. I tried furtively to give him a warning look, but in vain.

"Isn't he really too absurd for anything!" said Miss Mannersley, yet with a certain comfortable anticipation in her voice. "You know, I never saw anything like this before. I wouldn't have believed such a creature could have existed."

Even had I succeeded in warning him, I doubt if it would have been of any avail. For seizing a guitar from one of the musicians, he struck a few chords and suddenly began to zigzag into the center of the floor, swaying his body languishingly from side to side in time with the music and the pitch of a thin Spanish tenor. It was a gypsy love song. Possibly Miss Mannersley's lingual accomplishments did not include a knowledge of Castilian, but she could not fail to see that the gestures and illustrative pantomime were addressed to her. Passionately assuring her that she was the most favored daughter of the Virgin, that her eyes were like votive tapers, and yet in the same breath accusing her of being a "brigand" and "assassin" in her attitude toward "his heart," he balanced with quivering timidity toward her, threw an imaginary cloak in front of her neat boots as a carpet for her to tread on, and with a final astonishing pirouette and a languishing twang of his guitar, sank on one knee and blowing a kiss, threw a rose at her feet.

If I had been seriously angry with him before for his grotesque extravagance, I could have pitied him now for the young girl's absolute unconsciousness of anything but his utter ludicrousness. The applause of dancers and by-standers was instantaneous and hearty; her only contribution to it was a slight parting of her thin red lips in a half incredulous smile. In the silence that followed the applause, as Enríquez walked pantingly away I heard her saying, half to herself, "Certainly a most extraordinary creature!" In my indignation I could not help turning suddenly upon her and looking straight into her eyes. They were brown, with that peculiar velvet opacity common to the pupils of nearsighted persons, and seemed to defy internal scrutiny. She only repeated carelessly, "Isn't he?" and added, "Please see if you can find Jocasta. I suppose we ought to be going now, and I dare say he won't be doing it again. Ah! There she is. Good gracious, child! What have you got there?"

It was Enríquez's rose which Jocasta had picked up and was timidly holding out toward her mistress.

"Heavens! I don't want it. Keep it yourself."

I walked with them to the door, as I did not fancy a certain glitter in the black eyes of the Señoritas Manuela and Pepita, who were watching her curiously. But I think she was as oblivious of this as she was of Enríquez's particular attentions. As we reached the street I felt that I ought to say something more.

"You know," I began casually, "that although those poor people meet here in this public way, their gathering is really quite a homely pastoral and a national custom, and these girls are all honest hardworking peons or servants enjoying themselves in quite the old idyllic fashion."

"Certainly," said the young girl, half abstractedly. "Of course it's a Moorish dance, originally brought over, I suppose, by those old Andalusian immigrants two hundred years ago. It's quite Arabic in its suggestions. I have got something like it in an old *cancionero* I picked up at a bookstall in Boston. But," she added, with a gasp of reminiscent satisfaction, "that's not like *him!* Oh, no! *he* is decidedly original. Heavens, yes."

I turned away in some discomfiture to join Enríquez, who was calmly awaiting me with a cigarette in his mouth outside the *sala.* Yet he looked so unconscious of any previous absurdity that I hesitated in what I thought was a necessary warning. He, however, quickly precipitated it. Glancing after the retreating figures of the two women he said, "Thees mees from Boston is return to her house. You do not accompany her? I shall. Behold me—I am there."

But I linked my arm firmly in his. Then I pointed out first, that she was already accompanied by a servant; secondly, that if I who knew her had hesitated to offer myself as an escort it was hardly proper for him, a perfect stranger, to take that liberty; that Miss Mannersley was very punctilious of etiquette which he, as a Castilian gentleman, ought to appreciate.

"But will she not regard lofe—the admiration excessif?" he said, twirling his thin little mustache meditatively.

"No; she will not," I returned sharply, "and you ought to understand that she is on a different level from your Manuelas and Carmens."

"Pardon, my friend," he said gravely. "Thees women are ever the same. There is a proverb in my language. Listen: 'Whether the sharp blade of the Toledo pierce the satin or the goatskin, it shall find behind it ever the same heart to wound.' I am that Toledo blade—possibly it is you, my friend. Wherefore let us together pursue this girl of Boston on the instant."

But I kept my grasp on Enríquez's arm and succeeded in restraining his mercurial impulses for the moment. He halted and puffed vigorously at his cigarette, but the next instant he started forward again.

"Let us, however, follow with discretion in the rear; we shall pass her house; we shall gaze at it; it shall touch her heart."

Ridiculous as was this following of the young girl we had only just parted from I nevertheless knew that Enríquez was quite capable of attempting it alone. I thought it better to humor him by consenting to walk with him in that direction, but I felt it necessary to say:

"I ought to warn you that Miss Mannersley already looks upon your performances at the *sala* as something *outré* and peculiar, and if I were you I shouldn't do anything to deepen that impression."

"You are saying she ees shock?" said Enríquez gravely.

I felt I could not conscientiously say that she was shocked and he saw my hesitation.

"Then she have jealousy of the señoritas," he observed with insufferable complacency. "You observe! I have already said. It is ever so."

I could stand it no longer.

"Look here, Harry," I said, "if you must know it, she looks upon you as an acrobat—a paid performer."

"Ah"—his black eyes sparkled. "The torero, the man who fights the bull, he is also an acrobat."

"Yes, but she thinks you a clown!—a *gracioso de teatro*,—there!"

"Then I have make her laugh?" he said coolly.

I don't think he had but I shrugged my shoulders.

"*Bueno!*" he said cheerfully. "Lofe, he begin with a laugh, he make feenish with a sigh."

I turned to look at him in the moonlight. His face presented its habitual Spanish gravity, a gravity that was almost ironical. His small black eyes had their characteristic irresponsible audacity, the irresponsibility of the vivacious young animal. It could not be possible that he was really touched with the placid frigidities of Miss Mannersley. I remembered his equally elastic gallantries with Miss Pinkey Smith, a blonde western belle, from which both had harmlessly rebounded. As we walked on slowly I continued more persuasively:

"Of course this is only your nonsense, but don't you see, Miss Mannersley thinks it all in earnest and really your nature?" I hesitated, for it suddenly struck me that it *was* really his nature. "And hang it all! You don't want her to believe you a common buffoon or some intoxicated *muchacho*."

"Intoxicated?" repeated Enríquez, with exasperating languishment. "Yes, that is the word that shall express itself. My friend, you have made a shot in the center—you have ring the bell every time! It is intoxication—but not of *aguardiente*. Look! I have long time an ancestor of whom is a pretty story. One day in church he have seen a young girl, a mere peasant girl, pass to the confessional. He look her in her eye, he stagger"—here Enríquez wobbled pantomimically into the road—"he fall!"—he would have suited the action to the word if I had not firmly held him up. "They have take him home where he have remain without his clothes and have dance and sing. But it was the drunkenness of *love*. And look you, thees village girl was a nothing, not even pretty. The name of my ancestor was—"

"Don Quixote de la Mancha," I suggested maliciously. "I suspected as much. Come along. That will do."

"My ancestor's name," continued Enríquez gravely, "was Antonio Hermenegildo de Salvatierra, which is not the same. Thees Don Quixote of whom you speak exist not at all."

"Never mind. Only for Heaven's sake, we are nearing the house; don't make a fool of yourself again."

It was a wonderful moonlit night. The deep redwood porch of the Mannersley parsonage under the shadow of a great oak, the largest in the Encinal, was diapered in black and silver. As the women stepped upon the porch their shadows were silhouetted against the door. Miss Mannersley paused for an instant and turned to give a last look at the beauty of the night as Jocasta entered. Her glance fell upon us as we passed. She nodded carelessly and unaffectedly to me, but as she recognized Enríquez she looked a little longer at him with her previous cold and invincible curiosity. To my horror Enríquez began instantly to affect a slight tremulousness of gait and a difficulty of breathing, but I gripped his arm savagely and managed to get him past the house as the door closed finally on the young lady.

"You do not comprehend, friend Pancho," he said gravely, "but those eyes in their glass are as the *espejo ustorio*, the burning mirror. They burn, they consume me here like paper. Let us affix to ourselves thees tree. She will, without doubt, appear at her window. We shall salute her for good night."

"We will do nothing of the kind," I said sharply.

Finding that I was determined, he permitted me to lead him away. I was delighted to notice, however, that he had indicated the window which I knew was the minister's study, and that as the bedrooms were in the rear of the house, this later incident was probably not overseen by the young lady or the servant. But I did not part from Enríquez until I saw him safely back to the *sala* where I left him sipping chocolate, his arm alternating around the waists of his two previous partners in a delightful Arcadian and childlike simplicity and an apparent utter forgetfulness of Miss Mannersley.

The fandangos were usually held on Saturday night. The next day being Sunday I missed Enríquez; but as he was a devout Catholic I remembered that he was at mass in the morning and possibly at the bullfight at San Antonio in the afternoon. But I was somewhat surprised on the Monday morning following, as I was crossing the plaza, to have my arm taken by the Reverend Mr. Mannersley in the nearest approach to familiarity that was consistent with the reserve of this eminent divine. I looked at him inquiringly. Although scrupulously correct in his attire his features always had a singular resemblance to the national caricature known as "Uncle Sam," but with the humorous expression left out. Softly stroking his goatee with three fingers he began condescendingly:

"You are, I think, more or less familiar with the characteristics and customs of the Spanish as exhibited by the settlers here."

A thrill of apprehension went through me. Had he

heard of Enríquez's proceedings? Had Miss Mannersley cruelly betrayed him to her uncle?

"I have not given that attention myself to their language and social peculiarities," he continued with a large wave of the hand, "being much occupied with a study of their religious beliefs and superstitions"—it struck me that this was apt to be a common fault of people of the Mannersley type—"but I have refrained from a personal discussion of them. On the contrary, I have held somewhat broad views on the subject of their remarkable missionary work and have suggested a scheme of cooperation with them quite independent of doctrinal teaching, to my brethren of other Protestant Christian sects. These views I first incorporated in a sermon last Sunday week, which I am told has created considerable attention." He stopped and coughed slightly. "I have not yet heard from any of the Roman clergy but I am led to believe that my remarks were not ungrateful to Catholics generally."

I was relieved, although still in some wonder why he should address me on this topic. I had a vague remembrance of having heard that he had said something on Sunday which had offended some puritans of his flock, but nothing more.

He continued, "I have just said that I was unacquainted with the characteristics of the Spanish-American race. I presume, however, they have the impulsiveness of their Latin origin. They gesticulate—eh? They express their gratitude, their joy, their affection, their emotions generally, by spasmodic movements? They naturally dance—sing— eh?"

A horrible suspicion crossed my mind; I could only stare helplessly at him.

"I see," he said graciously. "Perhaps it is a somewhat general question. I will explain myself. A rather singular occurrence happened to me the other night. I had returned from visiting a parishioner and was alone in my study reviewing my sermon for the next day. It must have been quite late before I concluded, for I distinctly remember my niece had returned with her servant fully an hour before. Presently I heard the sounds of a musical instrument in the road, with the accents of someone singing or rehearsing some metrical composition in words that, although couched in a language foreign to me, in expression and modulation gave me the impression of being distinctly adulatory. For some little time, in the greater preoccupation of my task I paid little attention to the performance, but its persistency at length drew me in no mere idle curiosity to the window. From thence, standing in my dressing gown and believing myself unperceived, I noticed under the large oak in the roadside the figure of a young man, who by the imperfect light appeared to be of Spanish extraction. But I evidently miscalculated my own invisibility, for he moved rapidly forward as I came to the window, and in a series of the most extraordinary pantomimic gestures saluted me. Beyond my experience of a few Greek plays in earlier days, I confess I am not an adept in the understanding of gesticulation; but it struck me that the various phases of gratitude, fervor, reverence and exaltation were successively portrayed. He placed his hands upon his head, his heart, and even clasped them together in this manner."

To my consternation the reverend gentleman here imitated Enríquez's most extravagant pantomime.

"I am willing to confess," he continued, "that I was singularly moved by them, as well as by the highly creditable and Christian interest that evidently produced them. At last I opened the window. Leaning out, I told him that I regretted that the lateness of the hour prevented any further response from me than a grateful though hurried acknowledgment of his praiseworthy emotion, but that I should be glad to see him for a few moments in the vestry before service the next day, or at early candlelight before the meeting of the Bible class. I told him that as my sole purpose had been the creation of an evangelical brotherhood and the exclusion of merely doctrinal views, nothing could be more gratifying to me than this spontaneous and unsolicited testimony to my motives. He appeared for an instant to be deeply affected, and indeed quite overcome with emotion, and then gracefully retired, with some agility and a slight saltatory movement."

He paused. A sudden and overwhelming idea took possession of me, and I looked impulsively into his face. Was it possible that for once Enríquez's ironical extravagance had been understood, met and vanquished by a master hand? But the Reverend Mr. Mannersley's self-satisfied face betrayed no ambiguity or lurking humor. He was evidently in earnest; he had complacently accepted for himself the abandoned Enríquez's serenade to his niece. I felt an hysterical desire to laugh, but it was checked by my companion's next words.

"I informed my niece of the occurrence in the morning at breakfast. She had not heard anything of the strange performance, but she agreed with me as to its undoubted origin in a grateful recognition of my liberal efforts toward his co-religionists. It was she, in fact, who suggested that your knowledge of these people might corroborate my impressions."

I was dumbfounded. Had Miss Mannersley, who must have recognized Enríquez's hand in this, concealed the fact in a desire to shield him? But this was so inconsistent with her utter indifference to him, except as a grotesque study, that she would have been more likely to tell her uncle all about his previous performance. Nor could it be that she wished to conceal her visit to the fandango. She was far too independent for that, and it was even possible that the reverend gentleman in his desire to know more of Enríquez's compatriots would not have objected. In my confusion I meekly added my conviction to hers, congratulated him upon his evident success, and slipped away.

But I was burning with a desire to see Enríquez and know all. He was imaginative but not untruthful. Unfortunately, I learned that he was just then following one of his erratic impulses and had gone to a rodeo at his cousin's in the foothills, where he was alternately exercising his horsemanship in catching and breaking wild cattle, and delighting his relatives with his incomparable grasp of the American language and customs, and of the airs of a young man of fashion. Then my thoughts recurred to Miss Mannersley. Had she really been oblivious that night to Enríquez's serenade? I resolved to find out if I could without betraying Enríquez. Indeed it was possible, after all, that it might not have been he.

Chance favored me. The next evening I was at a party where Miss Mannersley by reason of her position and quality was a distinguished—I had almost written a popular—guest. But as I have formerly stated, although the youthful fair of the Encinal were flattered by her casual attentions and secretly admired her superior style and aristocratic calm, they were more or less uneasy under the dominance of her intelligence and education, and were afraid to attempt either confidence or familiarity. They were also singularly jealous of her, for although the average young man was equally afraid of her cleverness and candor he was not above paying a tremulous and timid court to her for its effect upon her humbler sisters. This evening she was surrounded by her usual satellites including, of course, the local notables and special guests of distinction. She had been discussing, I think, the existence of glaciers on Mount Shasta with a bespectacled geologist, and had participated with charming frankness in a conversation on anatomy with the local doctor and a learned professor, when she was asked to take a seat at the piano. She played with remarkable skill and wonderful precision, but coldly and brilliantly. As she sat there in her subdued but perfectly fitting evening dress, her regular profile and short but slender neck firmly set upon her high shoulders, exhaling an atmosphere of refined puritanism and provocative intelligence, the utter incongruity of Enríquez's extravagant attentions if ironical, and their equal hopelessness if not, seemed to me plainer than ever. What had this well-poised, coldly observant spinster to do with that quaintly ironic ruffler, that romantic cynic, that rowdy Don Quixote, that impossible Enríquez? Presently she ceased playing. Her slim narrow slipper, revealing her thin ankle, remained upon the pedal; her delicate fingers were resting idly on the keys; her head was slightly thrown back and her narrow eyebrows prettily knit toward the ceiling in an effort of memory.

"Something of Chopin's," suggested the geologist ardently.

"That exquisite sonata!" pleaded the doctor.

"Suthin' of Rubinstein. Heard him once," said a gentleman of Siskiyou. "He just made that pianner get up and howl. Play Rube."

She shook her head with parted lips and a slight touch of girlish coquetry in her manner. Then her fingers suddenly dropped upon the keys with a glassy tinkle; there were a few quick pizzicato chords, down went the low pedal with a monotonous strumming, and she presently began to hum to herself. I started, as well I might, for I recognized one of Enríquez's favorite and most extravagant guitar solos. It was audacious; it was barbaric; it was, I fear, vulgar. As I remembered it, as he sang it, it recounted the adventures of one Don Francisco, a provincial gallant and roisterer of the most objectionable type. It had one hundred and four verses, which Enríquez never spared me. I shuddered as in a pleasant quiet voice the correct Miss Mannersley warbled in musical praise of the *pellejo*, or wineskin, and a eulogy of the dicebox came caressingly from her thin red lips. But the company was far differently affected: the strange wild air and wilder accompaniment were evidently catching; people moved toward the piano; somebody whistled the air from a distant corner; even the faces of the geologist and doctor brightened.

"A tarantella, I presume?" suggested the doctor.

Miss Mannersley stopped, and rose from the piano.

"It is a Moorish gypsy song of the fifteenth century," she said dryly.

"It seemed sorter familiar, too," hesitated one of the young men timidly, "like as if—don't you know?—you had without knowing it, don't you know?"—he blushed slightly—"sorter picked it up somewhere."

"I 'picked it up' as you call it, in the collection of medieval manuscripts of the Harvard Library and copied it," returned Miss Mannersley coldly as she turned away.

But I was not inclined to let her off so easily. I presently made my way to her side.

"Your uncle was complimentary enough to consult me as to the meaning of the appearance of a certain exuberant Spanish visitor at his house the other night."

I looked into her brown eyes, but my own slipped off her velvety pupils without retaining anything.

Then she reinforced her gaze with a pince-nez, and said carelessly:

"Oh, it's you? How are you? Well, could you give him any information?"

"Only generally," I returned, still looking into her eyes. "These people are impulsive. The Spanish blood is a mixture of gold and quicksilver."

She smiled slightly. "That reminds me of your volatile friend. He was mercurial enough, certainly. Is he still dancing?"

"And singing sometimes," I responded pointedly.

But she only added casually, "A singular creature," without exhibiting the least consciousness, and drifted away leaving me none the wiser. I felt that Enríquez alone could enlighten me. I must see him.

I did, but not in the way I expected. There was a bullfight at San Antonio the next Saturday afternoon, the usual Sunday performance being changed in deference to the Sabbatical habits of the Americans. An additional attraction was offered in the shape of a bull and bear fight, also a concession to American taste which had voted the bullfight "slow," and had averred that the bull "did not get a fair show." I am glad that I am able to spare the reader the usual realistic horrors, for in the Californian performances there was very little of the brutality that distinguished this function in the mother country. The horses were not miserable worn-out hacks but young and alert mustangs, and the display of horsemanship by the picadors was not only wonderful but secured an almost absolute safety to horse and rider. I never saw a horse gored; although unskillful riders were sometimes thrown in wheeling quickly to avoid the bull's charge, they generally regained their animals without injury.

The Plaza de Toros was reached through the decayed and tile-strewn outskirts of an old Spanish village. It was a rudely built oval amphitheater with crumbling white-washed adobe walls and roofed only over portions of the gallery, reserved for the provincial "notables" but now occupied by a few shopkeepers and their wives with a sprinkling of American travelers and ranchmen. The impalpable adobe dust of the arena was being whirled into the air by the strong onset of the afternoon trade winds which happily, however, helped also to dissipate a reek of garlic and the acrid fumes of cheap tobacco rolled in cornhusk cigarettes. I was leaning over the second barrier waiting for the meagre and circuslike procession to enter with the keys of the bull pen, when my attention was attracted to a movement in the reserved gallery. A lady and gentleman of a quality that was evidently unfamiliar to the rest of the audience were picking their way along the rickety benches to a front seat. I recognized the geologist with some surprise, and the lady he was leading with still greater astonishment. For it was Miss Mannersley, in her precise well-fitting walking costume—a monotone of sober color among the parti-colored audience.

However, I was perhaps less surprised than the audience, for I was not only becoming as accustomed to the young girl's vagaries as I had been to Enríquez's extravagance, but I was also satisfied that her uncle might have given her permission to come as a recognition of the Sunday concession of the management, as well as to conciliate his supposed Catholic friends. I watched her sitting there until the first bull had entered, and after a rather brief play with the picadors and banderilleros, was dispatched. At the moment when the matador approached the bull with his lethal weapon I was not sorry for an excuse to glance at Miss Mannersley. Her hands were in her lap, her head slightly bent forward over her knees. I fancied that she too had dropped her eyes before the brutal situation; to my horror I saw that she had a drawing book in her hand and was actually sketching it. I turned my eyes in preference to the dying bull.

The second animal led out for this ingenious slaughter was, however, more sullen, uncertain and discomposing to his butchers. He accepted the irony of a trial with gloomy suspicious eyes, and he declined the challenge of whirling and insulting picadors. He bristled with banderillas like a hedgehog, but remained with his haunches backed against the barrier, at times almost hidden in the fine dust raised by the monotonous stroke of his sullenly pawing hoof—his one dull heavy protest. A vague uneasiness had infected his adversaries; the picadors held aloof; the banderilleros skirmished at a safe distance. The audience resented only the indecision of the bull. Galling epithets were flung at him, followed by cries of *"Espada!"* Curving his elbow under his short cloak the matador with his flashing blade in hand advanced and—stopped. The bull remained motionless.

For at that instant a heavier gust of wind than usual swept down upon the arena, lifting a suffocating cloud of dust and whirled it around the tiers of benches and the balcony, and for a moment seemed to stop the performance. I heard an exclamation from the geologist who had risen to his feet. I fancied I heard even a faint cry from Miss Mannersley, but the next moment, as the dust was slowly settling, we saw a sheet of paper in the air that had been caught up in this brief cyclone dropping, dipping from side to side on uncertain wings until it slowly descended in the very middle of the arena. It was a leaf from Miss Mannersley's sketchbook, the one on which she had been sketching.

In the pause that followed it seemed to be the one object that at last excited the bull's growing but tardy ire. He glanced at it with murky distended eyes; he snorted at it with vague yet troubled fury. Whether he detected his own presentiment in Miss Mannersley's sketch or whether he recognized it as an unknown and unfamiliar treachery in his surroundings I could not conjecture, for the next moment the matador, taking advantage of the bull's concentration, with a complacent leer at the audience advanced toward the paper. But at that instant a young man cleared the barrier into the arena with a single bound, shoved the matador to one side, caught up the paper, turned toward the balcony and Miss Mannersley with a gesture of apology, dropped gaily before the bull, knelt down before him with an exaggerated humility, and held up the drawing as if for his inspection.

A roar of applause broke from the audience, a cry of warning and exasperation from the attendants, as the goaded bull suddenly charged the stranger. But he sprang to one side with great dexterity, made a courteous gesture to the matador as if passing the bull over to him, and still holding the paper in his hand, re-leaped the barrier and rejoined the audience in safety. I did not wait to see the deadly dominant thrust with which the matador received the charging bull; my eyes were following the figure now bounding up the steps to the balcony, where with an exaggerated salutation he laid the drawing in Miss Mannersley's lap and vanished. There was no mistaking that thin lithe form, the narrow black mustache and gravely dancing eyes. The audacity of conception, the extravagance of execution, the quaint irony of the sequel could belong to no one but Enríquez.

I hurried up to her as the six yoked mules dragged the carcass of the bull away. She was placidly putting up her book, the unmoved focus of a hundred eager and curious eyes. She smiled slightly as she saw me.

"I was just telling Mr. Briggs what an extraordinary creature it was, and how you know him. He must have had great experience to do that sort of thing so cleverly and safely. Does he do it often? Of course, not just that. But does he pick up cigars and things that I see they throw to the matador? Does he belong to the management? Mr. Briggs thinks the whole thing was a feint to distract the bull," she added with a wicked glance at the geologist who, I fancied, looked disturbed.

"I am afraid," I said dryly, "that his act was as unpremeditated and genuine as it was unusual."

"Why afraid?"

It was a matter-of-fact question, but I instantly saw my mistake. What right had I to assume that Enríquez's attentions were any more genuine than her own easy indifference? And if I suspected that they were, was it fair to give my friend away to this heartless coquette?

"You are not very gallant," she said with a slight laugh as I was hesitating, and turned away with her escort before I could frame a reply.

But at least Enríquez was now accessible, and I should gain some information from him. I knew where to find him, unless he were still lounging about the building, intent upon more extravagance; but I waited until I saw Miss Mannersley and Briggs depart without further interruption.

The hacienda of Ramón Saltello, Enríquez's cousin, was on the outskirts of the village. When I arrived there I found Enríquez's pinto mustang steaming in the corral, and although I was momentarily delayed by these servants at the gateway, I was surprised to find Enríquez himself lying languidly on his back in a hammock in the patio. His arms were hanging down listlessly on each side as if in the greatest prostration, yet I could not resist the impression that the rascal had only just got into the hammock when he heard of my arrival.

"You have arrived, friend Pancho, in time," he said in accents of exaggerated weakness. "I am absolutely exhaust. I am bursted, caved in, kerflummoxed. I have behold you, my friend, at the barrier. I speak not, I make no sign at the first because I was on fire; I speak not at the feenish—for I am exhaust."

"I see; the bull made it lively for you."

He instantly bounded up in the hammock.

"The bull! *Caramba!* Not a thousand bulls! And thees one, look you, was a craven. I snap my fingers over his horn; I roll my cigarette under his nose."

"Well then—what was it?"

He instantly lay down again, pulling up the sides of the hammock. Presently his voice came from its depths, appealing in hollow tones to the sky.

"He asks me—thees friend of my soul, thees brother of my life, thees Pancho that I lofe—what it was? He would that I should tell him why I am game in the legs, why I shake in the hand, crack in the voice and am generally wipe out! And yet he, my pardner—thees Francisco—know that I have seen the mees from Boston! That I have gaze into the eye, touch the hand, and for the instant possess the picture that hand have drawn! It was a sublime picture, Pancho," he said, sitting up again suddenly, "and have kill the bull before our friend Pepe's sword have touch even the bone of hees back and make feenish of him."

"Look here, Enríquez," I said bluntly, "have you been serenading that girl?"

He shrugged his shoulders without the least embarrassment and said:

"Ah, yes. What would you? It is of a necessity."

"Well," I retorted, "then you ought to know that her uncle took it all to himself—thought you some grateful Catholic pleased with his religious tolerance."

He did not even smile. "*Bueno*," he said gravely. "That make something too. In thees affair it is well to begin with the duenna. He is the duenna."

"And," I went on relentlessly, "her escort told her just now that your exploit in the bull ring was only a trick to divert the bull, suggested by the management."

"Bah! her escort is a geologian. Naturally she is to him as a stone."

I would have continued, but a peon interrupted us at this moment with a sign to Enríquez, who leaped briskly from the hammock, bidding me wait his return from a messenger in the gateway.

Still unsatisfied of mind I waited, and sat down in the hammock that Enríquez had quitted. A scrap of paper was lying in its meshes, which at first appeared to be of the kind from which Enríquez rolled his cigarettes; but as I picked it up to throw it away I found it was of much firmer and stouter material. Looking at it more closely, I was surprised to recognize it as a piece of the tinted drawing paper torn off the "block" that Miss Mannersley had used. It had been deeply creased at right angles as if it had been folded; it looked as if it might have been the outer half of a sheet used for a note.

It might have been a trifling circumstance but it greatly excited my curiosity. I knew that he had returned the sketch to Miss Mannersley, for I had seen it in her hand. Had she given him another? And if so, why had it been folded to the destruction of the drawing? Or was it part of a note which he had destroyed? In the first impulse of discovery I walked quickly with it toward the gateway where Enríquez had disappeared, intending to restore it to him. He was just outside talking with a young girl. I started, for it was Jocasta—Miss Mannersley's maid.

With this added discovery came that sense of uneasiness and indignation with which we illogically are apt to resent the withholding of a friend's confidence, even in matters concerning only himself. It was no use for me to reason that it was no business of mine, that he was right in keeping a secret that concerned another—and a lady; but

I was afraid I was even more meanly resentful because the discovery quite upset my theory of his conduct and of Miss Mannersley's attitude toward him.

I continued to walk on to the gateway where I bade Enríquez a hurried good-by alleging the sudden remembrance of another engagement but without appearing to recognize the girl, who was moving away, when to my further discomfiture the rascal stopped me with an appealing wink, threw his arms around my neck, whispered hoarsely in my ear, "Ah! you see—you comprehend—but you are the mirror of discretion!" and returned to Jocasta. But whether this meant that he had received a message from Miss Mannersley or that he was trying to suborn her maid to carry one was still uncertain. He was capable of either.

During the next two or three weeks I saw him frequently, but as I had resolved to try the effect of ignoring Miss Mannersley in our conversation I gathered little further of their relations, and to my surprise, after one or two characteristic extravagances of allusion, Enríquez dropped the subject too. Only one afternoon, as we were parting, he said carelessly:

"My friend, you are going to the casa of Mannersley tonight. I too have the honor of the invitation. But you will be my Mercury—my Leporello—you will take of me a message to thees Mees Boston, that I am crushed, desolated, prostrate and flabbergasted—that I cannot arrive, for I have of that night to sit up with the grand aunt of my brother-in-law, who has a quinsy to the death. It is sad."

This was the first indication I had received of Miss Mannersley's advances. I was equally surprised at Enríquez's refusal.

"Nonsense!" I said bluntly. "Nothing keeps you from going."

"My friend," returned Enríquez with a sudden lapse into languishment that seemed to make him absolutely infirm, "it is everything that shall restrain me. I am not strong. I shall become weak of the knee and tremble under the eye of Mees Boston. I shall precipitate myself to the geologian by the throat. Ask me another conundrum that shall be easy."

He seemed idiotically inflexible, and did not go. But I did. I found Miss Mannersley exquisitely dressed and looking singularly animated and pretty. The lambent glow

of her inscrutable eye as she turned toward me might
have been flattering but for my uneasiness in regard to
Enríquez. I delivered his excuses as naturally as I could.
She stiffened for an instant, and seemed an inch higher.

"I am so sorry," she said at last in a level voice. "I
thought he would have been so amusing. Indeed, I had
hoped we might try an old Moorish dance together which
I have found and was practicing."

"He would have been delighted, I know. It's a great pity
he didn't come with me," I said quickly. "But," I could
not help adding with emphasis on her words, "he is such
an 'extraordinary creature,' you know."

"I see nothing extraordinary in his devotion to an aged
relative," returned Miss Mannersley quietly as she turned
away, "except that it justifies my respect for his character."

I do not know why I did not relate this to him. Possibly
I had given up trying to understand them; perhaps I was
beginning to have an idea that he could take care of
himself. But I was somewhat surprised a few days later
when after asking me to go with him to a rodeo at his
uncle's he added composedly, "You will meet Mees Boston."

I stared, and but for his manner would have thought it
part of his extravagance. For the rodeo, a yearly chase of
wild cattle for the purpose of lassoing and branding them,
was a rather brutal affair and purely a man's function; it
was also a family affair, a property stocktaking of the
great Spanish cattle owners, and strangers, particularly
Americans, found it difficult to gain access to its mysteries
and the *festa* that followed.

"But how did she get an invitation?" I asked. "You did
not dare to ask"—I began.

"My friend," said Enríquez with a singular deliber-
ation, "the great and respectable Boston herself, and her
serene venerable oncle and other Boston magnificoes have
of a truth done me the inexpressible honor to solicit of my
degraded papistical oncle that she shall come—that she
shall of her own superior eye behold the barbaric customs
of our race."

His tone and manner were so peculiar that I stepped
quickly before him, laid my hands on his shoulders, and
looked down into his face. But the actual devil which I
now for the first time saw in his eyes went out of them

suddenly, and he relapsed again in affected languishment in his chair.

"I shall be there, friend Pancho," he said with a preposterous gasp. "I shall nerve my arm to lasso the bull and tumble him before her at her feet. I shall throw the 'buck-jump' mustang at the same sacred spot. I shall pluck for her the buried chicken at full speed from the ground and present it to her. You shall see it, friend Pancho. I shall be there."

He was as good as his word. When Don Pedro Amador, his uncle, installed Miss Mannersley with Spanish courtesy on a raised platform in the long valley where the rodeo took place, the gallant Enríquez selected a bull from the frightened and galloping herd, and cleverly isolating him from the band, lassoed his hind legs and threw him exactly before the platform where Miss Mannersley was seated. It was Enríquez who caught the unbroken mustang, sprang from his own saddle to the bare back of his captive and with only the lasso for a bridle halted him on rigid haunches at Miss Mannersley's feet. It was Enríquez who in the sports that followed leaned from his saddle at full speed, caught up the chicken buried to its head in the sand without wringing its neck, and tossed it unharmed and fluttering toward his mistress. As for her, she wore the same look of animation that I had seen in her face at our previous meeting. Although she did not bring her sketchbook with her as at the bullfight, she did not shrink from the branding of the cattle, which took place under her very eyes.

Yet I had never seen her and Enríquez together; they had never to my actual knowledge even exchanged words. And now although she was the guest of his uncle, his duties seemed to keep him in the field and apart from her. Nor as far as I could detect, did either apparently make any effort to have it otherwise. The peculiar circumstance seemed to attract no attention from anyone else. But for what I alone knew, or thought I knew, of their actual relations, I should have thought them strangers.

But I felt certain that the *festa* which took place in the broad patio of Don Pedro's casa would bring them together. And later in the evening, as we were all sitting on the veranda watching the dancing of the Mexican women whose white-flounced *sayas* were monotonously rising and falling to the strains of two melancholy harps, Miss Mannersley rejoined us from the house. She seemed to be utterly absorbed and abstracted in the barbaric dances, and scarcely moved as she leaned over the railing with her cheek resting on her hand. Suddenly she arose with a little cry.

"What is it?" asked two or three.

"Nothing—only I have lost my fan."

She had risen and was looking abstractedly on the floor. Half a dozen men jumped to their feet. "Let me fetch it," they said.

"No thank you. I think I know where it is, and will go for it myself." She was moving away.

But Don Pedro interposed with Spanish gravity. Such a thing was not to be heard of in his casa. If the señorita would not permit *him*, an old man, to go for it, it must be brought by Enríquez, her cavalier of the day.

But Enríquez was not to be found. I glanced at Miss Mannersley's somewhat disturbed face and begged her to let me fetch it. I thought I saw a flush of relief come into her pale cheek as she said in a lower voice, "On the stone seat in the garden."

I hurried away leaving Don Pedro still protesting. I knew the gardens and the stone seat at an angle of the wall, not a dozen yards from the casa. The moon shone full upon it. There indeed lay the little gray-feathered fan. But close beside it also lay the crumpled black, gold-embroidered riding gauntlet that Enríquez had worn at the rodeo.

I thrust it hurriedly into my pocket and ran back. As I passed through the gateway I asked a peon to send Enríquez to me. The man stared. Did I not know that Don Enríquez had ridden away two minutes ago?

When I reached the veranda I handed the fan to Miss Mannersley without a word.

"*Bueno*," said Don Pedro gravely; "it is as well. There shall be no bones broken over the getting of it for Enríquez, I hear, has had to return to the Encinal this very evening."

Miss Mannersley retired early. I did not inform her of my discovery, nor did I seek in any way to penetrate her secret. There was no doubt that she and Enríquez had been together, perhaps not for the first time; but what was the result of their interview? From the young girl's demeanor and Enríquez's hurried departure, I could only fear the worst for him. Had he been tempted into some further extravagance and been angrily rebuked, or had he avowed a real passion concealed under his exaggerated mask, and been deliberately rejected? I tossed uneasily half the night, following in my dreams my poor friend's hurrying hoofbeats, and ever starting from my sleep at what I thought was the sound of galloping hoofs.

I rose early and lounged into the patio; but others were there before me, and a small group of Don Pedro's family were excitedly discussing something, and I fancied they turned away awkwardly and consciously as I approached. There was an air of indefinite uneasiness everywhere. A strange fear came over me with the chill of the early morning air. Had anything happened to Enríquez? I had always looked upon his extravagance as part of his playful humor. Could it be possible that under the sting of rejection he had made his grotesque threat of languishing effacement real? Surely Miss Mannersley would know or suspect something, if it were the case.

I approached one of the Mexican women and asked if the señorita had risen. The woman started, and looked covertly around before she replied. Did not Don Pancho know that Miss Mannersley and her maid had not slept in their beds that night but had gone, none knew where?

For an instant I felt an appalling sense of my own responsibility in this suddenly serious situation and hurried after the retreating family group. But as I entered the corridor a vaquero touched me on the shoulder. He had evidently just dismounted and was covered with the dust of the road. He handed me a note written in pencil on a leaf from Miss Mannersley's sketchbook. It was in Enríquez's hand, and his signature was followed by his most extravagant rubric.

FRIEND PANCHO: When you read this line you shall of a possibility think I am no more. That is where you shall slip up, my little brother! I am much more—I am two times as much, for I have marry Miss Boston. At the mission church, at five of the morning, sharp! No cards shall be left! I kiss the hand of my venerable uncle-in-law. You shall say to him that we fly to the south wilderness as the combined evangelical missionary to the heathen! Miss Boston herself say this. Ta-ta! How are you now?

Your own

ENRÍQUEZ.

Delmar of Pima

HAMLIN GARLAND

The county seat of Pima was an adobe Mexican town,
so far as its exterior went, and hugged close under the
semicircle formed by the turbid flow of the Rio Perco on
the left and the deep arroyo on the right, wherein Medicine Creek lost itself. The houses looked to be dens of
animals—and the life that went on within them was often
too cruel and too shameless for any beast to have a share
in it.

Andrew Delmar approached the river from the south,
and having been a long time on the road, was glad of the
gleam of water and the sight of a town. His little wagon
train was heavily laden with goods bought on credit in
Santa Fé, and it was his intention to set up a grocery in
San Felipe if he should safely arrive there.

As he drew down to the river bank he came upon a
bridge spanning the river, and at one end thereof stood a
gate and a small hut.

"I wonder what this means?" he said in Spanish to
José, who drove the team next to him.

"It is a toll-bridge, boss."

"Oh, I don't think so," Delmar replied.

At this moment a formidable person appeared at the
door of the hut and advanced to meet the train. He wore
a wide white hat and a big revolver swung at his hip. His
belt was well filled with cartridges.

"Good evenin', gentlemen," said he.

"Good evening. Is that a toll-bridge?" asked Delmar.

"You bet it is," was the decided reply.

"How much toll?"

The gate-keeper eyed the loads critically. "Fifteen dollars," he finally said.

Delmar turned his head and said in Spanish: "How about the river, José? it looks low. I believe we can ford it."

"I think so, too, boss."

Delmar turned his team and was moving away when the gate-keeper called out: "Don't you go to fording that river. I'll hold you up for the fifteen just the same. This bridge is a mighty accommodation ten months in the year, and you can't——"

"That's all right," said Delmar. "It don't accommodate me just now. Go on, Jack."

Delmar at this time was about thirty-five years old, and tall and thin; but his dark gray eyes had a keen hawk-like stare which could make a man feel uncomfortable. He carried two fine revolvers frankly ready for use, and the gate-keeper retired for reënforcements. Delmar put his teams into the shallow river, whose sandy bottom he found to be hard and smooth. As he emerged from the water on the town-side the gate-keeper, reënforced by another influential citizen of the town, confronted him.

"You'd better pony up the metal," he said menacingly. "We don't allow no funny business about it."

"Get out of my way," replied Delmar, and his hand fell with a swift flirt upon his revolver. "You'll repent any gun-play you start with me." There was something in his tone which ended the controversy, for the moment at least. The two tax-gatherers retired, muttering threats.

"We'll make this town hot for you."

"That's all right," he replied; "I'm used to a hot climate."

Delmar was a natural-born politician, and before he had covered his goods with a roof he had possessed himself of the situation in the county. First of all, the cattle element ("The Cowmen") held every office and controlled every election. Cowboys were privileged to "shoot up" the town and have roaring times without regard to the "greasers" or ordinary citizens. Law was for them license and the restraint to their opponents. To kill a Mexican was reprehensible, but not criminal. To stampede a herd of cattle through a drove of sheep was considered a useful, practical joke. It tended to keep the sheep-herders humble, and diminished the number of sheep who destroyed the range for cattle. Secondly, this element was "Democratic," and considered itself the aristocracy of the county in contradistinction to the Mexican, or "greaser" population.

In the eyes of these cattle barons and their retainers the greaser was a nuisance. He was given to cultivating the soil along the river-beds, and might be seen any day wading like a snipe in the red mud of his irrigating ditches. They were getting too plenty anyhow and needed to be discouraged. They interfered with the water-rights, and were coming to be so infernal sharp as to argue their rights, saying, "We have as good a claim to the government range as you cattlemen."

The Mexicans, as a matter of fact, knew very little about American politics or any other kind, but they were "agin the government," so far as they knew it. They collected, therefore, under the Republican banner, and made persistent but ineffectual efforts to gain their rights in the county. Numerically they were considerably in the lead, but as the cattlemen controlled all the election machinery, numbers did not count. At the time when Delmar crossed the river and became a citizen of Felipe, the cattlemen were calm and complacent in despotic control of the county.

Delmar at once lined up with the Mexicans. He was half-Spanish, and spoke the Mexican dialect perfectly; but he was also a shrewd trader and ambitious to rule. It was his opportunity, and he seized upon it. His two drivers went out among the Mexicans at once, telling them of Delmar's parentage, and that his sympathies were with them and against the cattlemen, and also that he was going into the sheep business himself. They also spread a knowledge of his reputation as a pistol-shot, and enumerated the men in Albuquerque County who had tried to "snuff him out" and failed.

As a result of this work, and by virtue of his own engaging manner, Delmar did a roaring trade from the start. He bought wool and sold goods, "catching 'em goin' and comin'," as the saying is. He was attentive, alert, and smiling, and withal exact in his dealings. He said frankly, "I'm here to make money, but I'll give you as good a deal as any other merchant and treat you like men, but right there I stop. I'm not selling goods for my health. What

I say I'll do, you may bank on, and I'm on your side in this fight against the cattle interest."

He invited leading citizens among the Mexicans to his house, and was hearty and unaffected with every man, woman, and child. The women chattered for hours about him, and came at last to trust him absolutely.

After a careful study of the situation Delmar said to a group of influential Mexicans, "What you want to do first is to get your votes counted."

This remark he made dispassionately, but he was considerably more insistent on the election day which followed. Not a single Republican vote appeared in the count of his voting precinct, though a dozen were known to have voted for the Republican candidate.

After the vote was announced, Delmar walked up to the desk behind which the judges sat smoking comfortably.

"Howdy, gentlemen?" said he.

"Howdy, Delmar? Come in."

"No, thank you. I just called to know where my Republican vote is. I voted the straight ticket, and it does not appear in the returns."

The chairman looked amused. "Is that so? Well, you know how it is—one vote that way—it must have got lost in the shuffle."

This pleased the other judges, and they laughed together most heartily.

With a deadly earnestness which stopped their gaping mouths in a distorted grin, Delmar said, "Gentlemen, at the next election my vote will not get lost in the shuffle. Good-night."

In the months which followed he set to work quietly to organize the Mexican vote, and a year later, at the head of seventy-five men, he marched to the polls, and walking up to the window, thrust his head in, and without greeting said:

"Gentlemen, last year my Republican vote got lost in the shuffle. I don't think it will this time."

The judges were insolent. "How are you going to help yourself?"

"I'm going to see that you count it," replied Delmar. He took a ticket and read it aloud to his men and to all the judges. He then handed it in and said, "I here deposit my vote. If that ballot does not appear on the returns I shall hold every man of you personally responsible for its loss."

He then called up his Mexican supporters one by one and read their ballots. One by one they deposited their ballots, and when they had finished, Delmar said:

"Seventy-six Republican ballots must appear in the returns or you will answer for them." The judges sat in silence, too amazed to formulate a sentence.

As the time for closing the polls came, Delmar was present, and the clerk said with insolent inflection:

"It is customary to clear the room during the counting of the ballots. Mr. Delmar, you must retire."

"This is a public room, and as I have no representative on your board I shall stay."

"Clear the room," called the chairman angrily.

Delmar stepped to the door and threw it open. Twenty swart and resolute Mexicans, armed and ready for battle, filed into the room, ominously silent, their eyes on their leader.

Delmar, calm with the calmness of the rattlesnake, walked toward the window and said: "Go on with your count, and if every one of those seventy-six ballots does not appear in the returns, we'll kill every man of you right where you sit. You can't count us out the way you do the niggers in Arkansas."

With trembling fingers the judges went on with their counting, and the Mexican vote was returned in full.

"Gentlemen, I am obliged to you. Before another election comes I shall make arrangements to have every other polling place in the county guarded, and I here publicly announce myself a candidate for the office of sheriff. If the Democrats of this county want war, they can have it to their complete satisfaction."

II

The lawlessness of the cattle element had become unbearable. As the sheep industry grew, the cattlemen resorted to every violence and abuse. Women were insulted, herders were fired upon, horses were stampeded through the sheep, drunken cowboys rode up and down the streets of the Mexican towns shooting at every head, and the sheriff could never seem to find these lawbreakers. He was always somewhere else when they passed by.

Under these conditions Delmar said to his followers, "We will make the fight on sheriff."

"But, señor, they will kill you," said old Pérez.

"I have the reputation of defending myself, Pérez. If you'll stand by me I'll take the risk. But we must be organized like an army. We must know where to find every man."

"Very good, señor; it shall be done."

By this time Delmar was known to every man in Pima County. He dressed in plain black like a minister, with a broad black hat and a little lawn tie. He made a point of going unarmed. He was always low-voiced and genial, but there was something formidable in the contrast between his grisly reputation and his pleasant and kindly presence. Only now and then did some inconsiderate person see the set glare of his blue-gray eyes. It was well understood also that he had seen service in the cattle wars of Texas.

Every effort was made to defeat him, but he was too strong for them. The Mexicans outnumbered the cattlemen nearly one hundred ballots, and by his personal efforts the returning boards of all the principal precincts had a Mexican representative, and the count promised to be fair. Just before election he heard that two hundred fraudulent names were to be added to the voting list, and he set forth to prevent this. He called on the recorder, and after some preliminary talk on the weather, said: "I understand that two hundred fraudulent votes have been added to the voting list. Those names are valuable to me. It will be a good deal of trouble to you to pick 'em out, and so I brought along some money to pay you. Deliver me those names, and you enable me to defeat a villainous conspiracy, and you earn five thousand dollars." He got the names.

He then went to the registrar and hired him to mix the names so that the real and the bogus were inextricable. Passing then to the judges of the precinct where the names were to be voted, he hired them to vote the names for his ticket. The other side would vote them too, but Delmar had made sure that the two fraudulent lists not merely offset each other, but also exposed the cattlemen—put the laugh on them. Delmar was elected. After the vote was announced he mounted the band-stand in the little plaza and made a speech, wherein he said:

"The people of Pima County have made me sheriff, and I wish to announce that after I take my office any law-breaker will be answerable to me till he is delivered over to the law. No cowboy can 'shoot up the town,' or outrage women, or kill sheep-herders, and escape punishment so long as I can sit a horse and hold a gun. The cattle interest has known no law, and the present sheriff is a cowardly hound who daren't show his head when a boozy cow-puncher yells. They may control the courts, but the cattlemen of Pima have no string on the sheriff-elect."

This was open-handed warfare—even the cowmen had to admit that—and there were those who professed admiration for him. "I like his grit," said Hutchison, of the "Double Arrow." "I won't sanction any underhand work with such a man."

The first test of his courage came shortly after his entering upon his duties. Word was brought to him that Jack Haley was "shooting up" the town of Paint Rock, and Delmar jumped a horse and galloped over the divide to bring the desperado in. Haley heard he was coming, and stuffing his Winchester throat full of cartridges, ran into the back parlor of the "Cowboy's Home," and stood ready with his gun at full-cock expecting Delmar to come in the front way.

But the sheriff ran swiftly and noiselessly round to a side door, and stealing close to the listening desperado, thrust his own Winchester against Haley's side and said, "Drop that gun!"

Haley gave one scared look at Delmar, and his gun clattered to the floor. His surprise and fear were so "comic" to the other cowboys that they roared over it for a whole day. Delmar mounted his horse, and with Haley meekly obeying every order, rode away. The desperado was taking no chances with a sheriff who poked Winchesters into his ribs.

Jail accommodations were not ample in San Felipe, and it was the custom to take the prisoners out to dinner at the hotel. They went in pairs handcuffed together, but were released upon entering the dining-room. Delmar called them all together one morning and said, "Now, boys, if you'll each give me your word of honor not to attempt to run I'll leave the handcuffs off."

No one saw any humor in the phrase "word of honor," and each man solemnly pledged himself to return promptly to his cell under all conditions, and thereafter the handcuffs were discarded, and the convicts moved to their dinner like gentlemen of a jury, with Delmar quietly bringing up the rear.

For a week or two all went well, but one noon as they

were returning from their dinner Haley broke away and ran. The wind was blowing a gale, and the streets were full of dust, and Delmar could only dimly see the flying figure. He shouted, "Back to your cells, boys!" and took after the dishonorable cowboy. The flight had been well planned. Haley's own horse, a fine bay, stood bridled and saddled at a street corner, and before Delmar could fire, the fugitive was mounted and sweeping out on the plain at arrow speed.

Running wildly, Delmar followed, hoping to intercept him at the bridge. Just as he was about to halt in despair he met a man driving a superb young mare in a cart. Delmar called, "Stop, drop the lines! I must have your horse—I'm the sheriff."

With three or four slashes of his knife he stripped the harness from the mare, and leaping upon her back was off after his man. The mare ran magnificently, and gained rapidly on Haley, who was heavier, and whose cow-saddle weighed nearly forty pounds. For four miles it was an even thing, then Delmar began to draw quite near. Haley was a perfect horseman, and sat his horse easily and rode with great judgment, and had Delmar been indifferently mounted, he would certainly have lost his man.

At last Haley's horse stumbled and nearly fell, and Delmar drew close enough to say pleasantly:

"Better surrender."

"Never, by God!" Haley replied, making a motion to shoot.

Delmar threw himself far over behind his horse and rode alongside. Haley did the same, slipping so far that his saddle turned and he went to the ground and stopped his horse.

Delmar rode on out of pistol-shot, for he had only a small revolver containing but four cartridges, while Haley had the regular six-inch cowboy "gun" and was desperate. The sheriff was sure his deputies would come scurrying down the trail in a few minutes, and studied how he might keep his man occupied. Both horses were trembling with fatigue and dripping with sweat. Haley was confident and glad of a chance to breathe his horse.

"You'd better clear the track," he said. "As soon as my horse gets his wind I'm going to ride right over ye."

"You'll be a dead man before you hit leather," replied Delmar. "You keep your distance, and don't attempt to mount your horse; if you do, you get hurt."

"I saw your gun, it ain't worth a cent at this distance," said Haley with a grin. "It's nothing but a popgun. I don't want to plug ye, but I'll have to if ye don't clear the track."

Both men were dismounted and looking at each other over the necks of their horses. Each was well versed in the tricks of the range, and neither was anxious to begin.

"See here, Delmar, I don't want to kill you—you've treated me white; you better let me go."

"That's mighty kind of you, Bill; but I reckon I'll stay right here. It's a black mark on me if you get away. I'm due to die or take you back. I tell you right now I'm going to have you dead or alive."

Haley smiled again, a wicked smile, but Delmar saw a cloud of dust far up on the rise, and his blood leaped. Tom, his deputy, was coming, riding Blaze, who had no equal in the county. Haley was nerving himself for his charge and suspected nothing of reënforcements.

Just as he was about to mount, Delmar threw himself on his horse and rode away up the trail.

Haley laughed and said, "Going to give it up?"

"Oh, no—I'm just keeping out o' range."

Haley was instantly suspicious, and looking around saw the oncoming horses. He threw himself into his saddle and spurred straight at the sheriff.

Delmar reined his horse out of the road and went to cover behind his neck, but Haley did not shoot for some reason.

Down the hill came the blaze-face sorrel, with neck outthrust and his wild eyes rolling, and on his back with a Winchester in his hands was Tom Pérez. He passed like a whirlwind, and a moment later threw his gun to his shoulder and fired.

Haley went down in a cloud of dust, and before he could rise Tom stood over him with the butt of his gun upraised, ready to brain the helpless desperado.

"Hold on! Don't kill him!" called Delmar in Spanish. "If you strike him I'll fire," he said, as he rode up and dismounted.

Haley appeared grateful, and as they helped him up he gave Delmar a look like that a dog might give on being released from a trap. The bullet had gone through the cantle of his saddle and into the fleshy part of his hip. He was not much hurt, but the fight was taken out of him, and he returned to jail without a word of protest.

Delmar was eager to know what happened to the other prisoners.

"They rounded themselves up and returned to jail, every man of them," the citizens reported.

"They are gentlemen," said Delmar, greatly relieved. "I'll stand treat to the crowd to-morrow."

III

Haley's case was made an issue by the cattlemen, and they rallied to his support. A cowboy jury acquitted him of the charges of "shooting with intent to kill" and "resisting an officer of the law." They decided that he was harmlessly amusing himself by "having a little Fourth of July all by hisself," and as for resisting the officer, he didn't know who Delmar was, and so was not guilty of that.

On the night of Haley's release the town filled up with cowboys, and in "Charley's Place" a gang collected to celebrate their victory over Delmar, and to threaten the sheriff with extinction. In the midst of it the door opened and Delmar walked in alone, looking very meek and mild in his black suit and white tie. He was apparently unarmed and perfectly serene. He called for a lemonade, and while it was being prepared turned to the amazed cowboys and said:

"Have all the fun you can, boys; but at midnight this place closes its doors and you leave town. Haley, I think the treat is on me. What will you have?"

Haley took a Chicago cocktail and grinned pleasantly.

"You done your duty, Cap, but I held better cards."

"I don't go back on the jury's verdict, Bill; but I notify you right now that when you resist arrest again you'll be meat for a coroner's jury."

"That's all right, Sheriff; I ain't a-monkeyin' with the buzz-saw twice in the same place."

It required courage to turn his back to these ruffians, but Delmar did it, and nothing was said till he closed the door behind him. Then Haley said:

"Say, boys, I like nerve, and that greaser sheriff has got it. If he didn't stand in with sheep men I'd say let him alone."

"He's got to be killed; he's too fresh," said Jim Tate. "If he comes fussin' 'round me I hand it to him, now you hear me! I won't have no greaser walkin' around on my neck."

"You better let him alone," persisted Haley. "He's a bad man to dodge. I know, for I tried it."

At twelve o'clock Dutch Charley nervously approached, and most apologetically explained: "Boys—I peg you vill oxcoose me—put dot Delmar has ordered me to glose up already. You must bull your freight right away. Sure ting, poys. I tondt vant no druck mit dot sheriff."

They grumbled and swore, but moved out one by one and rode away quietly. No one yelled or fired a gun till he was well out of town and safe.

Delmar met every test. He proved himself fearless and cool and adroit. No man ever got the drop on him. When he went after a criminal he got him. Twice he brought in his man in a blanket, and once the coroner's services were required. After that no cattleman openly spoke of resisting him, though a half-dozen began to plan his undoing in other ways. They opposed his reëlection, but without success. He held every Mexican vote in his hand, and added a few Democrats who were tired of lawlessness and wanted the county cleared of its cutthroats and robbers. Naturally, the sheep industry throve under his rule.

During his second term the opposition found its opportunity. Delmar had established a trading post on the neighboring Indian reservation, and found it necessary to spend a good deal of time there. The county was quiet, there were few prisoners, and with his brother as deputy, Delmar felt safe in leaving the county temporarily during the time when court was not in session, especially as he was always within call.

One morning just as the dawn was breaking, Tom Pérez rode up to his trading post on a reeking, panting, trembling horse, bringing a message from Carlos, his brother.

"Come, quick as God'll let ye! Court meets to-morrow. The judge has declared the office of sheriff vacant, and has appointed Abe Snively to fill it. Hell's to pay."

Delmar had the blaze-face sorrel in game condition for just such emergencies as this, and in two minutes was mounted and riding south. San Felipe was seventy-five miles away, but just as the sun was setting he rode into the jail-yard, and his brother with shining face rushed to meet him.

"I'm glad to see you, old man. We haven't a minute to spare."

Within the jail Delmar found several of his most trusted friends among the Mexicans, and after a few minutes' talk with them each rode away in an opposite direction, without signs of haste, but with eyes hot and lips firm-set.

In "Charley's Place" some seventy-five cowboys and cattlemen were gathered to celebrate their anticipated victory over "the greaser sheriff." The judge, a big slouch of a man, was playing "cinch" with the county attorney and Snively, the man they had united to make sheriff. They were all pretty drunk when Delmar walked in quietly, without hurry and without bluster. Every man in the room was his enemy, and every one was armed but himself. He moved straight toward the group at the table, and as he came their faces set in surprise and fear. His approach was as sinister as the movement of a wildcat, but his smoothly-shaven face was fair as a boy's, and his broad hat sat gracefully on his head. His small hands seemed to glisten like those of a woman, and his black suit suggested priests and undertakers.

The room was absolutely silent as he reached the table, and every word he spoke could be heard in the farthest corner of the room.

"Judge Murdock, I understand you have declared the office of sheriff vacant. I give notice that I am still the Sheriff of Pima County, and will be until I am impeached by a jury of my peers and after a fair, open trial. I shall open court to-morrow morning." Turning, he said, "Boys, take a drink with me."

A few straggled hesitatingly up to the bar and drank. The others remained stupidly, sullenly silent.

Again Delmar turned his back and walked out with seventy-five armed and angry men behind him. His safety lay in the fact that he was unarmed.

IV

The court-room occupied one quarter of an adobe block. The jail formed the south half, and the northeast corner contained the judge's room and the jury-room. The building was one story high, and a piazza ran round the end and across the side of the court-room, which had three windows to the north and one window and a door to the east. It was filled with rude benches seating about one hundred people, and when Delmar and his brother Carl led the prisoners into the room next day, every seat was occupied by an armed retainer of the cattlemen. The room was noisy with the loud witticisms of these men, who were confident, jocular, and "aching for trouble."

Delmar found Snively in the sheriff's place. The judge was in his seat joking with the attorneys and trying to appear at ease. Delmar sent Carl into the prisoners' pen with his charges, and drawing a chair close beside Snively gently took a seat and fixed his penetrating glance upon the judge, who was chewing tobacco nervously while retaining his attitude of easy confidence.

At last, taking the bull by the horns, the judge turned and said in an affectedly easy tone, "Mr. Snively, open court."

Snively started to obey, but Delmar's small hand pressed upon his arm, and his menacing eyes pierced to the man's cowardly soul.

"If you move, I'll kill you," he said. Then he rose. As his tall form lifted, the door leading to the judge's room opened, as if upon signal, and twenty Mexicans with repeating rifles in their arms entered silently, two by two, and filed down the wall. Their swart faces were resolute, and their dark eyes were balefully agleam. As they lined up, elbow to elbow, the noise of hurrying feet on the porch outside arose. The cattlemen turned, and as they looked their faces grew gray with fear. Every window bristled with Winchesters, and in the doorway knelt Tom Pérez and old Juan Mendoza with magazine guns ready, while over their shoulders peered three sinister and determined sheep-herders, their rifles at full cock. There was something appalling in the suddenness of this beleaguerment, but deadlier still was the look on the faces of these brown men. They were there to kill and to die if need be, and in their silence, their exaltation of bearing, the cattlemen saw annihilation. They were like rats in a trap. The Mexicans could pump them full of lead, killing them at ease and instantly.

The judge was no fool. He comprehended his danger and felt the power of the sheriff. His hands shook, and his face was like yellow paper as he looked to left and right. Not a word was spoken till Delmar, stepping before the bench, began sternly to speak.

"Judge Murdock, you put up a plot to oust me. You declared the office of sheriff vacant, and appointed a man to fill the vacancy. I want to know by what right? I was elected sheriff by the people of Pima County. By what process of law did you remove me? Is there a line of ink as a record of an investigation or trial? Will you quote the statute by virtue of which you set me aside?"

After each question he waited for a reply, but none came. His voice rang through the room, which was perfectly silent save for the labored breathing of the excited men. The judge cowered on his bench, all his assumed complacency gone.

"I will not take my dismissal from a scoundrel of your stripe. You are a blackguard and a loafer. You are indictable at this minute for a dastardly crime. You left Arkansas between two days—but your career in this county is nearly ended. I will never rest till you leave here, the low-lived hound I know you to be." Then turning to the spectators he said, "I was elected Sheriff of Pima—I am sheriff now, and shall continue to be until removed by due process of law. *Oyez, Oyez,* the County Court of Common Pleas of Pima is now open."

Turning to Carl, he said, "Remove the prisoners."

Carl led his charges back to jail, and Delmar, taking his seat beside the appointee-sheriff, waited the further action of the judge.

The Mexicans never for a moment relaxed their vigilance. Every Winchester remained at full cock, every hand was close upon the trigger—a word, a sign from Delmar, and the slaughter would begin—every cattleman knew it. The county attorney said in a low voice to the terrified magistrate:

"Dismiss the court, you fool!"

The judge looked around him at the rifles, at Delmar, at the empty prisoners' dock, and at last in a weak, flat, dry voice said:

"The court is adjourned till to-morrow morning."

"Open up, boys, but keep your guard!" called Delmar to the men at the door. "Keep the drop on every man."

They opened up, and slowly, almost sedately, the cattlemen and their hustlers filed out and down the street. Delmar was in command of the empty court-room.

V

The cowboys withdrew to the mesa above the town, and there intrenched themselves. All the inhabitants of that end of the village fled to Delmar, reporting many threats uttered by the cattlemen, who had entered the saloons and were carrying away liquor. Battle seemed unavoidable.

Mounted on a fine black horse, and totally unarmed, Delmar rode up the street and began climbing the hill— one man against a hundred. The women moaned and prayed, and the men stood on the roofs of the houses watching, expecting each moment to see a white puff of smoke and—but the black horse climbed steadily up and up, and at last stood upon the level ground.

A group of men rode forward from the cattlemen's camp and met the sheriff. Hutchison, of the "Double Arrow," was among the group, but Snively was spokesman.

"What do you want here?" he asked angrily.

Delmar ignored him. "Mr. Hutchison," he said politely and calmly, "I ask your aid to help dispose of this mob of armed men. Some of them are your hired hands, others are your friends. As sheriff of the county, I order you to proceed quietly to your homes."

Hutchison remained silent with his eyes on the ground, and leaving him and Snively behind him, Delmar rode straight toward the camp. His body was curiously numb, and the skin of his cheeks felt stiff and dry, but his head was clear. As he rode up, several reckless ruffians drew their revolvers, but their companions beat them down with warning oaths.

Delmar lifted his voice: "Boys, you are unlawfully assembled and likely to make trouble. As Sheriff of the County of Pima, I order you to disperse."

A chorus of scornful outcries answered him, and when he spoke again his voice came through set teeth.

"I give you just one hour to clear this mesa; at the end of that time I will clear it at the mouths of a hundred Winchesters."

Turning his horse, he rode away slowly. He did not put his horse to the gallop till he reached the street level.

Meanwhile the word had gone out to all the ranches that war had come, and the Mexicans, hatless, with trousers rolled to the knees, and stained with mud of the fields, came trotting into town. Nearly every man owned a gun (a weapon was considered one of the prime necessities of life), and all were ready to charge the hill at the word of command.

Delmar, seated upon his horse, with his eyes upon the mob, looked often at his watch, and spoke often to say,

"Wait, wait," to his excited little army. Between two such mobs the slaughter would be appalling. One by one he swore in his deputies, until nearly eighty men of all ages but of equal bravery were assembled at his back.

About fifteen minutes before the hour was up a squad of the cattlemen drew apart from the rest and swept down upon the town howling like wolves.

"Hide. Hunt your holes. Don't fire till I tell you," shouted Delmar.

Instantly the main body of his supporters disappeared, leaving him in the middle of the street, but every chimney-pot seemed to sprout a shining steel tube.

The reckless cowboys swept round in a wide circle through the edge of the town. Twice they crossed the main street, and seeing no one but Delmar and Tom Pérez and Carl, they came to a halt and shouted:

"Come and take us, you ——— greaser!"

Delmar held up his hand, and all about him the clicking of locks that followed his movement was like the sounds of hidden insects.

"You are covered by eighty guns. Fire one shot, and not one of you will breathe another breath." His voice was not loud, but it reached and made them pause and confer. Some of them were still for fight, but others said, "He's called our bluff; let's skin back up the hill."

"Four to one is too many—and us mounted. I'm for retreat."

As they were slowly withdrawing, one of them raised a shout and pointed to the mesa top. A band of fifteen cattlemen led by Hutchison on his pinto pony were riding away. The mob was beginning to disintegrate. By the time the bluffing party reached the mesa top, only a half-dozen remained, and they were preparing to leave. Haley and Hutchison had each said, "Boys, I'm done. Delmar holds the most cards. Not only now, but hereafter. He's boss—and I like his grit. I'm going home, and you politicians can fight your own battles with the sheriff. Good evening."

That night a coyote clamored in hunger and fear round the deserted camp of the cattlemen. Their power was broken.

Hutchison, riding homeward, met an old gray-haired Mexican, trotting along with a shot-gun in his arms, his eyes agleam.

"Where are you going?" asked Hutchison.

"I hear Andy is having a fight," replied the old man,

breathing hard, "and I am hurrying for fear I shall miss it."

Hutchison turned to Haley:

"We can't whip a man who commands men like that. He's right and we're wrong. That's what's the matter with us. We cattlemen are on the losing side. I'm going to quit."

The Mexican

JACK LONDON

I

Nobody knew his history—they of the Junta least of all. He was their "little mystery," their "big patriot," and in his way he worked as hard for the coming Mexican Revolution as did they. They were tardy in recognizing this, for not one of the Junta liked him. The day he first drifted into their crowded, busy rooms they all suspected him of being a spy—one of the bought tools of the Díaz secret service. Too many of the comrades were in civil and military prisons scattered over the United States, and others of them, in irons, were even then being taken across the border to be lined up against adobe walls and shot.

At the first sight the boy did not impress them favorably. Boy he was, not more than eighteen and not over-large for his years. He announced that he was Felipe Rivera, and that it was his wish to work for the revolution. That was all—not a wasted word, no further explanation. He stood waiting. There was no smile on his lips, no geniality in his eyes. Big, dashing Paulino Vera felt an inward shudder. Here was something forbidding, terrible, inscrutable. There was something venomous and snakelike in the boy's black eyes. They burned like cold fire, as with a vast, concentrated bitterness. He flashed them from the faces of the conspirators to the typewriter which little Mrs. Sethby was industriously operating. His eyes rested on hers but an instant—she had chanced to look up—and she, too, sensed the nameless something that made her pause. She was compelled to read back in order to regain the swing of the letter she was writing.

Paulino Vera looked questioningly at Arrellano and Ramos, and questioningly they looked back and to each other. The indecision of doubt brooded in their eyes. This slender boy was the Unknown, vested with all the menace of the Unknown. He was unrecognizable, something quite beyond the ken of honest, ordinary revolutionists whose fiercest hatred for Díaz and his tyranny after all was only that of honest and ordinary patriots. Here was something else, they knew not what. But Vera, always the most impulsive, the quickest to act, stepped into the breach.

"Very well," he said coldly. "You say you want to work for the revolution. Take off your coat. Hang it over there. I will show you—come—where are the buckets and cloths. The floor is dirty. You will begin by scrubbing it, and by scrubbing the floors of the other rooms. The spittoons need to be cleaned. Then there are the windows."

"Is it for the revolution?" the boy asked.

"It is for the revolution," Vera answered.

Rivera looked cold suspicion at all of them, then proceeded to take off his coat.

"It is well," he said.

And nothing more. Day after day he came to his work—sweeping, scrubbing, cleaning. He emptied the ashes from the stoves, brought up the coal and kindling, and lighted the fires before the most energetic one of them was at his desk.

"Can I sleep here?" he asked once.

Aha! So that was it—the hand of Díaz showing through! To sleep in the rooms of the Junta meant access to their secrets, to the lists of names, to the addresses of comrades down on Mexican soil. The request was denied, and Rivera never spoke of it again. He slept they knew not where, and ate they knew not where nor how. Once Arrellano offered him a couple of dollars. Rivera declined the money with a shake of the head. When Vera joined in and tried to press it upon him, he said:

"I am working for the revolution."

It takes money to raise a modern revolution, and always the Junta was pressed. The members starved and toiled, and the longest day was none too long, and yet there were times when it appeared as if the revolution stood or fell on no more than the matter of a few dollars.

Once, the first time, when the rent of the house was two
months behind and the landlord was threatening dispossession,
it was Felipe Rivera, the scrub boy in the poor, cheap
clothes, worn and threadbare, who laid sixty dollars in
gold on May Sethby's desk. There were other times. Three
hundred letters, clicked out on the busy typewriters (appeals
for assistance, for sanctions from the organized
labor groups, requests for square news deals to the editors
of newspapers, protests against the highhanded treatment
of revolutionists by the United States courts), lay unmailed,
awaiting postage. Vera's watch had disappeared—
the old-fashioned gold repeater that had been his father's.
Likewise had gone the plain gold band from May Sethby's
third finger. Things were desperate. Ramos and Arrellano
pulled their long mustaches in despair. The letters must go
off, and the post office allowed no credit to purchasers of
stamps. Then it was that Rivera put on his hat and went
out. When he came back he laid a thousand two-cent
stamps on May Sethby's desk.

"I wonder if it is the cursed gold of Díaz?" said Vera
to the comrades.

They elevated their brows and could not decide. And
Felipe Rivera, the scrubber for the revolution, continued,
as occasion arose, to lay down gold and silver for the
Junta's use.

And still they could not bring themselves to like him.
They did not know him. His ways were not theirs. He
gave no confidences. He repelled all probing. Youth that
he was, they could never nerve themselves to dare to
question him.

"A great and lonely spirit, perhaps, I do not know, I do
not know," Arrellano said helplessly.

"He is not human," said Ramos.

"His soul has been seared," said May Sethby. "Light
and laughter have been burned out of him. He is like one
dead, and yet he is fearfully alive."

"He has been through hell," said Vera. "No man could
look like that who has not been through hell—and he is
only a boy."

Yet they could not like him. He never talked, never
inquired, never suggested. He would stand listening, expressionless,
a thing dead, save for his eyes, coldly burning,
while their talk of the revolution ran high and warm.
From face to face and speaker to speaker his eyes would

turn, boring like gimlets of incandescent ice, disconcerting and perturbing.

"He is no spy," Vera confided to May Sethby. "He is a patriot—mark me, the greatest patriot of us all. I know it, I feel it, here in my heart and head I feel it. But him I know not at all."

"He has a bad temper," said May Sethby.

"I know," said Vera with a shudder. "He has looked at me with those eyes of his. They do not love; they threaten; they are savage as a wild tiger's. I know, if I should prove unfaithful to the cause, that he would kill me. He has no heart. He is pitiless as steel, keen and cold as frost. He is like moonshine in a winter night when a man freezes to death on some lonely mountaintop. I am not afraid of Díaz and all his killers; but this boy, of him am I afraid. I tell you true. I am afraid. He is the breath of death."

Yet Vera it was who persuaded the others to give the first trust to Rivera. The line of communication between Los Angeles and Lower California had broken down. Three of the comrades had dug their own graves and been shot into them. Two more were United States prisoners in Los Angeles. Juan Alvarado, the federal commander, was a monster. All their plans did he checkmate. They could no longer gain access to the active revolutionists, and the incipient ones, in Lower California.

Young Rivera was given his instructions and dispatched south. When he returned, the line of communication was re-established, and Juan Alvarado was dead. He had been found in bed, a knife hilt-deep in his breast. This had exceeded Rivera's instructions, but they of the Junta knew the times of his movements. They did not ask him. He said nothing. But they looked at one another and conjectured.

"I have told you," said Vera. "Díaz has more to fear from this youth than from any man. He is implacable. He is the hand of God."

The bad temper, mentioned by May Sethby, and sensed by them all, was evidenced by physical proofs. Now he appeared with a cut lip, a blackened cheek, or a swollen ear. It was patent that he brawled, somewhere in that outside world where he ate and slept, gained money, and moved in ways unknown to them. As the time passed he had come to set type for the little revolutionary sheet they published weekly. There were occasions when he was unable to set type, when his knuckles were bruised and battered, when his thumbs were injured and helpless, when one arm or the other hung wearily at his side while his face was drawn with unspoken pain.

"A wastrel," said Arrellano.

"A frequenter of low places," said Ramos.

"But where does he get the money?" Vera demanded. "Only today, just now, have I learned that he paid the bill for white paper—one hundred and forty dollars."

"There are his absences," said May Sethby. "He never explains them."

"We should set a spy upon him," Ramos propounded.

"I should not care to be that spy," said Vera. "I fear you would never see me again, save to bury me. He has a terrible passion. Not even God would he permit to stand between him and the way of his passion."

"I feel like a child before him," Ramos confessed.

"To me he is power—he is the primitive, the wild wolf, the striking rattlesnake, the stinging centipede," said Arrellano.

"He is the revolution incarnate," said Vera. "He is the flame and the spirit of it, the insatiable cry for vengeance that makes no cry but that slays noiselessly. He is a destroying angel moving through the still watches of the night."

"I could weep over him," said May Sethby. "He knows nobody. He hates all people. Us he tolerates, for we are the way of his desire. He is alone ... lonely." Her voice broke in a half sob and there was dimness in her eyes.

Rivera's ways and times were truly mysterious. There were periods when they did not see him for a week at a time. Once he was away a month. These occasions were always capped by his return, when, without advertisement or speech, he laid gold coins on May Sethby's desk. Again, for days and weeks, he spent all his time with the Junta. And yet again, for irregular periods, he would disappear through the heart of each day, from early morning until late afternoon. At such times he came early and remained late. Arrellano had found him at midnight, setting type with fresh-swollen knuckles, or mayhap it was his lip, new-split, that still bled.

II

The time of the crisis approached. Whether or not the revolution would be depended upon the Junta, and the

Junta was hard-pressed. The need for money was greater than ever before, while money was harder to get. Patriots had given their last cent and now could give no more. Section-gang laborers—fugitive peons from Mexico—were contributing half their scanty wages. But more than that was needed. The heartbreaking, conspiring, undermining toil of years approached fruition. The time was ripe. The revolution hung on the balance. One shove more, one last heroic effort, and it would tremble across the scales to victory. They knew their Mexico. Once started, the revolution would take care of itself. The whole Díaz machine would go down like a house of cards. The border was ready to rise. One Yankee, with a hundred I.W.W. men, waited the word to cross over the border and begin the conquest of Lower California. But he needed guns. And clear across to the Atlantic, the Junta in touch with them all and all of them needing guns, mere adventurers, soldiers of fortune, bandits, disgruntled American union men, socialists, anarchists, roughnecks, Mexican exiles, peons escaped from bondage, whipped miners from the bullpens of Cœur d'Alene and Colorado who desired only the more vindictively to fight—all the flotsam and jetsam of wild spirits from the madly complicated modern world. And it was guns and ammunition, ammunition and guns—the unceasing and eternal cry.

Fling this heterogeneous, bankrupt, vindictive mass across the border, and the revolution was on. The custom-house, the northern ports of entry, would be captured. Díaz could not resist. He dared not throw the weight of his armies against them, for he must hold the south. And through the south the flame would spread despite. The people would rise. The defenses of city after city would crumple up. State after state would totter down. And at last, from every side, the victorious armies of the revolution would close in on the city of Mexico itself, Díaz's last stronghold.

But the money. They had the men, impatient and urgent, who would use the guns. They knew the traders who would sell and deliver the guns. But to culture the revolution thus far had exhausted the Junta. The last dollar had been spent, the last resource and the last starving patriot milked dry, and the great adventure still trembled on the scales. Guns and ammunition! The ragged battalions must be armed. But how? Ramos lamented his confiscated estates. Arrellano bewailed the spendthriftness of his youth.

May Sethby wondered if it would have been different had they of the Junta been more economical in the past.

"To think that the freedom of Mexico should stand or fall on a few paltry thousands of dollars," said Paulino Vera.

Despair was in all their faces. José Amarillo, their last hope, a recent convert who had promised money, had been apprehended at his hacienda in Chihuahua and shot against his own stable wall. The news had just come through.

Rivera, on his knees, scrubbing, looked up, with suspended brush, his bare arms flecked with soapy, dirty water.

"Will five thousand do it?" he asked.

They looked their amazement. Vera nodded and swallowed. He could not speak, but he was on the instant invested with a vast faith.

"Order the guns," Rivera said, and thereupon was guilty of the longest flow of words they had ever heard him utter. "The time is short. In three weeks I shall bring you the five thousand. It is well. The weather will be warmer for those who fight. Also, it is the best I can do."

Vera fought his faith. It was incredible. Too many fond hopes had been shattered since he had begun to play the revolution game. He believed this threadbare scrubber of the revolution, and yet he dared not believe.

"You are crazy," he said.

"In three weeks," said Rivera. "Order the guns."

He got up, rolled down his sleeves, and put on his coat.

"Order the guns," he said. "I am going now."

III

After hurrying and scurrying, much telephoning and bad language, a night session was held in Kelly's office. Kelly was rushed with business; also, he was unlucky. He had brought Danny Ward out from New York, arranged the fight for him with Billy Carthey, the date was three weeks away, and for two days now, carefully concealed from the sporting writers, Carthey had been lying up, badly injured. There was no one to take his place. Kelly had been burning the wires east to every eligible lightweight, but they were tied up with dates and contracts. And now hope had revived, though faintly.

"You've got a hell of a nerve," Kelly addressed Rivera, after one look, as soon as they got together.

Hate that was malignant was in Rivera's eyes, but his face remained impassive.

"I can lick Ward," was all he said.

"How do you know? Ever see him fight?"

Rivera shook his head.

"He can beat you up with one hand and both eyes closed."

Rivera shrugged his shoulders.

"Haven't you got anything to say?" the fight promoter snarled.

"I can lick him."

"Who'd you ever fight, anyway?" Michael Kelly demanded. Michael was the promoter's brother, and ran the Yellowstone Poolrooms, where he made goodly sums on the fight game.

Rivera favored him with a bitter, unanswering stare.

The promoter's secretary, a distinctively sporty young man, sneered audibly.

"Well, you know Roberts." Kelly broke the hostile silence. "He ought to be here. I've sent for him. Sit down and wait, though from the looks of you, you haven't got a chance. I can't throw the public down with a bum fight. Ringside seats are selling at fifteen dollars, you know that."

When Roberts arrived it was patent that he was mildly drunk. He was a tall, lean, slack-jointed individual, and his walk, like his talk, was a smooth and languid drawl.

Kelly went straight to the point.

"Look here, Roberts, you've been braggin' you discovered this little Mexican. You know Carthey's broke his arm. Well, this little yellow streak has the gall to blow in today and say he'll take Carthey's place. What about it?"

"It's all right, Kelly," came the slow response. "He can put up a fight."

"I suppose you'll be sayin' next that he can lick Ward," Kelly snapped.

Roberts considered judicially.

"No, I won't say that. Ward's a topnotcher and a ring general. But he can't hash-house Rivera in short order. I know Rivera. Nobody can get his goat. He ain't got a goat that I could ever discover. And he's a two-handed fighter. He can throw in the sleep-makers from any position."

"Never mind that. What kind of a show can he put up?

You've been conditioning and training fighters all your life. I take off my hat to your judgment. Can he give the public a run for its money?"

"He sure can, and he'll worry Ward a mighty heap on top of it. You don't know that boy. I do. I discovered him. He ain't got a goat. He's a devil. He's a wizzy-wooz if anybody should ask you. He'll make Ward sit up with a show of local talent that'll make the rest of you sit up. I won't say he'll lick Ward, but he'll put up such a show that you'll all know he's a comer."

"All right." Kelly turned to his secretary. "Ring up Ward. I warned him to show up if I thought it worth while. He's right across at the Yellowstone, throwin' chests and doing the popular." Kelly turned back to the conditioner. "Have a drink?"

Roberts sipped his highball and unburdened himself.

"Never told you how I discovered the little cuss. It was a couple of years ago he showed up out at the quarters. I was getting Prayne ready for his fight with Delaney. Prayne's wicked. He ain't got a tickle of mercy in his make-up. He'd chopped up his pardners something cruel, and I couldn't find a willing boy that'd work with him. I'd noticed this little starved Mexican kid hanging around, and I was desperate. So I grabbed him, slammed on the gloves, and put him in. He was tougher'n rawhide, but weak. And he didn't know the first letter in the alphabet of boxing. Prayne chopped him to ribbons. But he hung on for two sickening rounds, when he fainted. Starvation, that was all. Battered? You couldn't have recognized him. I gave him half a dollar and a square meal. You oughta seen him wolf it down. He hadn't had a bite for a couple of days. That's the end of him, thinks I. But next day he showed up, stiff an' sore, ready for another half and a square meal. And he done better as time went by. Just a born fighter, and tough beyond belief. He hasn't a heart. He's a piece of ice. And he never talked eleven words in a string since I know him. He saws wood and does his work."

"I've seen 'm," the secretary said. "He's worked a lot for you."

"All the big little fellows has tried out on him," Roberts answered. "And he's learned from 'em. I've seen some of them he could lick. But his heart wasn't in it. I reckoned he never liked the game. He seemed to act that way."

"He's been fighting some before the little clubs the last few months," Kelly said.

"Sure. But I don't know what struck 'm. All of a sudden his heart got into it. He just went out like a streak and cleaned up all the little local fellows. Seemed to want the money, and he's won a bit, though his clothes don't look it. He's peculiar. Nobody knows his business. Nobody knows how he spends his time. Even when he's on the job, he plumb up and disappears most of each day soon as his work is done. Sometimes he just blows away for weeks at a time. But he don't take advice. There's a fortune in it for the fellow that gets the job of managin' him, only he won't consider it. And you watch him hold out for the cash money when you get down to terms."

It was at this stage that Danny Ward arrived. Quite a party it was. His manager and trainer were with him, and he breezed in like a gusty draft of geniality, good nature, and all-conqueringness. Greetings flew about, a joke here, a retort there, a smile or a laugh for everybody. Yet it was his way, and only partly sincere. He was a good actor, and he had found geniality a most valuable asset in the game of getting on in the world. But down underneath he was the deliberate, cold-blooded fighter and business-man. The rest was a mask. Those who knew him or trafficked with him said that when it came to brass tacks he was Danny on the Spot. He was invariably present at all business discussions, and it was urged by some that his manager was a blind whose only function was to serve as Danny's mouthpiece.

Rivera's way was different. Indian blood, as well as Spanish, was in his veins, and he sat back in a corner, silent, immobile, only his black eyes passing from face to face and noting everything.

"So that's the guy," Danny said, running an appraising eye over his proposed antagonist. "How de do, old chap."

Rivera's eyes burned venomously, but he made no sign of acknowledgment. He disliked all gringos, but this gringo he hated with an immediacy that was unusual even in him.

"Gawd!" Danny protested facetiously to the promoter. "You ain't expectin' me to fight a deef mute." When the laughter subsided he made another hit. "Los Angeles must be on the dink when this is the best you can scare up. What kindergarten did you get 'm from?"

"He's a good little boy, Danny, take it from me," Roberts defended. "Not as easy as he looks."

"And half the house is sold already," Kelly pleaded. "You'll have to take 'm on, Danny. It's the best we can do."

Danny ran another careless and unflattering glance over Rivera and sighed.

"I gotta be easy with 'm, I guess. If only he don't blow up."

Roberts snorted.

"You gotta be careful," Danny's manager warned. "No taking chances with a dub that's likely to sneak a lucky one across."

"Oh, I'll be careful all right, all right," Danny smiled. "I'll get 'm at the start an' nurse 'm along for the dear public's sake. What d'ye say to fifteen rounds, Kelly—an' then the hay for him?"

"That'll do," was the answer. "As long as you make it realistic."

"Then let's get down to biz." Danny paused and calculated. "Of course, sixty-five per cent of gate receipts, same as with Carthey. But the split'll be different. Eighty will just about suit me." And to his manager, "That right?"

The manager nodded.

"Here, you, did you get that?" Kelly asked Rivera.

Rivera shook his head.

"Well, it's this way," Kelly exposited. "The purse'll be sixty-five per cent of the gate receipts. You're a dub, and an unknown. You and Danny split, twenty per cent goin' to you, an' eighty to Danny. That's fair, isn't it, Roberts?"

"Very fair, Rivera," Roberts agreed. "You see, you ain't got a reputation yet."

"What will sixty-five per cent of the gate receipts be?" Rivera demanded.

"Oh, maybe five thousand, maybe as high as eight thousand," Danny broke in to explain. "Something like that. Your share'll come to something like a thousand or sixteen hundred. Pretty good for takin' a licking from a guy with my reputation. What d'ye say?"

Then Rivera took their breaths away.

"Winner takes all," he said with finality.

A dead silence prevailed.

"It's like candy from a baby," Danny's manager proclaimed.

Danny shook his head.

"I've been in the game too long," he explained. "I'm not casting reflections on the referee or the present company.

I'm not sayin' nothing about bookmakers an' frame-ups that sometimes happen. But what I do say is that it's poor business for a fighter like me. I play safe. There's no tellin'. Mebbe I break my arm, eh? Or some guy slips me a bunch of dope." He shook his head solemnly. "Win or lose, eighty is my split. What d'ye say, Mexican?"

Rivera shook his head.

Danny exploded. He was getting down to brass tacks now.

"Why, you dirty little greaser! I've a mind to knock your block off right now."

Roberts drawled his body to interposition between hostilities.

"Winner takes all," Rivera repeated sullenly.

"Why do you stand out that way?" Danny asked.

"I can lick you," was the straight answer.

Danny half started to take off his coat. But, as his manager knew, it was a grandstand play. The coat did not come off, and Danny allowed himself to be placated by the group. Everybody sympathized with him. Rivera stood alone.

"Look here, you little fool," Kelly took up the argument. "You're nobody. We know what you've been doing the last few months—putting away little local fighters. But Danny is class. His next fight after this will be for the championship. And you're unknown. Nobody ever heard of you out of Los Angeles."

"They will," Rivera answered with a shrug, "after this fight."

"You think for a second you can lick me?" Danny blurted in.

Rivera nodded.

"Oh, come; listen to reason," Kelly pleaded. "Think of the advertising."

"I want the money," was Rivera's answer.

"You couldn't win from me in a thousand years," Danny assured him.

"Then what are you holding out for?" Rivera countered. "If the money's that easy, why don't you go after it?"

"I will, so help me!" Danny cried with abrupt conviction. "I'll beat you to death in the ring, my boy—you monkeyin' with me this way. Make out the articles, Kelly. Winner take all. Play it up in the sportin' columns. Tell 'em it's a grudge fight. I'll show this fresh kid a few."

Kelly's secretary had begun to write, when Danny interrupted.

"Hold on!" He turned to Rivera. "Weights?"

"Ringside," came the answer.

"Not on your life, fresh kid. If winner takes all, we weigh in at 10 A.M."

"And winner takes all?" Rivera queried.

Danny nodded. That settled it. He would enter the ring in his full ripeness of strength.

"Weigh in at ten," Rivera said.

The secretary's pen went on scratching.

"It means five pounds," Roberts complained to Rivera. "You've given too much away. You've thrown the fight right there. Danny'll be as strong as a bull. You're a fool. He'll lick you sure. You ain't got the chance of a dewdrop in hell."

Rivera's answer was a calculated look of hatred. Even this gringo he despised, and him had he found the whitest gringo of them all.

IV

Barely noticed was Rivera as he entered the ring. Only a very slight and very scattering ripple of halfhearted handclapping greeted him. The house did not believe in him. He was the lamb led to slaughter at the hands of the great Danny. Besides, the house was disappointed. It had expected a rushing battle between Danny Ward and Billy Carthey, and here it must put up with this poor little tyro. Still further, it had manifested its disapproval of the change by betting two, and even three, to one on Danny. And where a betting audience's money is, there is its heart.

The Mexican boy sat down in his corner and waited. The slow minutes lagged by. Danny was making him wait. It was an old trick, but ever it worked on the young, new fighters. They grew frightened, sitting thus and facing their own apprehensions and a callous, tobacco-smoking audience. But for once the trick failed. Roberts was right. Rivera had no goat. He, who was more delicately coordinated, more finely nerved and strung than any of them, had no nerves of this sort. The atmosphere of foredoomed defeat in his own corner had no effect on him. His handlers were gringos and strangers. Also they were scrubs—the dirty driftage of the fight game, without honor, without efficiency. And they were chilled, as well, with certitude that theirs was the losing corner.

"Now you gotta be careful," Spider Hagerty warned him. Spider was his chief second. "Make it last as long as you can—them's my instructions from Kelly. If you don't, the papers'll call it another bum fight and give the game a bigger black eye in Los Angeles."

All of which was not encouraging. But Rivera took no notice. He despised prize fighting. It was the hated game of the hated gringo. He had taken up with it, as a chopping block for others in the training quarters, solely because he was starving. The fact that he was marvelously made for it had meant nothing. He hated it. Not until he had come in to the Junta had he fought for money, and he had found the money easy. Not first among the sons of men had he been to find himself successful at a despised vocation.

He did not analyze. He merely knew that he must win this fight. There could be no other outcome. For behind him, nerving him to this belief, were profounder forces than any the crowded house dreamed. Danny Ward fought for money and for the easy ways of life that money would bring. But the things Rivera fought for burned in his brain—blazing and terrible visions, that, with eyes wide open, sitting lonely in the corner of the ring and waiting for his tricky antagonist, he saw as clearly as he had lived them.

He saw the white-walled water-power factories of Rio Blanco. He saw the six thousand workers, starved and wan, and the little children, seven and eight years of age, who toiled long shifts for ten cents a day. He saw the perambulating corpses, the ghastly death's heads of men who labored in the dye rooms. He remembered that he had heard his father call the dye rooms the "suicide holes," where a year was death. He saw the little patio, and his mother cooking and moiling at crude housekeeping and finding time to caress and love him. And his father he saw, large, big-mustached, and deep-chested, kindly above all men, who loved all men and whose heart was so large that there was love to overflowing still left for the mother and the little *muchacho* playing in the corner of the patio. In those days his name had not been Felipe Rivera. It had been Fernández, his father's and mother's name. Him had they called Juan. Later he had changed it himself, for he had found the name of Fernández hated by prefects of police, *jefes políticos*, and *rurales*.

Big, hearty Joaquín Fernández! A large place he occupied in Rivera's visions. He had not understood at the time, but, looking back, he could understand. He could see him setting type in the little printery, or scribbling endless hasty, nervous lines on the much-cluttered desk. And he could see the strange evenings, when workmen, coming secretly in the dark like men who did ill deeds, met with his father and talked long hours where he, the *muchacho*, lay not always asleep in the corner.

As from a remote distance he could hear Spider Hagerty saying to him: "No layin' down at the start. Them's instructions. Take a beatin' an' earn your dough."

Ten minutes had passed, and he still sat in his corner. There were no signs of Danny, who was evidently playing the trick to the limit.

But more visions burned before the eye of Rivera's memory. The strike, or, rather, the lockout, because the workers of Rio Blanco had helped their striking brothers of Puebla. The hunger, the expeditions in the hills for berries, the roots and herbs that all ate and that twisted and pained the stomachs of all of them. And then the nightmare; the waste of ground before the company's store; the thousands of starving workers; General Rosalio Martínez and the soldiers of Porfirio Díaz; and the death-spitting rifles that seemed never to cease spitting, while the workers' wrongs were washed and washed again in their own blood. And that night! He saw the flatcars, piled high with the bodies of the slain, consigned to Vera Cruz, food for the sharks of the bay. Again he crawled over the grisly heaps, seeking and finding, stripped and mangled, his father and his mother. His mother he especially remembered—only her face projecting, her body burdened by the weight of dozens of bodies. Again the rifles of the soldiers of Porfirio Díaz cracked, and again he dropped to the ground and slunk away like some hunted coyote of the hills.

To his ears came a great roar, as of the sea, and he saw Danny Ward, leading his retinue of trainers and seconds, coming down the center aisle. The house was in wild uproar for the popular hero who was bound to win. Everybody proclaimed him. Everybody was for him. Even Rivera's own seconds warmed to something akin to cheerfulness when Danny ducked jauntily through the ropes and entered the ring. His face continually spread to an unending succession of smiles, and when Danny smiled he smiled in every feature, even to the laughter wrinkles of the corners of the eyes and into the depths of the eyes themselves. Never was there so genial a fighter. His face was a running advertisement of good feeling, of goodfellowship. He knew everybody. He joked, and laughed, and greeted his friends through the ropes. Those farther away, unable to suppress their admiration, cried loudly: "Oh, you Danny!" It was a joyous ovation of affection that lasted a full five minutes.

Rivera was disregarded. For all that the audience noticed, he did not exist. Spider Hagerty's bloated face bent down close to his.

"No gettin' scared," the Spider warned. "An' remember instructions. You gotta last. No layin' down. If you lay down, we got instructions to beat you up in the dressing rooms. Savvy? You just gotta fight."

The house began to applaud. Danny was crossing the ring to him. Danny bent over, caught Rivera's right hand in both his own and shook it with impulsive heartiness. Danny's smile-wreathed face was close to his. The audience yelled its appreciation of Danny's display of sporting spirit. He was greeting his opponent with the fondness of a brother. Danny's lips moved, and the audience, interpreting the unheard words to be those of a kindly-natured sport, yelled again. Only Rivera heard the low words.

"You little Mexican rat," hissed from between Danny's gaily smiling lips, "I'll fetch the yellow outa you."

Rivera made no move. He did not rise. He merely hated with his eyes.

"Get up, you dog!" some man yelled through the ropes from behind.

The crowd began to hiss and boo him for his unsportsmanlike conduct, but he sat unmoved. Another great outburst of applause was Danny's as he walked back across the ring.

When Danny stripped, there were ohs! and ahs! of delight. His body was perfect, alive with easy suppleness and health and strength. The skin was white as a woman's, and as smooth. All grace, and resilience, and power resided therein. He had proved it in scores of battles. His photographs were in all the physical-culture magazines.

A groan went up as Spider Hagerty peeled Rivera's sweater over his head. His body seemed leaner because of the swarthiness of the skin. He had muscles, but they made no display like his opponent's. What the audience neglected to see was the deep chest. Nor could it guess the toughness of the fiber of the flesh, the instantaneousness of the cell explosions of the muscles, the fineness of the nerves that wired every part of him into a splendid fighting mechanism. All the audience saw was a brown-skinned boy of eighteen with what seemed the body of a boy. With Danny it was different. Danny was a man of twenty-four, and his body was a man's body. The contrast was still more striking as they stood together in the center of the ring receiving the referee's last instructions.

Rivera noticed Roberts sitting directly behind the newspapermen. He was drunker than usual, and his speech was correspondingly slower.

"Take it easy, Rivera," Roberts drawled. "He can't kill you, remember that. He'll rush you at the go-off, but don't get rattled. You just cover up, and stall, and clinch. He can't hurt you much. Just make believe to yourself that he's choppin' out on you at the trainin' quarters."

Rivera made no sign that he had heard.

"Sullen little devil," Roberts muttered to the man next to him. "He always was that way."

But Rivera forgot to look his usual hatred. A vision of countless rifles blinded his eyes. Every face in the audience, far as he could see, to the high dollar seats, was transformed into a rifle. And he saw the long Mexican border arid and sun-washed and aching, and along it he saw the ragged bands that delayed only for the guns.

Back in his corner he waited, standing up. His seconds had crawled out through the ropes, taking the canvas stool with them. Diagonally across the squared ring, Danny faced him. The gong struck, and the battle was on. The audience howled its delight. Never had it seen a battle open more convincingly. The papers were right. It was a grudge fight. Three quarters of the distance Danny covered in the rush to get together, his intention to eat up the Mexican lad plainly advertised. He assailed with not one blow, nor two, nor a dozen. He was a gyroscope of blows, a whirlwind of destruction. Rivera was nowhere. He was overwhelmed, buried beneath avalanches of punches delivered from every angle and position by a past master in the art. He was overborne, swept back against the ropes, separated by the referee, and swept back against the ropes again.

It was not a fight. It was a slaughter, a massacre. Any audience, save a prize-fighting one, would have exhausted its emotions in that first minute. Danny was certainly showing what he could do—a splendid exhibition. Such was the certainty of the audience, as well as its excitement and favoritism, that it failed to take notice that the Mexican still stayed on his feet. It forgot Rivera. It rarely saw him, so closely was he enveloped in Danny's man-eating attack. A minute of this went by, and two minutes. Then, in a separation, it caught a clear glimpse of the Mexican. His lip was cut, his nose was bleeding. As he turned and staggered into a clinch the welts of oozing blood, from his contacts with the ropes, showed in red bars across his back. But what the audience did not notice was that his chest was not heaving and that his eyes were coldly burning as ever. Too many aspiring champions, in the cruel welter of the training camps, had practiced this man-eating attack on him. He had learned to live through for a compensation of from half a dollar a go up to fifteen dollars a week—a hard school, and he was schooled hard.

Then happened the amazing thing. The whirling, blurring mix-up ceased suddenly. Rivera stood alone. Danny, the redoubtable Danny, lay on his back. His body quivered as consciousness strove to return to it. He had not staggered and sunk down, nor had he gone over in a long slumping fall. The right hook of Rivera had dropped him in mid-air with the abruptness of death. The referee shoved Rivera back with one hand and stood over the fallen gladiator counting the seconds. It is the custom of prize-fighting audiences to cheer a clean knockdown blow. But this audience did not cheer. The thing had been too unexpected. It watched the toll of seconds in tense silence, and through this silence the voice of Roberts rose exultantly:

"I told you he was a two-handed fighter!"

By the fifth second Danny was rolling over on his face, and when seven was counted he rested on one knee, ready to rise after the count of nine and before the count of ten. If his knee still touched the floor at "ten" he was considered "down" and also "out." The instant his knee left the floor he was considered "up," and in that instant it was Rivera's right to try and put him down again. Rivera took no chances. The moment that knee left the floor he would strike again. He circled around, but the referee circled in between, and Rivera knew that the seconds he counted were very slow. All gringos were against him, even the referee.

At "nine" the referee gave Rivera a sharp thrust back. It was unfair, but it enabled Danny to rise, the smile back on his lips. Doubled partly over, with arms wrapped about face and abdomen, he cleverly stumbled into a clinch. By all the rules of the game the referee should have broken it, but he did not, and Danny clung on like a surf-battered barnacle and moment by moment recuperated. The last minute of the round was going fast. If he could live to the end he would have a full minute in his corner to revive. And live to the end he did, smiling through all desperateness and extremity.

"The smile that won't come off!" somebody yelled, and the audience laughed loudly in its relief.

"The kick that greaser's got is something God-awful," Danny gasped in his corner to his adviser while his handlers worked frantically over him.

The second and third rounds were tame. Danny, a tricky and consummate ring general, stalled and blocked and held on, devoting himself to recovering from that dazing first-round blow. In the fourth round he was himself again. Jarred and shaken, nevertheless his good condition had enabled him to regain his vigor. But he tried no man-eating tactics. The Mexican had proved a tartar. Instead he brought to bear his best fighting powers. In tricks and skill and experience he was the master, and though he could land nothing vital, he proceeded scientifically to chop and wear down his opponent. He landed three blows to Rivera's one, but they were punishing blows only, and not deadly. It was the sum of many of them that constituted deadliness. He was respectful of this two-handed dub with the amazing short-arm kicks in both his fists.

In defense Rivera developed a disconcerting straight left. Again and again, attack after attack he straight-lefted away from him with accumulated damage to Danny's mouth and nose. But Danny was protean. That was why he was the coming champion. He could change from style to style of fighting at will. He now devoted himself to in-fighting. In this he was particularly wicked, and it enabled him to avoid the other's straight left. Here he set the house wild repeatedly, capping it with a marvelous lock-break and lift of an inside uppercut that raised the Mexican in the air and dropped him to the mat. Rivera rested on one knee, making the most of the count, and in the soul of him he knew the referee was counting short seconds on him.

Again, in the seventh, Danny achieved the diabolical inside uppercut. He succeeded only in staggering Rivera, but in the ensuing moment of defenseless helplessness he smashed him with another blow through the ropes. Rivera's body bounced on the heads of the newspapermen below, and they boosted him back to the edge of the platform outside the ropes. Here he rested on one knee, while the referee raced off the seconds. Inside the ropes, through which he must duck to enter the ring, Danny waited for him. Nor did the referee intervene or thrust Danny back.

The house was beside itself with delight.

"Kill 'm, Danny, kill 'm!" was the cry.

Scores of voices took it up until it was like a war chant of wolves.

Danny did his best, but Rivera, at the count of eight, instead of nine, came unexpectedly through the ropes and safely into a clinch. Now the referee worked, tearing him away so that he could be hit, giving Danny every advantage that an unfair referee can give.

But Rivera lived, and the daze cleared from his brain. It was all of a piece. They were the hated gringos and they were all unfair. And in the worst of it visions continued to flash and sparkle in his brain—long lines of railroad track that simmered across the desert; *rurales* and American constables; prisons and calabooses; tramps at water tanks—all the squalid and painful panorama of his odyssey after Rio Blanco and the strike. And, resplendent and glorious, he saw the great red revolution sweeping across his land. The guns were there before him. Every hated face was a gun. It was for the guns he fought. He was the guns. He was the revolution. He fought for all Mexico.

The audience began to grow incensed with Rivera. Why didn't he take the licking that was appointed him? Of course he was going to be licked, but why should he be so obstinate about it? Very few were interested in him, and they were the certain, definite percentage of a gambling crowd that plays long shots. Believing Danny to be the winner, nevertheless they had put their money on the Mexican at four to ten and one to three. More than a trifle was up on the point of how many rounds Rivera could last. Wild money had appeared at the ringside proclaiming that he could not last seven rounds, or even six. The winners of this, now that their cash risk was happily settled, had joined in cheering on the favorite.

Rivera refused to be licked. Through the eighth round his opponent strove vainly to repeat the uppercut. In the ninth Rivera stunned the house again. In the midst of a clinch he broke the lock with a quick, lithe movement, and in the narrow space between their bodies his right lifted from the waist. Danny went to the floor and took the safety of the count. The crowd was appalled. He was being bested at his own game. His famous right uppercut had been worked back on him. Rivera made no attempt to catch him as he arose at "nine." The referee was openly blocking that play, though he stood clear when the situation was reversed and it was Rivera who was required to rise.

Twice in the tenth Rivera put through the right uppercut, lifted from waist to opponent's chin. Danny grew desperate. The smile never left his face, but he went back to his man-eating rushes. Whirlwind as he would, he could not damage Rivera, while Rivera through the blur and whirl, dropped him to the mat three times in succession. Danny did not recuperate so quickly now, and by the eleventh round he was in a serious way. But from then till the fourteenth he put up the gamest exhibition of his career. He stalled and blocked, fought parsimoniously, and strove to gather strength. Also he fought as foully as a successful fighter knows how. Every trick and device he employed, butting in the clinches with the seeming of accident, pinioning Rivera's glove between arm and body, heeling his glove on Rivera's mouth to clog his breathing. Often, in the clinches, through his cut and smiling lips he snarled insults unspeakable and vile in Rivera's ear. Everybody, from the referee to the house, was with Danny and was helping Danny. And they knew what he had in mind. Bested by this surprise box of an unknown, he was pinning all on a single punch. He offered himself for punishment, fished, and feinted, and drew, for that one opening that would enable him to whip a blow through with all his strength and turn the tide. As another and greater fighter had done before him, he might do—a right and left, to solar plexus and across the jaw. He could do it, for he was noted for the strength of punch that remained in his arms as long as he could keep his feet.

Rivera's seconds were not half caring for him in the intervals between rounds. Their towels made a showing but drove little air into his panting lungs. Spider Hagerty talked advice to him, but Rivera knew it was wrong advice. Everybody was against him. He was surrounded by treachery. In the fourteenth round he put Danny down again, and himself stood resting, hands dropped at side, while the referee counted. In the other corner Rivera had been noting suspicious whisperings. He saw Michael Kelly make his way to Roberts and bend and whisper. Rivera's ears were a cat's, desert-trained, and he caught snatches of what was said. He wanted to hear more, and when his opponent arose he maneuvered the fight into a clinch over against the ropes.

"Got to," he could hear Michael, while Roberts nodded. "Danny's got to win—I stand to lose a mint. I've got a ton of money covered—my own. If he lasts the fifteenth I'm bust. The boy'll mind you. Put something across."

And thereafter Rivera saw no more visions. They were trying to job him. Once again he dropped Danny and stood resting, his hands at his side. Roberts stood up.

"That settled him," he said. "Go to your corner."

He spoke with authority, as he had often spoken to Rivera at the training quarters. But Rivera looked hatred at him and waited for Danny to rise. Back in his corner in the minute interval, Kelly, the promoter, came and talked to Rivera.

"Throw it, damn you," he rasped in a harsh low voice. "You gotta lay down, Rivera. Stick with me and I'll make your future. I'll let you lick Danny next time. But here's where you lay down."

Rivera showed with his eyes that he heard, but he made neither sign of assent nor dissent.

"Why don't you speak?" Kelly demanded angrily.

"You lose anyway," Spider Hagerty supplemented. "The referee'll take it away from you. Listen to Kelly and lay down."

"Lay down, kid," Kelly pleaded, "and I'll help you to the championship."

Rivera did not answer.

"I will, so help me, kid."

At the strike of the gong Rivera sensed something impending. The house did not. Whatever it was, it was there inside the ring with him and very close. Danny's earlier surety seemed returned to him. The confidence of his advance frightened Rivera. Some trick was about to be worked. Danny rushed, but Rivera refused the encounter. He side-stepped away into safety. What the other wanted was a clinch. It was in some way necessary to the trick. Rivera backed and circled away, yet he knew, sooner or later, the clinch and the trick would come. Desperately he resolved to draw it. He made as if to effect the clinch with Danny's next rush. Instead, at the last instant, just as their bodies should have come together, Rivera darted nimbly back. And in the same instant Danny's corner raised a cry of foul. Rivera had fooled them. The referee paused irresolutely. The decision that trembled on his lips was never uttered, for a shrill, boy's voice from the gallery piped, "Raw work!"

Danny cursed Rivera openly, and forced him, while Rivera danced away. Also Rivera made up his mind to strike no more blows at the body. In this he threw away half his chance of winning, but he knew if he was to win at all it was with the outfighting that remained to him. Given the least opportunity, they would lie a foul on him. Danny threw all caution to the winds. For two rounds he tore after and into the boy who dared not meet him at close quarters. Rivera was struck again and again; he took blows by the dozens to avoid the perilous clinch. During this supreme final rally of Danny's the audience rose to its feet and went mad. It did not understand. All it could see was that its favorite was winning after all.

"Why don't you fight?" it demanded wrathfully of Rivera. "You're yellow! You're yellow!" "Open up, you cur! Open up!" "Kill 'm, Danny! Kill 'm!" "You sure got 'm! Kill 'm!"

In all the house, bar none, Rivera was the only cold man. By temperament and blood he was the hottest-passioned there; but he had gone through such vastly greater heats that this collective passion of ten thousand throats, rising surge on surge, was to his brain no more than the velvet cool of a summer twilight.

Into the seventeenth round Danny carried his rally. Rivera, under a heavy blow, drooped and sagged. His hands dropped helplessly as he reeled backward. Danny thought it was his chance. The boy was at his mercy. Thus Rivera, feigning, caught him off his guard, lashing out a clean drive to the mouth. Danny went down. When he arose Rivera felled him with a down-chop of the right on neck and jaw. Three times he repeated this. It was impossible for any referee to call these blows foul.

"Oh, Bill! Bill!" Kelly pleaded to the referee.

"I can't," that official lamented back. "He won't give me a chance."

Danny, battered and heroic, still kept coming up. Kelly and others near to the ring began to cry out to the police to stop it, though Danny's corner refused to throw in the towel. Rivera saw the fat police captain starting awkwardly to climb through the ropes, and was not sure what it meant. There were so many ways of cheating in this game of the gringos. Danny, on his feet, tottered groggily and helplessly before him. The referee and the captain were both reaching for Rivera when he struck the last blow. There was no need to stop the fight, for Danny did not rise.

"Count!" Rivera cried hoarsely to the referee.

And when the count was finished Danny's seconds gathered him up and carried him to his corner.

"Who wins?" Rivera demanded.

Reluctantly the referee caught his gloved hand and held it aloft.

There were no congratulations for Rivera. He walked to his corner unattended, where his seconds had not yet placed his stool. He leaned backward on the ropes and looked his hatred at them, swept it on and about him till the whole ten thousand gringos were included. His knees trembled under him, and he was sobbing from exhaustion. Before his eyes the hated faces swayed back and forth in the giddiness of nausea. Then he remembered they were the guns. The guns were his. The revolution could go on.

II.

THROUGH THE
DEPRESSION TO 1940:

Realistic Profiles

With a Hey Nonny Nonny

WILLIAM SAROYAN

Within the Sunday night silence of the place he moved
along the sleeping street toward the house where Maria
lived, feeling through his movement the sharp certainty of
his life. He was glad about this, which was private, and it
was a gladness of inward smiling, but deeper within than
his smiling was his bitterness about his people, laboring in
the valley, and still deeper was his violent hatred for that
in life which made his people suffer, and he said to
himself, repeating Agunaga's words, *Tomorrow we will
make a beginning. All of us will go from the fields to our
houses and we will not pick their cotton and we will not
harvest their crops of melons and peaches and grapes, and
we will stand idle in our houses, waiting for anything. We
will go from the fields and stand in our houses.*

Agunaga was the orator, the organizer.

Walking, he felt himself reaching fully the moment of
his mortality, the clear and clean moment of his movement, to Maria, of his thought and remembrance, and he
breathed deeply, breathing the name and the substance of
the girl, grateful to God for the quiet and strong life
within himself, and breathing, he prayed, using the vocab-
ulary of simple souls, the wordless language of being, and
each intake of breath was the equivalent of a pious exclamation, devotion to God.

From a distance he heard faintly the jangling of the
player-piano that stood in the entrance way to the Hollywood Picture House. The music came to him through the

115

quietness of the night as a universal sadness in the heart of man, a strange yearning for the precise and ineffable, a melancholy longing for the grace of a solid and more precise life, for love and truth and dignity, and even if the music itself was nervous, fidgety as men had been made fidgety by the feverishness of the time, it was still somehow glorious.

He paused in the darkness of the street, listening, feeling that his own life was related to the abstract life of the jangling music, seeking to understand the meaning of himself in the street and the strange music with him there. Somewhere it seemed that he had heard the music before, only then the music had been wholly beautiful, rising from the earth itself, from the warm earth before his coming, from plants growing and streams flowing and men singing and women dancing, coming up from the truth of the earth to the warmth of the heart of man, flowing there, and now, years afterwards, returning again to the weary silence of the street as a jangling of a player-piano, an American song, the way Americans made their songs, the music nervous and the words foolish: *with a hey nonny nonny and a ha-cha-cha.*

Agunaga was sad and he was angry, and he said, We must do this. We must make this beginning. No matter what happens, no matter what they do to us, we must do it. In the morning, from the fields to our houses.

He walked on, thinking, *I am now almost seventeen and I have lived all these years upon the earth,* thinking, *no matter what happens, I shall be somewhere upon this earth forever,* thinking, *it is because of Maria, because I love her and am now walking to her,* thinking, *tomorrow all of us will turn away from the fields, our earth, and go to our houses, waiting for their wrath.*

As a small boy, going with his mother and father and his sisters and brothers from one place of laboring to another, he had dreamed Maria, feeling that she must be alive somewhere upon the earth since the thought of her was in him, of itself, as if it had been there always, time and time again, through many births and many deaths, a timelessness of heart, and on long afternoons, deep beneath the heat of a summer universe, he had seen her rise from some bright plain like a splendid flower, suddenly whole with the sun's love and miraculously mortal, of face and form, able to move and talk and laugh and sing and be silent, and he had leapt inwardly with joy and awe at the knowledge that he would someday find her, fully formed and mortal and breathing, and himself of a sufficient strength and piety to go to her, though his heart died in him with adoration, and speak to her or merely stand in her presence, saying no word, but somehow carrying with him the truth of his love, of his timeless need of her, his ancient seeking after her.

He walked on, feeling the strange rhythm of the player-piano music in his blood.

On the front porch of her house he spoke to the girl. Tomorrow, he said, Agunaga says that we must not work to make them rich.

He told her all that Agunaga had said, and the girl listened but did not speak.

She was a year younger than Rivas, lovelier and more perfect even than his dream of her, being real, and although he had known her only a month it seemed to him that he had known her always, from the first, that he had always been near her, beside her, within her, the fulfillment of herself and himself, the completion of themselves, their truth and reality, the finality of all mortality, of each as each and of each as one.

Speaking to her, he saw himself with the girl in the good house, in a quiet place of the good earth, beneath the sun, their lives quiet and timeless, and he wondered if they would let him earn enough to buy the house and a small part of the earth and be alive with her there. Would they let him live this life he wanted to live, instead of the wasteful life?

He remembered with bitterness the inevitable events of tomorrow: the going from the fields to the houses, the cessation of his labor on the earth, the singing of his body there, and he said again this time almost sadly, *Tomorrow all of us are going to leave the fields and go to the houses,* and while he spoke he could see the consequent ugliness of the performance, the rich ones angry and the poor ones angry, and then bitter hate, and then perhaps running and shouting and killing: and his blood sang *with a hey nonny nonny*.

Going from the girl, he felt himself remaining beside her, her shadow, the fullness of her being, emerging from life with her to sleep, the good sleep of the innocent and poor, his inward shape moving with her over the hidden earth, the place where he was timeless with her, where ugliness could not exist.

He was with the men in the morning, working in the field, sensing the quiet sullenness of everyone there, feeling remotely within himself that the inevitable ugliness of the event would mar his dream, perhaps destroy it, change the course of his blood and thought, and unconsciously he began to think of Maria as if he or she were dead, saying her name over and over again, breathing the bitterness of a violent and unknown frustration, his blood foolishly remarking *with a hey nonny nonny*, doing it in English, while the rest of it, more deeply inward, spoke in Mexican, saying the name, his anger coming up to his mouth because it was known in him that the event of the morning would end monstrously, in some stupid frustration, smashing the good house to pieces, annihilating the good earth, effacing the good sun, stifling his speech, stopping his laughter, mangling the inward form of Maria, killing him.

He could feel all this within himself deeply, and it was so much of an evil truth to him that he wanted to stand tall on the earth, as tall as a great tree, and shout at all who brought about such things. But he could do nothing and in desperation he turned to the man beside him, and then decided not to speak, since there was nothing to say.

Suddenly it was known among all the men that the time had come. Moving helplessly, he walked with the men from the field, his heart crying out against the performance, saying that it was evil, that they should labor because of the goodness of labor, the goodness of muscle in opposition to the inert, in relation with the whole universe.

If they speak to you, said an older man, say that you know nothing. Tell them to see Agunaga.

Yes, said the boy.

From the dirt road he turned and saw the desolating scene, his heart sickening within him, the endless field empty of man, all the cotton ready to be picked, everyone sullen and angry, and the good sun, quietly in the sky, unaware of them, and far down the road hundreds of them walking away from their labor, silently turning from the earth, refusing any longer to be of it, wanting more, wanting all, each man nourishing within himself the green, warty passion of greed, of hatred and defiance, and his own heart violent with despair and bewilderment, crying out that it was wrong, knowing that the whole thing would end foolishly, in some foolish waste of strength, and blood, and life and dream.

He saw Agunaga, slim and quiet and sorrowful, leading his people from the earth, and the man on the horse hurrying to him, dust rising from the places where the horse had run. He turned suddenly and ran down the road to Agunaga, wanting to hear what Agunaga would say, and he heard someone shout, *Rivas, come back here,* but he did not even pause or turn around, and he reached Agunaga just as the man on the horse reached him. The man's face was hideous with amazement and anger.

What do you call this? said the man on the horse, the horse stamping down the soft hot dust, the dust rising.

Agunaga answered quietly. We planted the cotton, he said. We led water to it. We killed the weeds. Now it is ready for picking and we will pick it, but we must be paid for our labor. We are going to our houses.

The man began to swear and he said he would have other workers in the field in less than an hour, and he said Agunaga and his people would have to get out of the company's houses. Or else, said the man, we will force you out.

Agunaga said nothing and the man turned on the horse and went away. Then Agunaga said, *Stay in your houses,* and from the quiet way he said this Rivas knew how bitter and angry Agunaga was.

In the afternoon, when the real trouble began, Rivas was sitting on the porch of his house, his two younger brothers and his younger sister inside with his mother. He could feel that the whole thing would turn out foolishly, something almost glorious, but like the American music foolish, and he did not know what to do or what to think because he could feel himself being torn from all that he wanted of life, and it seemed to him that he was losing Maria, which was all that he wanted since she was all, the meadow, the sky, the tree, fire, air, water.

The real trouble began when workers were brought from Bakersfield, from the pool rooms and the gambling joints, men who were not really of the earth, who were not really workers, and the trouble grew when these men, carrying shovels and clubs and guns, and urged by the company to do so, came to the houses of the Mexicans and told them to get out, many men, low and vicious and wanting to do vicious things, and the Mexicans would not get out.

The houses were simple and they weren't worth fighting about, but the Mexicans had lived in them many months,

and Agunaga had told them not to leave the houses, and
when the men from Bakersfield swore at the Mexicans
and threatened to drive them away, the big trouble began
and there was running, and Rivas, knowing that the whole
thing would end in his own death, but angry because his
brothers and his sisters and his mother were inside the
house, frightened and weeping, ran with the others, against
the men from Bakersfield, and running his blood sprang
upward madly, and he knew they would kill him since he
was fearless, and would throw himself into danger, and he
struck them, and they knocked him down, and he jumped
to his feet, swearing sullenly with his blood, knowing that
his dream would be marred forever, and there was one
man with a shovel and Rivas knocked this man down and
began swinging the shovel at the others, and he could hear
the player-piano of the Hollywood Picture House jangling
out the sad and weary music of the heart of man, *with a
hey nonny nonny*, and he stumbled and fell, and he got up
insane with rage, and just before he was shot he heard his
mother shout from the porch of his house, JUAN JUAN
JUAN, and as he fell into the blackness he knew that she
had fainted and that it was mangled, all of it, the whole
earth effaced, and his body sank into the warm earth,
blood spurting from his head, and the sun ended, and
Maria perished, and he had no thought and no dream, but
his blood was still angry and still warm and it kept leaping
upward, high as a tree, shouting her name, *Maria*, and it
was all foolish, and he knew it would be stupid like the
American music, *with a hey nonny nonny*, the whole thing
ending pathetically with his body mangled and his spirit
destroyed, as a ghastly frustration, his blood wanting
Maria and the good house and the good earth and the
warm sun, and saying over and over again, *Maria, Maria,*
and humming to him, as he turned to rock.

The Surgeon and the Nun

PAUL HORGAN

Here you are. I haven't thought of this for thirty years.
I don't know what called it to mind. I'll tell you anyway.

When I was a young doctor just out of internship I left
Chicago to come West, oh, for several reasons. I'd worked
hard and they were afraid my lungs might be a little
weakened, and then besides, I've always been independent,
and wanted to get out on my own, and I'd seen enough of
the society doctors back there. Anyway, I came on, and
heard of a new section of country in New Mexico, opening up, down toward Texas, and thinks I, I'll just go and
see about it. The hottest day I ever spent, yes, and the
next night, and the next day, too, as you'll see.

The railroad spur had been pushing down South
through the Pecos Valley, a few miles a week, and it was
in July that I got on the train and bought a ticket for
Eddy, the town I was thinking about trying.

The track was completed all the way, by then, but they
had a lot of repairing to do all the time, and no train
schedule was maintained, because we'd move, and crawl,
and then stop, baking; with nothing but dust to breathe,
white dust like filtered sunlight; outside the car window
was naked land—with freckles, I remember thinking:
spotty bushes and gravel. Above, a blue sky like hot
metal. The heat swam on the ground.

You couldn't sleep or read or think.

There was nobody to talk to in the car.

Two seats across the aisle from me was a Sister of

121

Mercy, sitting there in her black robes, skirts and sleeves, and heavy starch, and I wondered at the time, How on earth can she stand it? The car was an oven. She sat there looking out the window, calm and strengthened by her philosophy. It seemed to me she had expressive hands; I recalled the sisters in the hospital in Chicago, and how they had learned to say so much and do so much with their skilled hands. When my traveling nun picked up a newspaper and fanned herself slowly, it was more as if she did it in grace than to get cool.

She was in her early thirties, I thought, plump, placid and full of a wise delicacy and yes, independence, with something of the unearthly knowingness in her steady gaze that I used to see in the Art Institute—those portraits of ladies of the fifteenth century, who look at you sideways, with their eyebrows up.

She wore glasses, very bright, with gold bars to them.

Well, the train stopped again.

I thought I couldn't stand it. When we moved, there was at least a stir of air, hot and dusty, but at that, we felt as if we were getting some place, even though slowly. We stopped, and the cars creaked in the heat, and I felt thick in the head. I put my face out the window and saw that we had been delayed by a work gang up ahead. They were Mexican laborers. Aside from them, and their brown crawlings up and down the little road-bed embankment, there was nothing, no movement, no life, no comfort, for miles. A few railroad sheds painted dusty red stood by the trackside.

I sat for ten minutes; nothing happened. I couldn't even hear the sounds of work, ringing pickaxes or whatnot; I felt indignant. This was no way to maintain a public conveyance!

It was around one o'clock in the afternoon.

Mind you, this was 1905, it isn't a wilderness any more out here. Oh, it was then. Every time I looked out at the white horizon my heart sank, I can tell you. Why had I ever left Chicago?

Then I wondered where the Sister was traveling to.

It was strange how comforting she was, all of a sudden. I had a flicker of literary amusement out of the Chaucerian flavor of her presence—a nun, traveling, alone, bringing her world with her no matter where she might be, or in what circumstance; sober, secure, indifferent to anything but the green branches of her soul; benign about the blistering heat and the maddening delay; and withal, an object of some archaic beauty, in her medieval habit, her sidelong eyes, her plump and frondy little hands. I almost spoke to her several times, in that long wait of the train; but she was so classic in her repose that I finally decided not to. I got up instead and went down to the platform of the car, which was floury with dust all over its iron floor and coupling chains, and jumped down to the ground.

How immense the sky was, and the sandy plains that shuddered with the heat for miles and miles! And how small and oddly desirable the train looked!

It was all silent until I began to hear the noises that framed that midsummer midday silence . . . bugs droning, the engine breathing up ahead, a whining hum in the telegraph wires strung along by the track, and then from the laborers a kind of subdued chorus.

I went to see what they were all huddled about each other for.

There wasn't a tree for fifty miles in any direction.

In the heat-reflecting shade of one of the grape red sheds the men were standing around and looking at one of their number who was lying on the ground with his back up on the lowest boards.

The men were mostly little, brown as horses, sweating and smelling like leather, and in charge of them was a big American I saw squatting down by the recumbent Mexican.

"Come on, come on," he was saying, when I came up.

"What's the matter?" I asked.

The foreman looked up at me. He had his straw hat off, and his forehead and brows were shad-belly white where the sunburn hadn't reached. The rest of his face was apple colored, and shiny. He had little eyes, squinted, and the skin around them was white, too. His lips were chapped and burnt powdery white.

"Says he's sick."

The Mexicans nodded and murmured.

"Well, I'm a doctor, maybe I can tell."

The foreman snorted.

"They all do it. Nothin' matter with him. He's just play-actin'. Come on, Pancho, you get, by God, t'hell up, now!"

He shoved his huge dusty shoe against the little Mexican's side. The Mexican drooled a weak cry. The other laborers made operatic noises in chorus. They were clearly afraid of the foreman.

"Now hold on," I said to him. "Let me look him over, anyway."

I got down on the prickly ground.

It took a minute or less to find out. The little cramped up Mexican had an acute attack of appendicitis, and he was hot and sick and when I touched his side, he wept like a dog and clattered on his tongue without words.

"This man is just about ready to pop off," I told the foreman. "He's got acute appendicitis. He'll die unless he can be operated on."

The heat; the shimmering land; something to do; all changed me into feeling cool and serious, quite suddenly.

"I can perform an emergency operation, somehow, though it may be too late. Anyway, it can't do more'n kill him, and he'll die if I don't operate, that's sure!"

"Oh, no. *Oh*-ho, no, you don't," said the foreman, standing up and drawling. He was obviously a hind, full of some secret foremanship, some plainsman's charm against the evil eye, or whatever he regarded civilization as. "I ain't got no authority for anythin' like that on my section gang! And ennyhow, they all take on like that when they're tarred of workin'!"

Oh, it was the same old thing.

All my life I've got my back up over something no more my business than the man in the moon, but seems to me when it's a matter of right and wrong, or good and bad, or the like, thinks I, there's no choice but to go to work and fight.

That blasted foreman infuriated me. And I can swear when I have to. Well, I set to and gave him such a dressing down as you never heard.

I called him everything I ever heard and then I made up some more pretty ones for good measure.

I told him I'd have him up before the nearest district territorial judge for criminal negligence. I told him I was a personal friend of John J. Summerdown, the president of the new railroad, and I'd, by God, have his job so fast he wouldn't know what hit him. I told him that anybody'd stand by and let a man die instead of taking every chance there was to save him, I said was lower'n— Anyway, you can't go through medical school without picking up a few fancy words.

He cocked his elbows and fists at me a couple of times.

But when I'm right, I know I'm right, and that's all you need to handle a peasant like that.

He got scared, and we both wiped the sweat off our brows at the same minute, the same gesture, and glared at each other, and I wondered if I looked as hot and messy and ignorant as he did, and I laughed.

The Mexicans were curious and asking questions and clawing at him. I turned around, like a nervous old maid, or a scared child, to see if the train was still there.

It had become a symbol of safety to me, the only way out of that yellow, yellow plain streaming with sunlight. Yes, it was still there, dusty black, and dusty white where the light rested.

The foreman talked to the men . . . there must have been about three dozen of them.

He may have been a fool but he was a crafty one.

He was talking in Mexican and telling them what I wanted to do to Pancho, their brother and friend. He pantomimed surgery—knife in fist and slash and finger-scissors and then grab at belly, and then tongue out, and eyes rolled out of sight, and slump, and dead man: all this very intently, like a child doing a child's powerful ritual of play.

"Oh, yo, yo, yo," went all the Mexicans, and shook their fists at me, and showed their white teeth in rage. No sir, there'd be no cutting on Pancho!

"You see?" said the foreman, "I told 'em what I had to do, and they won't have it."

I am no actor, and certainly no orator, but I turned to those poor peons and tried to show them as best I could how the only way to save Pancho, lying there like a baked peanut, was to operate right now.

The foreman kept up a musical kind of antiphony to my arguments.

You know? It was something like the old lyric struggle between good and evil—enlightenment and superstition.

There we were, miles from everything, on that plain where the heat went up from the fried ground in sheets; nothing but a rickety line of tracks to keep us in the world, so to speak; and a struggle going on over the theory of life or death, as exemplified in the person of a perfectly anonymous wretch who'd eaten too many beans once too often!

I'd be damned if I'd quit.

I went back to the train and had more on my mind now than chivalry and Chaucer and Clouet.

She was still sitting there in her heavy starch and her yards and yards of black serge.

Her face was pink with the heat and her glasses a little moist. But she was like a calm and shady lake in that blistering wilderness, and her hands rested like ferns on the itchy plush of the seat which gave off a miniature dust storm of stifling scent whenever anything moved on it.

I could hear the argument and mutual reinforcement in cries and threats going on and gathering force out there in the little mob. It was like the manifest sound of some part of the day, the heat, the desert life, which being disturbed now filled the quavering air with protest.

When I stopped in the aisle beside her, she looked up sideways. Of course, she didn't mean it to, but it looked sly and humorous, and her glasses flashed.

"Excuse me, Sister," I said. "Have you ever had any hospital experience?"

"Is someone ill?"

Her voice was oddly doleful, but not because she was; no, it had the faintest trace of a German tone, and her words an echo of German accent, that soft, trolling, ach-Gott-in-Himmel charm that used to be the language of the old Germany, a comfortable sweetness that is gone now.

"There's a Mexican laborer out there who's doubled up with appendicitis. I am a surgeon, by the way."

"Yes, for a long time I was dietitian at Mount Mercy Hospital, that's in Clefeland?"

"Well, you see what I think I ought to do."

"So, you should operate?"

"It's the only thing'd save him, and maybe that'll be too late."

"Should we take him in the train and take care of him so? And operate when we reach town?"

Yes, you must see how placid she was, how instantly dedicated to the needs of the present, at the same time. She at once talked of what "we" had to do. She owned responsibility for everything that came into her life. I was young then, and I'm an old man now, but I still get the same kind of pride in doctors and those in holy orders when they're faced with something that has to be done for somebody else. The human value, mind you.

"I don't think they'll let us touch him. They're all Mexicans, and scared to death of surgery. You should've heard them out there a minute ago."

"Yess, I hear them now."

"What I think we'd better do is get to work right here. The poor wretch wouldn't last the ride to Eddy, God knows how long the train'd take."

"But *where*, doctor!"

"Well, maybe one of those sheds."

"So, and the train would wait?"

"Oh! I don't know. I can find out."

I went and asked the conductor up in the next car. He said no, the train wouldn't wait, provided they ever got a chance to go.

"We'd have to take a chance on the train," I told Sister. "Also, those men out there are not very nice about it. Maybe if you came out?"

At that she did hesitate a little; just a moment; probably the fraction it takes a celibate lady to adjust her apprehensions over the things she has heard about men, all of them, the very authors of sin, ancestors of misery, and custodians of the forbidden fruit.

"It would have been more convenient," I said, "if I'd never got off the train. That groaning little animal would die, and when the train went, we'd be on it; but we cannot play innocent now. The Mexican means nothing to me. Life is not that personal to a doctor. But if there's a chance to save it, you have to do it, I suppose."

Her response to this was splendid. She flushed and gave me a terrific look, full of rebuke and annoyance at my flippancy. She gathered her great serge folds up in handfuls and went down the car walking angrily. I followed her and together we went over to the shed. The sunlight made her weep a little and blink.

The men were by now sweating with righteous fury. Their fascinating language clattered and threatened. Pancho was an unpleasant sight, sick and uncontrolled. The heat was unnerving. They saw me first and made a chorus. Then they saw Sister and shut up in awe, and pulled their greasy hats off.

She knelt down by Pancho and examined him superficially and the flow of her figure, the fine robes kneeling in the dust full of ants, was like some vision to the Mexicans, in all the familiar terms of their Church. To me, it gave one of my infrequent glimpses into the nature of religious feeling.

She got up.

She turned to the foreman, and crossed her palms together. She was majestic and ageless, like any true authority.

"Doctor sayss there must be an op*e*ration on this man. He is very sick. I am ready to help."

"W', lady," said the foreman, "you just *try* an' cut on that Messican and see what happens!"

He ducked his head toward the laborers to explain this.

She turned to the men. Calmly, she fumbled for her long rosary at her discipline and held up the large crucifix that hung on its end. The men murmured and crossed themselves.

"Tell them what you have to do," she said to me coldly. She was still angry at the way I'd spoken in the train.

"All right, foreman, translate for me. Sister is going to assist me at an appendectomy. We'll move the man into the larger shed over there. I'd be afraid to take him to town, there isn't time. No: listen, this is better. What I *will* do: we could move him into the train, and operate while the train was standing still, and then let the train go ahead after the operation is over. That way, we'd get him to town for proper care!"

The foreman translated and pantomimed.

A threatening cry went up.

"They say you can't take Pancho off and cut on 'im on the train. They want him here."

Everybody looked at Pancho. He was like a little monkey with eyes screwed shut and leaking tears.

The little corpus of man never loses its mystery, even to a doctor, I suppose. What it is, we are; what we are, must serve it; in anyone. My professor of surgery used to say, "Hold back your pity till after the operation. You'll work better, and then the patient will be flattered to have it, and it might show up in the bill."

"Very well, we'll operate here. Sister, are you willing to help me? It'll mean staying here till tomorrow's train."

"*Ja*, doctor, of course."

I turned to the foreman.

"Tell them."

He shrugged and began to address them again.

They answered him, and he slapped his knee and

h'yucked a kind of hound dog laugh in his throat and said to us,

"W', if you go ahaid, these Mexicans here say *they'll sure 'nough kill you if you kill Pancho!*"

Yes, it was worse than I could have expected.

This was like being turned loose among savages.

You might have thought the searing heat of that light steel sky had got everybody into fanciful ways.

"Why, that's ridiculous!" I said to him. "He's nearly dead now! Osler himself might not save him! Nobody can ever guarantee an operation, but I can certainly guarantee that that man will die unless I take this one chance!"

"W', I dunno. See? That's what they *said* . . ."

He waved at the Mexicans.

They were tough and growling.

Sister was waiting. Her face was still as wax.

"Can't you *explain*," I said.

"Man, you never can 'splain *nothin'* to this crew! You better take the church lady there, and just get back on that train, that's what you better do!"

Well, there it was.

"You go to hell!" I said.

I looked at Sister. She nodded indignantly at me, and then smiled, sideways, that same sly look between her cheek and her lens, which she never meant that way; but from years of convent discretion she had come to perceive things obliquely and tell of them in whispers with many sibilants.

"Come on, we'll move him. Get some help there."

The Mexicans wouldn't budge. They stood in the way.

"Give me your pistol!"

The foreman handed it over. We soon got Pancho moved.

Sister helped me to carry him.

She was strong. I think she must have been a farm girl from one of the German communities of the Middle West somewhere. She knew how to work, the way to lift, where her hands would do the most good. Her heavy thick robes dragged in the dust. We went into the tool shed and it was like strolling into a furnace.

I hurried back to the train and got my bags and then went back again for hers. I never figured out how she could travel with so little and be so clean and comfortable. She had a box of food. It was conventional, in its odors, bananas, waxed paper, oranges, something spicy. Aside from that she had a little canvas bag with web straps binding it. I wondered what, with so little allowed her, she had chosen out of all the desirable objects of the world to have with her and to own.

My instrument case had everything we needed, even to two bottles of chloroform.

I got back into the dusty red shed by flashing the foreman's pistol at the mob. Inside I gave it back to him through the window with orders to keep control over the peasants.

What they promised to do to me if Pancho died began to mean something, when I saw those faces, like clever dogs, like smooth-skinned apes, like long-whiskered mice. I thought of having the engineer telegraph to some town and get help, soldiers, or something; but that was nervously romantic.

It was dark in the shed, for there was only one window. The heat was almost smoky there, it was so dim. There was a dirt floor. We turned down two big tool cases on their sides and laid them together. They were not quite waist high. It was our operating table.

When we actually got started, then I saw how foolish it was to try it, without any hospital facilities. But I remembered again that it was this chance or death for the little Mexican. Beyond that, it was something of an ethical challenge. Yes, we went ahead.

I remember details, but now so long after, maybe not in the right order.

I remember a particular odor, an oily smell of greasy sand, very powerful in the shed; the heat made the very dirt floor sweat these odors up, and they made me ill at ease in the stomach.

It was early afternoon. The sky was so still and change-less that it seemed to suspend life in a bowl of heat. The tin roof of the shed lowered a very garment of heat over us.

Faces clouded up at the window, to see: to threaten: to enjoy. We shook them away with the pistol. The foreman was standing in the doorway. Beyond him we had glimpses of the slow dancing silvery heat on the scratchy earth, and the diamond melt of light along the rails of the track.

The camp cook boiled a kettle of water.

Sister turned her back and produced some white rags from her petticoats.

She turned her heavy sleeves back and pinned her veils aside.

The invalid now decided to notice what was going on and he tried to sit up and began to scream.

Sister flicked me a glance and at once began to govern him with the touch of her hands, and a flow of comforting melody in *Deutsch* noises. I got a syringe ready with morphine. And the mob appeared at the door, yelling and kicking up the stifling dust which drifted in and tasted bitter in the nose.

I shot the morphine and turned around.

I began to swear.

That's all I recall; not *what* I said. But I said plenty. Pancho yelled back at his friends who would rescue him. It was like a cat concert for a minute or so.

Then the morphine heavied the little man down again, and he fell silent.

Then I shut up, and got busy with the chloroform. Sister said she could handle that. It was suddenly very quiet.

My instruments were ready and we had his filthy rags off Pancho. Sister had an instinctive adroitness, though she had never had surgical experience. Yet her hospital service had given her a long awareness of the sometimes trying terms of healing. In fascinated silence we did what had to be done before the operation actually started.

There was a locust, or a cicada, some singing bug outside somewhere, just to make the day sound hotter.

The silence cracked.

"He is dead!" they cried outside.

A face looked in at the window.

Now the threats began again.

I said to the foreman,

"Damn you, get hold of that crowd and make them shut up! You tell them he isn't dead! You tell them—"

I began to talk his language again, very fancy and fast. It worked on him. I never cussed so hard in my life.

Then I turned back and took up my knife.

There's a lot of dramatic nonsense in real life; for example: my hand was trembling like a wet dog, with that knife; and I came down near the incisionary area, and just before I made the first cut, steady? that hand got as steady as a stone!

I looked at Sister in that slice of a second, and she was biting her lips and staring hard at the knife. The sweat stood on her face and her face was bright red. Her light eyebrows were puckered. But she was ready.

In another second things were going fast.

I once told this story to someone, and later heard it repeated to someone else. I hardly recognized the events as my friend described them, because he made it all sound so dramatic and somehow like a scene in the opera, grand and full of high notes. No, it seems to me that the facts are more wonderful than all the things time and playgoing can do to a person's imagination. The whole situation couldn't have been meaner; more dangerous from forces like dirt and stupidity, instead of forces like fate or fascinating Mexican bandits. There was the hazard, too, of my own youth, my inexperience as a surgeon. There was my responsibility for Sister, in case any trouble might start. There was the heat and a patient with temperature and no way to cool off boiled water in a hurry, and the dust rising through the cracks of the door and window and walls of the shed, as the outraged men kicked and shuffled outside. We could see the sheets of dusty light standing in the room's dusk, sliced from the gloom by a crack of that sunlight and its abstract splendor.

Oh, my surgery professor and my colleagues would've been shocked to see some of the things I did, and didn't do, that day!

I tried to hum a little tune instead of talk.

But now and then the noise outside would get worse.

Or the foreman would creak the door open and stick his varlet face in to peer.

Or the patient would almost swallow his tongue making a noise like a hot sleeping baby.

So I'd swear.

Sister said nothing all the time.

She obeyed my instructions. Her face was pale, from so many things that she wasn't used to—the odors, the wound, manipulation of life with such means as knives and skill, the strain of seeing Pancho weaken gradually; she was glassy with perspiration. Her starched linen was melted. There was some intuitive machinery working between us. Aside from having to point occasionally at what I needed, things she didn't know the name of, I've never had a more able assistant at an operation in all my long life of practice.

I think it was because both she and I, in our professions, somehow belonged to a system of life which knew men and women at their most vulnerable, at times when they came face to face with the mysteries of the body and the soul, and could look no further, and needed help then.

Anyway, she showed no surprise. She showed none even at my skill, and I will admit that I looked at her now and then to see what she thought of my performance. For if I do say it myself, it was good.

She looked up only once, with a curious expression, and I thought it was like that of one of the early saints, in the paintings, her eyes filmed with some light of awareness and yet readiness, the hour before martyrdom; and this was when we heard the train start to go.

She looked rueful and forlorn, yet firm.

The engine let go with steam and then hooted with the exhaust, and the wheels ground along the hot tracks.

If I had a moment of despair, it was then; the same wavy feeling I'd had when the train had stopped here a couple of hours before.

The train receded in sound.

It died away in the plainy distance.

Shortly after there was a rush of voices and cries and steps toward the shack.

It was the laborers again, many of whom had been put back to work on the track ahead of the engine, in order to let the train proceed. Now they were done. Now they were crazy with menace.

It was about four o'clock, I suppose.

Fortunately, I was just finishing up. The door screeched on its shaken hinges and latch. I heard the foreman shouting at the men.

Then there was a shot.

"Most sacred Heart!" said Sister, on her breath, softly. It was a prayer, of course.

Then the door opened, and the foreman came in and closed it and leaned back on it.

He said they sent him in to see if Pancho were still living. I told him he was. He said he had to see. I said he was a blankety-blank meddling and low-down blank to come bothering me now; but that I was just done, and if he had to smell around he could come.

I showed him the pulse in the little old Mexican's neck, beating fast, and made him listen to the running rapid breath, like a dog's.

Then he looked around.

He was sickened, first, I suppose; then he got mad. The place *was* dreadful. There were unpleasant evidences of surgery around, and the heat was absolutely weakening, and the air was stifling with a clash of odors. Sister had gone to sit on a box in the corner, watching. She, too, must have looked like a challenge, an alien force, to him.

He grew infuriated again at the mysterious evidences of civilization.

He began to wave his gun and shout that next time, by God, he'd fire on us, and not on them Messicans out yander. He declared that he, too, was agin cuttin' on anybody. He was bewildered and sick to his stomach and suffering most of all from a fool's bafflement.

He bent down and tried to grab back the meager sheeting and the dressing on Pancho's abdomen. He was filthy beyond words. I butted him with my shoulder (to keep my hands away and reasonably clean) and he backed up and stood glaring and his mouth, which was heavy and thick, sagged and contracted in turn, like loose rubber.

Sister came forward and without comment, knelt down by the wretched operating table which might yet be, for all I knew, a bier, and began to pray, in a rich whisper, full of hisses and soft impacts of r's upon her palate, and this act of hers brought some extraordinary power into the room; it was her own faith, of course; her own dedication to a simple alignment of life along two channels, one leading to good, and the other to evil.

I was beginning to feel very tired.

I had the weakness after strain and the almost querulous relief at triumph over hazard.

I'd been thinking of her all along as a woman, in spite of her ascetic garb, for that was natural to me then. Now for the first time, listening to her pray, I was much touched, and saw that she was like a doctor who thinks enough of his own medicine to take some when he needs a lift.

The foreman felt it all too, and what it did to him was to make him shamble sullenly out of the shed to join the enemy.

We watched all night.

It got hardly any cooler.

Late at night Sister opened her lunch box with little delicate movements and intentions of sociability, and we made a little meal.

I felt intimate with her.

I had a sense of what, together, we had accomplished, and over and over I tried to feel her response to this. But none came. We talked rather freely of what we still had to do, and whether we thought the Mexicans *meant* it, and whether the train crew knew what was going on, and if they'd report it when they reached Eddy.

We had an oil lamp that the foreman gave us.

When I'd get drowsy, my lids would drop and it seemed to me that the flame of the wick was going swiftly down and out; then I'd jerk awake and the flame would be going on steadily, adding yet another rich and melancholy odor to our little surgery.

I made Sister go to sleep, on her corner box, sitting with her back against the wall.

She slept in state, her hands folded, her body inarticulated under the volume of her robes, which in the dim lamplight looked like wonderful masses carved from some dark German wood by trolls of the Bavarian forests . . . so fancifully ran my mind through that vigil.

I saw morning come, like a cobweb, on the little window; then steal the whole sky that I could see; and then just as a flavor of cool sweetness had begun to lift into the air off the plains, the sun appeared (rapidly, I thought, but then it was I, not the sun, whose fever hurried life along that day).

Early that day Pancho became conscious.

We talked to him and he answered.

He was enclosed in the mystery of pain and the relief of weakness.

When he identified Sister by her habit, he tried to cross himself, and she smiled and crowed at him and made the sign of the cross over him herself.

I examined him carefully, and he was all right. He had stood the shock amazingly well. It was too early for infection to show to any degree, but I began to have a certain optimism, a settling of the heart. It had come off. I began to think the day was cooler. You know: the sweetness over everything that seems to follow a feeling of honest satisfaction.

Then the crowd got busy again.

They saw Pancho through the window, his eyes open, his lips moving, smiling faintly, and staring at Sister with a child's wonder toward some manifest loveliness, hitherto known only in dream and legend.

In a second they were around the door, and pushing in, babbling like children, crying his name aloud, and eager to get at him and kiss him and gabble and marvel and felicitate.

They were filthy and enthusiastic, flowing like life itself toward that which feeds it. They were, then, infection personified.

I shouted at them and made them stay back. I let them see Pancho, but from a distance of three feet.

He spoke to them, thinly, and they cried "Aiee!" with astonishment, and nodded their heads as if sagely, and blinked their eyes at me, ducking their little bodies in homage. They couldn't have been more friendly now. They went yes-yes, and my-my, and how wonderful to have such a man! and he is my friend, and so forth.

But their very presence was dangerous, for they kicked up the dirt floor, and they hawked and spat on their words, and I finally put them out.

The foreman's mood was opposite to theirs.

He was now surly and disgruntled that we had pulled it off successfully.

He knew, as I had known, that the Mexicans really would kill if Pancho died.

We had the unpleasant impression that he felt cheated of a diverting spectacle.

We watched Pancho carefully all morning; he grew uncomfortable as the heat arose. But then, so did we. It rose and rose, and the bugs sang, and the tin roof seemed to hum too, but that must have been dramatic imagination. I had all our plans made. When the noon train came along, we would flag it, and carefully move Pancho on board, and take him down the valley to Eddy, where he could spend two weeks in the company hospital.

Mid-morning, I stepped outside and called the men together and the foreman, and made them a speech. Now they had their hats off, listening to me. Their little eyes couldn't have looked more kindly and earnest. *Sure*, I could take Pancho off on the train. *Sure*, they wanted him to get well. *By all means* the señor medico must do what he thought best. So with a great show of love for them, I shook hands with myself at the little mob, feeling like a gifted politician.

The train finally arrived, and as it first showed, standing down the tracks in the wavering heat, it looked like a machine of rescue.

There was only one more thing there.

When we went to take Pancho on the train, the foreman refused to help.

"I won't he'p you," he declared. "I ain't got no authority t' move none of my men, and I won't he'p you."

I picked out two of the less earthy natives and they helped me to bring the patient on board the train. We carried him on a camp cot. It belonged to the foreman. When he saw that, he got so mad he threw down his hat and jumped on it. The dust flew. His fish-white brow broke into sweat. Then he came running to stop us. We barely got Pancho on the train in time, and the door closed and latched. It was a state of siege until the train went again. It must have been ten minutes. Fortunately I'd brought my bags on board the first thing, and Sister's.

We finally pulled out.

We looked out the rear window, and saw our desert hospital recede into the slow pulsing glassy air.

We could see the little figures, most of them waving.

Just at the last, one of them held forth his arm, and we saw a puff of smoke, and heard an explosion in our imagination, and then heard the actual ring and sing-off of a bullet as it struck the rear of the car.

It was the foreman's farewell, the last, and futile, opinion of the ignorant.

The afternoon passed slowly in the train.

The heat and the dust were hard on everyone, and especially Pancho. I kept wetting down the cracks of the windows, and the doors, to keep the dust out if I could.

But soon the water was gone, and we had to sit there and hope.

We reached Eddy in the evening, and it was like a garden, after the endless plains and their sear life. We found green trees and artesian wells and fields of alfalfa.

There is little more to tell, and what there is, is not about Pancho, except that he made a recovery in the proper time.

It is about my saying good-by to Sister.

It seemed to me we had been through a good deal together.

Now we were going to separate, for she was taking a stagecoach from Eddy on down into Texas somewhere, and I was going to stay a few days and see my patient out of the woods.

So we said good-by in the lobby of the wooden hotel there, where she was going to spend the night.

Nobody knew what a good job I had done except Sister, and after we shook hands, and I thanked her for her wonderful help, I waited a moment, just a little moment.

She knew I was nervous and tired, and it was vanity of course, but I needed the little lift she could give me.

But she didn't say anything, while I waited, and then as I started to turn off and go, she did speak.

"I will pray for you, doctor."

"What?"

"That you may overcome your habit of profanity."

She bowed and smiled in genuine kindliness, and made her way to the stairs and disappeared.

Duty is an ideal and it has several interpretations, and these are likely to be closely involved with the character that makes them.

You might say that Sister and I represented life eternal and life temporal.

I never saw her again, of course, but if she's still alive, I have no doubt that she's one of the happiest people in the world.

Flight

JOHN STEINBECK

About fifteen miles below Monterey, on the wild coast, the Torres family had their farm, a few sloping acres above a cliff that dropped to the brown reefs and to the hissing white waters of the ocean. Behind the farm the stone mountains stood up against the sky. The farm buildings huddled like little clinging aphids on the mountain skirts, crouched low to the ground as though the wind might blow them into the sea. The little shack, the rattling, rotting barn were gray-bitten with sea salt, beaten by the damp wind until they had taken on the color of the granite hills. Two horses, a red cow and a red calf, half a dozen pigs and a flock of lean, multi-colored chickens stocked the place. A little corn was raised on the sterile slope, and it grew short and thick under the wind, and all the cobs formed on the landward side of the stalks.

Mama Torres, a lean, dry woman with ancient eyes, had ruled the farm for ten years, ever since her husband tripped over a stone in the field one day and fell full length on a rattlesnake. When one is bitten on the chest there is not much that can be done.

Mama Torres had three children, two undersized black ones of twelve and fourteen, Emilio and Rosy, whom Mama kept fishing on the rocks below the farm when the sea was kind and when the truant officer was in some distant part of Monterey County. And there was Pepé, the tall smiling son of nineteen, a gentle, affectionate boy, but very lazy. Pepé had a tall head, pointed at the top, and from its peak, coarse black hair grew down like a thatch all around. Over his smiling little eyes Mama cut a straight bang so he could see. Pepé had sharp Indian cheekbones and an eagle nose, but his mouth was as sweet and shapely as a girl's mouth, and his chin was fragile and chiseled. He was loose and gangling, all legs and feet and wrists, and he was very lazy. Mama thought him fine and brave, but she never told him so. She said, "Some lazy cow must have got into thy father's family, else how could I have a son like thee." And she said, "When I carried thee, a sneaking lazy coyote came out of the brush and looked at me one day. That must have made thee so."

Pepé smiled sheepishly and stabbed at the ground with his knife to keep the blade sharp and free from rust. It was his inheritance, that knife, his father's knife. The long heavy blade folded back into the black handle. There was a button on the handle. When Pepé pressed the button, the blade leaped out ready for use. The knife was with Pepé always, for it had been his father's knife.

One sunny morning when the sea below the cliff was glinting and blue and the white surf creamed on the reef, when even the stone mountains looked kindly, Mama Torres called out the door of the shack, "Pepé, I have a labor for thee."

There was no answer. Mama listened. From behind the barn she heard a burst of laughter. She lifted her full long skirt and walked in the direction of the noise.

Pepé was sitting on the ground with his back against a box. His white teeth glistened. On either side of him stood the two black ones, tense and expectant. Fifteen feet away a redwood post was set in the ground. Pepé's right hand lay limply in his lap, and in the palm the big black knife rested. The blade was closed back into the handle. Pepé looked smiling at the sky.

Suddenly Emilio cried, "Ya!"

Pepé's wrist flicked like the head of a snake. The blade seemed to fly open in mid-air, and with a thump the point dug into the redwood post, and the black handle quivered. The three burst into excited laughter. Rosy ran to the post and pulled out the knife and brought it back to Pepé. He closed the blade and settled the knife carefully in his listless palm again. He grinned self-consciously at the sky.

"Ya!"

The heavy knife lanced out and sunk into the post

again. Mama moved forward like a ship and scattered the play.

"All day you do foolish things with the knife, like a toy-baby," she stormed. "Get up on thy huge feet that eat up shoes. Get up!" She took him by one loose shoulder and hoisted at him. Pepé grinned sheepishly and came half-heartedly to his feet. "Look!" Mama cried. "Big lazy, you must catch the horse and put on him thy father's saddle. You must ride to Monterey. The medicine bottle is empty. There is no salt. Go thou now, Peanut! Catch the horse."

A revolution took place in the relaxed figure of Pepé. "To Monterey, me? Alone? *Sí*, Mama."

She scowled at him. "Do not think, big sheep, that you will buy candy. No, I will give you only enough for the medicine and the salt."

Pepé smiled. "Mama, you will put the hatband on the hat?"

She relented then. "Yes, Pepé. You may wear the hatband."

His voice grew insinuating, "And the green handkerchief, Mama?"

"Yes, if you go quickly and return with no trouble, the silk green handkerchief will go. If you make sure to take off the handkerchief when you eat so no spot may fall on it. . . ."

"*Sí*, Mama. I will be careful. I am a man."

"Thou? A man? Thou art a peanut."

He went into the rickety barn and brought out a rope, and he walked agilely enough up the hill to catch the horse.

When he was ready and mounted before the door, mounted on his father's saddle that was so old that the oaken frame showed through torn leather in many places, then Mama brought out the round black hat with the tooled leather band, and she reached up and knotted the green silk handkerchief about his neck. Pepé's blue denim coat was much darker than his jeans, for it had been washed much less often.

Mama handed up the big medicine bottle and the silver coins. "That for the medicine," she said, "and that for the salt. That for a candle to burn for the papa. That for *dulces* for the little ones. Our friend Mrs. Rodríguez will give you dinner and maybe a bed for the night. When you go to the church say only ten Paternosters and only

twenty-five Ave Marias. Oh! I know, big coyote. You
would sit there flapping your mouth over Aves all day
while you looked at the candles and the holy pictures.
That is not good devotion to stare at the pretty things."

The black hat, covering the high pointed head and
black thatched hair of Pepé, gave him dignity and age.
He sat the rangy horse well. Mama thought how handsome he was, dark and lean and tall. "I would not send
thee now alone, thou little one, except for the medicine,"
she said softly. "It is not good to have no medicine, for
who knows when the toothache will come, or the sadness
of the stomach. These things are."

"Adiós, Mama," Pepé cried. "I will come back soon.
You may send me often alone. I am a man."

"Thou art a foolish chicken."

He straightened his shoulders, flipped the reins against
the horse's shoulder and rode away. He turned once and
saw that they still watched him, Emilio and Rosy and
Mama. Pepé grinned with pride and gladness and lifted
the tough buckskin horse to a trot.

When he had dropped out of sight over a little dip in
the road, Mama turned to the black ones, but she spoke to
herself. "He is nearly a man now," she said. "It will be a
nice thing to have a man in the house again." Her eyes
sharpened on the children. "Go to the rocks now. The tide
is going out. There will be abalones to be found." She put
the iron hooks into their hands and saw them down the
steep trail to the reefs. She brought the smooth stone
metate to the doorway and sat grinding her corn to flour
and looking occasionally at the road over which Pepé
had gone. The noonday came and then the afternoon,
when the little ones beat the abalones on a rock to make
them tender and Mama patted the tortillas to make them
thin. They ate their dinner as the red sun was plunging
down toward the ocean. They sat on the doorsteps and
watched the big white moon come over the mountain
tops.

Mama said, "He is now at the house of our friend Mrs.
Rodríguez. She will give him nice things to eat and maybe
a present."

Emilio said, "Some day I too will ride to Monterey for
medicine. Did Pepé come to be a man today?"

Mama said wisely, "A boy gets to be a man when a
man is needed. Remember this thing. I have known boys
forty years old because there was no need for a man."

Soon afterwards they retired, Mama in her big oak bed on one side of the room, Emilio and Rosy in their boxes full of straw and sheepskins on the other side of the room.

The moon went over the sky and the surf roared on the rocks. The roosters crowed the first call. The surf subsided to a whispering surge against the reef. The moon dropped toward the sea. The roosters crowed again.

The moon was near down to the water when Pepé rode on a winded horse to his home flat. His dog bounced out and circled the horse yelping with pleasure. Pepé slid off the saddle to the ground. The weathered little shack was silver in the moonlight and the square shadow of it was black to the north and east. Against the east the piling mountains were misty with light; their tops melted into the sky.

Pepé walked wearily up the three steps and into the house. It was dark inside. There was a rustle in the corner.

Mama cried out from her bed. "Who comes? Pepé, is it thou?"

"*Sí*, Mama."

"Did you get the medicine?"

"*Sí*, Mama."

"Well, go to sleep, then. I thought you would be sleeping at the house of Mrs. Rodríguez." Pepé stood silently in the dark room. "Why do you stand there, Pepé? Did you drink wine?"

"*Sí*, Mama."

"Well, go to bed then and sleep out the wine."

His voice was tired and patient, but very firm. "Light the candle, Mama. I must go away into the mountains."

"What is this, Pepé? You are crazy." Mama struck a sulphur match and held the little blue burr until the flame spread up the stick. She set light to the candle on the floor beside her bed. "Now, Pepé, what is this you say?" She looked anxiously into his face.

He was changed. The fragile quality seemed to have gone from his chin. His mouth was less full than it had been, the lines of the lips were straighter, but in his eyes the greatest change had taken place. There was no laughter in them any more nor any bashfulness. They were sharp and bright and purposeful.

He told her in a tired monotone, told her everything just as it had happened. A few people came into the kitchen of Mrs. Rodríguez. There was wine to drink. Pepé drank wine. The little quarrel—the man started toward Pepé and then the knife—it went almost by itself. It flew, it darted before Pepé knew it. As he talked, Mama's face grew stern, and it seemed to grow more lean. Pepé finished. "I am a man now, Mama. The man said names to me I could not allow."

Mama nodded. "Yes, thou art a man, my poor little Pepé. Thou art a man. I have seen it coming on thee. I have watched thee throwing the knife into the post, and I have been afraid." For a moment her face had softened, but now it grew stern again. "Come! We must get you ready. Go. Awaken Emilio and Rosy. Go quickly."

Pepé stepped over to the corner where his brother and sister slept among the sheepskins. He leaned down and shook them gently. "Come, Rosy! Come, Emilio! The mama says you must arise."

The little black ones sat up and rubbed their eyes in the candlelight. Mama was out of bed now, her long black skirt over her nightgown. "Emilio," she cried. "Go up and catch the other horse for Pepé. Quickly, now! Quickly." Emilio put his legs in his overalls and stumbled sleepily out the door.

"You heard no one behind you on the road?" Mama demanded.

"No, Mama. I listened carefully. No one was on the road."

Mama darted like a bird about the room. From a nail on the wall she took a canvas water bag and threw it on the floor. She stripped a blanket from her bed and rolled it into a tight tube and tied the ends with string. From a box beside the stove she lifted a flour sack half full of black stringy jerky. "Your father's black coat, Pepé. Here, put it on."

Pepé stood in the middle of the floor watching her activity. She reached behind the door and brought out the rifle, a long 38-56, worn shiny the whole length of the barrel. Pepé took it from her and held it in the crook of his elbow. Mama brought a little leather bag and counted the cartridges into his hand. "Only ten left," she warned. "You must not waste them."

Emilio put his head in the door. " 'Qui 'st 'l caballo, Mama."

"Put on the saddle from the other horse. Tie on the blanket. Here, tie the jerky to the saddle horn."

Still Pepé stood silently watching his mother's frantic activity. His chin looked hard, and his sweet mouth was drawn and thin. His little eyes followed Mama about the room almost suspiciously.

Rosy asked softly, "Where goes Pepé?"

Mama's eyes were fierce. "Pepé goes on a journey. Pepé is a man now. He has a man's thing to do."

Pepé straightened his shoulders. His mouth changed until he looked very much like Mama.

At last the preparation was finished. The loaded horse stood outside the door. The water bag dripped a line of moisture down the bay shoulder.

The moonlight was being thinned by the dawn and the big white moon was near down to the sea. The family stood by the shack. Mama confronted Pepé. "Look, my son! Do not stop until it is dark again. Do not sleep even though you are tired. Take care of the horse in order that he may not stop of weariness. Remember to be careful with the bullets—there are only ten. Do not fill thy stomach with jerky or it will make thee sick. Eat a little jerky and fill thy stomach with grass. When thou comest to the high mountains, if thou seest any of the dark watching men, go not near to them nor try to speak to them. And forget not thy prayers." She put her lean hands on Pepé's shoulders, stood on her toes and kissed him formally on both cheeks, and Pepé kissed her on both cheeks. Then he went to Emilio and Rosy and kissed both of their cheeks.

Pepé turned back to Mama. He seemed to look for a little softness, a little weakness in her. His eyes were searching, but Mama's face remained fierce. "Go now," she said. "Do not wait to be caught like a chicken."

Pepé pulled himself into the saddle. "I am a man," he said.

It was the first dawn when he rode up the hill toward the little canyon which let a trail into the mountains. Moonlight and daylight fought with each other, and the two warring qualities made it difficult to see. Before Pepé had gone a hundred yards, the outlines of his figure were misty; and long before he entered the canyon, he had become a gray, indefinite shadow.

Mama stood stiffly in front of her doorstep, and on either side of her stood Emilio and Rosy. They cast furtive glances at Mama now and then.

When the gray shape of Pepé melted into the hillside

and disappeared, Mama relaxed. She began the high, whining keen of the death wail. "Our beautiful—our brave," she cried. "Our protector, our son is gone." Emilio and Rosy moaned beside her. "Our beautiful—our brave, he is gone." It was the formal wail. It rose to a high piercing whine and subsided to a moan. Mama raised it three times and then she turned and went into the house and shut the door.

Emilio and Rosy stood wondering in the dawn. They heard Mama whimpering in the house. They went out to sit on the cliff above the ocean. They touched shoulders. "When did Pepé come to be a man?" Emilio asked.

"Last night," said Rosy. "Last night in Monterey." The ocean clouds turned red with the sun that was behind the mountains.

"We will have no breakfast," said Emilio. "Mama will not want to cook." Rosy did not answer him. "Where is Pepé gone?" he asked.

Rosy looked around at him. She drew her knowledge from the quiet air. "He has gone on a journey. He will never come back."

"Is he dead? Do you think he is dead?"

Rosy looked back at the ocean again. A little steamer, drawing a line of smoke, sat on the edge of the horizon. "He is not dead," Rosy explained. "Not yet."

Pepé rested the big rifle across the saddle in front of him. He let the horse walk up the hill and he didn't look back. The stony slope took on a coat of short brush so that Pepé found the entrance to a trail and entered it.

When he came to the canyon opening, he swung once in his saddle and looked back, but the houses were swallowed in the misty light. Pepé jerked forward again. The high shoulder of the canyon closed in on him. His horse stretched out its neck and sighed and settled to the trail.

It was a well-worn path, dark soft leaf-mold earth strewn with broken pieces of sandstone. The trail rounded the shoulder of the canyon and dropped steeply into the bed of the stream. In the shallows the water ran smoothly, glinting in the first morning sun. Small round stones on the bottom were as brown as rust with sun moss. In the sand along the edges of the stream the tall, rich wild mint grew, while in the water itself the cress, old and tough, had gone to heavy seed.

The path went into the stream and emerged on the

other side. The horse sloshed into the water and stopped. Pepé dropped his bridle and let the beast drink of the running water.

Soon the canyon sides became steep and the first giant sentinel redwoods guarded the trail, great round red trunks bearing foliage as green and lacy as ferns. Once Pepé was among the trees, the sun was lost. A perfumed and purple light lay in the pale green of the underbrush. Gooseberry bushes and blackberries and tall ferns lined the stream, and overhead the branches of the redwoods met and cut off the sky.

Pepé drank from the water bag, and he reached into the flour sack and brought out a black string of jerky. His white teeth gnawed at the string until the tough meat parted. He chewed slowly and drank occasionally from the water bag. His little eyes were slumberous and tired, but the muscles of his face were hard set. The earth of the trail was black now. It gave up a hollow sound under the walking hoofbeats.

The stream fell more sharply. Little waterfalls splashed on the stones. Five-fingered ferns hung over the water and dripped spray from their fingertips. Pepé rode half over in his saddle, dangling one leg loosely. He picked a bay leaf from a tree beside the way and put it into his mouth for a moment to flavor the dry jerky. He held the gun loosely across the pommel.

Suddenly he squared in his saddle, swung the horse from the trail and kicked it hurriedly up behind a big redwood tree. He pulled up the reins tight against the bit to keep the horse from whinnying. His face was intent and his nostrils quivered a little.

A hollow pounding came down the trail, and a horseman rode by, a fat man with red cheeks and a white stubble beard. His horse put down its head and blubbered at the trail when it came to the place where Pepé had turned off. "Hold up!" said the man and he pulled up his horse's head.

When the last sound of the hoofs died away, Pepé came back into the trail again. He did not relax in the saddle any more. He lifted the big rifle and swung the lever to throw a shell into the chamber, and then he let down the hammer to half cock.

The trail grew very steep. Now the redwood trees were smaller and their tops were dead, bitten dead where the wind reached them. The horse plodded on; the sun went slowly overhead and started down toward the afternoon.

Where the stream came out of a side canyon, the trail left it. Pepé dismounted and watered his horse and filled up his water bag. As soon as the trail had parted from the stream, the trees were gone and only the thick brittle sage and manzanita and chaparral edged the trail. And the soft black earth was gone, too, leaving only the light tan broken rock for the trail bed. Lizards scampered away into the brush as the horse rattled over the little stones.

Pepé turned in his saddle and looked back. He was in the open now: he could be seen from a distance. As he ascended the trail the country grew more rough and terrible and dry. The way wound about the bases of great square rocks. Little gray rabbits skittered in the brush. A bird made a monotonous high creaking. Eastward the bare rock mountaintops were pale and powder-dry under the dropping sun. The horse plodded up and up the trail toward a little V in the ridge which was the pass.

Pepé looked suspiciously back every minute or so, and his eyes sought the tops of the ridges ahead. Once, on a white barren spur, he saw a black figure for a moment, but he looked quickly away, for it was one of the dark watchers. No one knew who the watchers were, nor where they lived, but it was better to ignore them and never to show interest in them. They did not bother one who stayed on the trail and minded his own business.

The air was parched and full of light dust blown by the breeze from the eroding mountains. Pepé drank sparingly from his bag and corked it tightly and hung it on the horn again. The trail moved up the dry shale hillside, avoiding rocks, dropping under clefts, climbing in and out of old water scars. When he arrived at the little pass he stopped and looked back for a long time. No dark watchers were to be seen now. The trail behind was empty. Only the high tops of the redwoods indicated where the stream flowed.

Pepé rode on through the pass. His little eyes were nearly closed with weariness, but his face was stern, relentless and manly. The high mountain wind coasted sighing through the pass and whistled on the edges of the big blocks of broken granite. In the air, a red-tailed hawk sailed over close to the ridge and screamed angrily. Pepé went slowly through the broken jagged pass and looked down on the other side.

The trail dropped quickly, staggering among broken

rock. At the bottom of the slope there was a dark crease, thick with brush, and on the other side of the crease a little flat, in which a grove of oak trees grew. A scar of green grass cut across the flat. And behind the flat another mountain rose, desolate with dead rocks and starving little black bushes. Pepé drank from the bag again for the air was so dry that it encrusted his nostrils and burned his lips. He put the horse down the trail. The hooves slipped and struggled on the steep way, starting little stones that rolled off into the brush. The sun was gone behind the westward mountain now, but still it glowed brilliantly on the oaks and on the grassy flat. The rocks and the hillsides still sent up waves of the heat they had gathered from the day's sun.

Pepé looked up to the top of the next dry withered ridge. He saw a dark form against the sky, a man's figure standing on top of a rock, and he glanced away quickly not to appear curious. When a moment later he looked up again, the figure was gone.

Downward the trail was quickly covered. Sometimes the horse floundered for footing, sometimes set his feet and slid a little way. They came at last to the bottom where the dark chaparral was higher than Pepé's head. He held up his rifle on one side and his arm on the other to shield his face from the sharp brittle fingers of the brush.

Up and out of the crease he rode, and up a little cliff. The grassy flat was before him, and the round comfortable oaks. For a moment he studied the trail down which he had come, but there was no movement and no sound from it. Finally he rode out over the flat, to the green streak, and at the upper end of the damp he found a little spring welling out of the earth and dropping into a dug basin before it seeped out over the flat.

Pepé filled his bag first, and then he let the thirsty horse drink out of the pool. He led the horse to the clump of oaks, and in the middle of the grove, fairly protected from sight on all sides, he took off the saddle and the bridle and laid them on the ground. The horse stretched his jaws sideways and yawned. Pepé knotted the lead rope about the horse's neck and tied him to a sapling among the oaks, where he could graze in a fairly large circle.

When the horse was gnawing hungrily at the dry grass, Pepé went to the saddle and took a black string of jerky from the sack and strolled to an oak tree on the edge of the grove, from under which he could watch the trail. He sat down in the crisp dry oak leaves and automatically felt for his big black knife to cut the jerky, but he had no knife. He leaned back on his elbow and gnawed at the tough strong meat. His face was blank, but it was a man's face.

The bright evening light washed the eastern ridge, but the valley was darkening. Doves flew down from the hills to the spring, and the quail came running out of the brush and joined them, calling clearly to one another.

Out of the corner of his eye Pepé saw a shadow grow out of the bushy crease. He turned his head slowly. A big spotted wildcat was creeping toward the spring, belly to the ground, moving like thought.

Pepé cocked his rifle and edged the muzzle slowly around. Then he looked apprehensively up the trail and dropped the hammer again. From the ground beside him he picked an oak twig and threw it toward the spring. The quail flew up with a roar and the doves whistled away. The big cat stood up: for a long moment he looked at Pepé with cold yellow eyes, and then fearlessly walked back into the gulch.

The dusk gathered quickly in the deep valley. Pepé muttered his prayers, put his head down on his arm and went instantly to sleep.

The moon came up and filled the valley with cold blue light, and the wind swept rustling down from the peaks. The owls worked up and down the slopes looking for rabbits. Down in the brush of the gulch a coyote gabbled. The oak trees whispered softly in the night breeze.

Pepé started up, listening. His horse had whinnied. The moon was just slipping behind the western ridge, leaving the valley in darkness behind it. Pepé sat tensely gripping his rifle. From far up the trail he heard an answering whinny and the crash of shod hooves on the broken rock. He jumped to his feet, ran to his horse and led it under the trees. He threw on the saddle and cinched it tight for the steep trail, caught the unwilling head and forced the bit into the mouth. He felt the saddle to make sure the water bag and the sack of jerky were there. Then he mounted and turned up the hill.

It was velvet dark. The horse found the entrance to the trail where it left the flat, and started up, stumbling and slipping on the rocks. Pepé's hand rose up to his head. His hat was gone. He had left it under the oak tree.

The horse had struggled far up the trail when the first change of dawn came into the air, a steel grayness as light mixed thoroughly with dark. Gradually the sharp snaggled edge of the ridge stood out above them, rotten granite tortured and eaten by the wind of time. Pepé had dropped his reins on the horn, leaving direction to the horse. The brush grabbed at his legs in the dark until one knee of his jeans was ripped.

Gradually the light flowed down over the ridge. The starved brush and rocks stood out in the half light, strange and lonely in high perspective. Then there came warmth into the light. Pepé drew up and looked back, but he could see nothing in the darker valley below. The sky turned blue over the coming sun. In the waste of the mountainside, the poor dry brush grew only three feet high. Here and there, big outcroppings of unrotted granite stood up like moldering houses. Pepé relaxed a little. He drank from his water bag and bit off a piece of jerky. A single eagle flew over, high in the light.

Without warning Pepé's horse screamed and fell on its side. He was almost down before the rifle crash echoed up from the valley. From a hole behind the struggling shoulder, a stream of bright crimson blood pumped and stopped and pumped and stopped. The hooves threshed on the ground. Pepé lay half stunned beside the horse. He looked slowly down the hill. A piece of sage clipped off beside his head and another crash echoed up from side to side of the canyon. Pepé flung himself frantically behind a bush.

He crawled up the hill on his knees and on one hand. His right hand held the rifle up off the ground and pushed it ahead of him. He moved with the instinctive care of an animal. Rapidly he wormed his way toward one of the big outcroppings of granite on the hill above him. Where the brush was high he doubled up and ran, but where the cover was slight he wriggled forward on his stomach, pushing the rifle ahead of him. In the last little distance there was no cover at all. Pepé poised and then he darted across the space and flashed around the corner of the rock.

He leaned panting against the stone. When his breath came easier he moved along behind the big rock until he came to a narrow split that offered a thin section of vision down the hill. Pepé lay on his stomach and pushed the rifle barrel through the slit and waited.

The sun reddened the western ridges now. Already the buzzards were settling down toward the place where the horse lay. A small brown bird scratched in the dead sage leaves directly in front of the rifle muzzle. The coasting eagle flew back toward the rising sun.

Pepé saw a little movement in the brush far below. His grip tightened on the gun. A little brown doe stepped daintily out on the trail and crossed it and disappeared into the brush again. For a long time Pepé waited. Far below he could see the little flat and the oak trees and the slash of green. Suddenly his eyes flashed back at the trail again. A quarter of a mile down there had been a quick movement in the chaparral. The rifle swung over. The front sight nestled in the V of the rear sight. Pepé studied for a moment and then raised the rear sight a notch. The little movement in the brush came again. The sight settled on it. Pepé squeezed the trigger. The explosion crashed down the mountain and up the other side, and came rattling back. The whole side of the slope grew still. No more movement. And then a white streak cut into the granite of the slit and a bullet whined away and a crash sounded up from below. Pepé felt a sharp pain in his right hand. A sliver of granite was sticking out from between his first and second knuckles and the point protruded from his palm. Carefully he pulled out the sliver of stone. The wound bled evenly and gently. No vein nor artery was cut.

Pepé looked into a little dusty cave in the rock and gathered a handful of spider web, and he pressed the mass into the cut, plastering the soft web into the blood. The flow stopped almost at once.

The rifle was on the ground. Pepé picked it up, levered a new shell into the chamber. And then he slid into the brush on his stomach. Far to the right he crawled, and then up the hill, moving slowly and carefully, crawling to cover and resting and then crawling again.

In the mountains the sun is high in its arc before it penetrates the gorges. The hot face looked over the hill and brought instant heat with it. The white light beat on the rocks and reflected from them and rose up quivering from the earth again, and the rocks and bushes seemed to quiver behind the air.

Pepé crawled in the general direction of the ridge peak, zig-zagging for cover. The deep cut between his knuckles began to throb. He crawled close to a rattlesnake before he saw it, and when it raised its dry head and made a soft beginning whirr, he backed up and took another way. The quick gray lizards flashed in front of him, raising a tiny line of dust. He found another mass of spider web and pressed it against his throbbing hand.

Pepé was pushing the rifle with his left hand now. Little drops of sweat ran to the ends of his coarse black hair and rolled down his cheeks. His lips and tongue were growing thick and heavy. His lips writhed to draw saliva into his mouth. His little dark eyes were uneasy and suspicious. Once when a gray lizard paused in front of him on the parched ground and turned its head sideways he crushed it flat with a stone.

When the sun slid past noon he had not gone a mile. He crawled exhaustedly a last hundred yards to a patch of high sharp manzanita, crawled desperately, and when the patch was reached he wriggled in among the tough gnarly trunks and dropped his head on his left arm. There was little shade in the meager brush, but there was cover and safety. Pepé went to sleep as he lay and the sun beat on his back. A few little birds hopped close to him and peered and hopped away. Pepé squirmed in his sleep and he raised and dropped his wounded hand again and again.

The sun went down behind the peaks and the cool evening came, and then the dark. A coyote yelled from the hillside, Pepé started awake and looked about with misty eyes. His hand was swollen and heavy; a little thread of pain ran up the inside of his arm and settled in a pocket in his armpit. He peered about and then stood up, for the mountains were black and the moon had not yet risen. Pepé stood up in the dark. The coat of his father pressed on his arm. His tongue was swollen until it nearly filled his mouth. He wriggled out of the coat and dropped it in the brush, and then he struggled up the hill, falling over rocks and tearing his way through the brush. The rifle knocked against stones as he went. Little dry avalanches of gravel and shattered stone went whispering down the hill behind him.

After a while the old moon came up and showed the jagged ridge top ahead of him. By moonlight Pepé traveled more easily. He bent forward so that his throbbing arm hung away from his body. The journey uphill was made in dashes and rests, a frantic rush up a few yards and then a rest. The wind coasted down the slope rattling the dry stems of the bushes.

The moon was at meridian when Pepé came at last to the sharp backbone of the ridge top. On the last hundred yards of the rise no soil had clung under the wearing winds. The way was on solid rock. He clambered to the top and looked down on the other side. There was a draw like the last below him, misty with moonlight, brushed with dry struggling sage and chaparral. On the other side the hill rose up sharply and at the top the jagged rotten teeth of the mountain showed against the sky. At the bottom of the cut the brush was thick and dark.

Pepé stumbled down the hill. His throat was almost closed with thirst. At first he tried to run, but immediately he fell and rolled. After that he went more carefully. The moon was just disappearing behind the mountains when he came to the bottom. He crawled into the heavy brush feeling with his fingers for water. There was no water in the bed of the stream, only damp earth. Pepé laid his gun down and scooped up a handful of mud and put it in his mouth, and then he spluttered and scraped the earth from his tongue with his finger, for the mud drew at his mouth like a poultice. He dug a hole in the stream bed with his fingers, dug a little basin to catch water; but before it was very deep his head fell forward on the damp ground and he slept.

The dawn came and the heat of the day fell on the earth, and still Pepé slept. Late in the afternoon his head jerked up. He looked slowly around. His eyes were slits of wariness. Twenty feet away in the heavy brush a big tawny mountain lion stood looking at him. Its long thick tail waved gracefully, its ears erect with interest, not laid back dangerously. The lion squatted down on its stomach and watched him.

Pepé looked at the hole he had dug in the earth. A half inch of muddy water had collected in the bottom. He tore the sleeve from his hurt arm, with his teeth ripped out a little square, soaked it in the water and put it in his mouth. Over and over he filled the cloth and sucked it.

Still the lion sat and watched him. The evening came down but there was no movement on the hills. No birds visited the dry bottom of the cut. Pepé looked occasionally at the lion. The eyes of the yellow beast dropped as though he were about to sleep. He yawned and his long thin red tongue curled out. Suddenly his head jerked around and his nostrils quivered. His big tail lashed. He stood up and slunk like a tawny shadow into the thick brush.

A moment later Pepé heard the sound, the faint far crash of horses' hooves on gravel. And he heard something else, a high whining yelp of a dog.

Pepé took his rifle in his left hand and he glided into the brush almost as quietly as the lion had. In the darkening evening he crouched up the hill toward the next ridge. Only when the dark came did he stand up. His energy was short. Once it was dark he fell over the rocks and slipped to his knees on the steep slope, but he moved on and on up the hill, climbing and scrabbling over the broken hillside.

When he was far up toward the top, he lay down and slept for a little while. The withered moon, shining on his face, awakened him. He stood up and moved up the hill. Fifty yards away he stopped and turned back, for he had forgotten his rifle. He walked heavily down and poked about in the brush, but he could not find his gun. At last he lay down to rest. The pocket of pain in his armpit had grown more sharp. His arm seemed to swell out and fall with every heartbeat. There was no position lying down where the heavy arm did not press against his armpit.

With the effort of a hurt beast, Pepé got up and moved again toward the top of the ridge. He held his swollen arm away from his body with his left hand. Up the steep hill he dragged himself, a few steps and a rest, and a few more steps. At last he was nearing the top. The moon showed the uneven sharp back of it against the sky.

Pepé's brain spun in a big spiral up and away from him. He slumped to the ground and lay still. The rock ridge top was only a hundred feet above him.

The moon moved over the sky. Pepé half turned on his back. His tongue tried to make words, but only a thick hissing came from between his lips.

When the dawn came, Pepé pulled himself up. His eyes were sane again. He drew his great puffed arm in front of him and looked at the angry wound. The black line ran up from his wrist to his armpit. Automatically he reached in his pocket for the big black knife, but it was not there. His eyes searched the ground. He picked up a sharp blade of stone and scraped at the wound, sawed at the proud flesh and then squeezed the green juice out in big drops. Instantly he threw back his head and whined like a dog. His whole right side shuddered at the pain, but the pain cleared his head.

In the gray light he struggled up the last slope to the ridge and crawled over and lay down behind a line of rocks. Below him lay a deep canyon exactly like the last, waterless and desolate. There was no flat, no oak trees, not even heavy brush in the bottom of it. And on the other side a sharp ridge stood up, thinly brushed with starving sage, littered with broken granite. Strewn over the hill there were giant outcroppings, and on the top the granite teeth stood out against the sky.

The new day was light now. The flame of sun came over the ridge and fell on Pepé where he lay on the ground. His coarse black hair was littered with twigs and bits of spider web. His eyes had retreated back into his head. Between his lips the tip of his black tongue showed.

He sat up and dragged his great arm into his lap and nursed it, rocking his body and moaning in his throat. He threw back his head and looked up into the pale sky. A big black bird circled nearly out of sight, and far to the left another was sailing near.

He lifted his head to listen, for a familiar sound had come to him from the valley he had climbed out of; it was the crying yelp of hounds, excited and feverish, on a trail.

Pepé bowed his head quickly. He tried to speak rapid words but only a thick hiss came from his lips. He drew a shaky cross on his breast with his left hand. It was a long struggle to get to his feet. He crawled slowly and mechanically to the top of a big rock on the ridge peak. Once there, he arose slowly, swaying to his feet, and stood erect. Far below he could see the dark brush where he had slept. He braced his feet and stood there, black against the morning sky.

There came a ripping sound at his feet. A piece of stone flew up and a bullet droned off into the next gorge. The hollow crash echoed up from below. Pepé looked down for a moment and then pulled himself straight again.

His body jarred back. His left hand fluttered helplessly toward his breast. The second crash sounded from below. Pepé swung forward and toppled from the rock. His body struck and rolled over and over, starting a little avalanche. And when at last he stopped against a bush, the avalanche slid slowly down and covered up his head.

III.

FROM WORLD WAR II
TO THE PRESENT:

*Portraits and Self-Portraits
of the Awakening Minority*

THE ANGLO VIEW:

Señor Payroll

WILLIAM E. BARRETT

Larry and I were Junior Engineers in the gas plant, which means that we were clerks. Anything that could be classified as paper work came to the flat double desk across which we faced each other. The Main Office downtown sent us a bewildering array of orders and rules that were to be put into effect.

Junior Engineers were beneath the notice of everyone except the Mexican laborers at the plant. To them we were the visible form of a distant, unknowable paymaster. We were Señor Payroll.

Those Mexicans were great workmen; the aristocrats among them were the stokers, big men who worked Herculean eight-hour shifts in the fierce heat of the retorts. They scooped coal with huge shovels and hurled it with uncanny aim at tiny doors. The coal streamed out from the shovels like black water from a high pressure nozzle, and never missed the narrow opening. The stokers worked stripped to the waist, and there was pride and dignity in them. Few men could do such work, and they were the few.

The Company paid its men only twice a month, on the fifth and on the twentieth. To a Mexican, this was absurd. What man with money will make it last fifteen days? If he hoarded money beyond the spending of three days, he was a miser—and when, Señor, did the blood of Spain flow in the veins of misers? Hence it was the custom for our stokers to appear every third or fourth day to draw the money due to them.

There was a certain elasticity in the Company rules, and Larry and I sent the necessary forms to the Main Office and received an "advance" against a man's pay check. Then, one day, Downtown favored us with a memorandum:

"There have been too many abuses of the advance-against-wages privilege. Hereafter, no advance against wages will be made to any employee except in a case of genuine emergency."

We had no sooner posted the notice when in came stoker Juan García. He asked for an advance. I pointed to the notice. He spelled it through slowly, then said, "What does this mean, this 'genuine emergency'?"

I explained to him patiently that the Company was kind and sympathetic, but that it was a great nuisance to have to pay wages every few days. If someone was ill or if money was urgently needed for some other good reason, then the Company would make an exception to the rule.

Juan García turned his hat over and over slowly in his big hands. "I do not get my money?"

"Next payday, Juan. On the twentieth."

He went out silently and I felt a little ashamed of myself. I looked across the desk at Larry. He avoided my eyes.

In the next hour two other stokers came in, looked at the notice, had it explained and walked solemnly out; then no more came. What we did not know was that Juan García, Pete Mendoza and Francisco González had spread the word, and that every other Mexican in the plant was explaining the order to every other Mexican. "To get the money now, the wife must be sick. There must be medicine for the baby."

The next morning Juan García's wife was practically dying, Pete Mendoza's mother would hardly last the day, there was a veritable epidemic among the children, and, just for variety, there was one sick father. We always suspected that the old man was really sick; no Mexican would otherwise have thought of him. At any rate, nobody paid Larry and me to examine private lives; we made out our forms with an added line describing the "genuine emergency." Our people got paid.

That went on for a week. Then came a new order, curt and to the point: "Hereafter, employees will be paid

ONLY on the fifth and the twentieth of the month. No exceptions will be made except in the cases of employees leaving the service of the Company."

The notice went up on the board, and we explained its significance gravely. "No, Juan García, we cannot advance your wages. It is too bad about your wife and your cousins and your aunts, but there is a new rule."

Juan García went out and thought it over. He thought out loud with Mendoza and González and Ayala, then, in the morning, he was back. "I am quitting this company for different job. You pay me now?"

We argued that it was a good company and that it loved its employees like children, but in the end we paid off, because Juan García quit. And so did González, Mendoza, Obregón, Ayala and Ortez, the best stokers, men who could not be replaced.

Larry and I looked at each other; we knew what was coming in about three days. One of our duties was to sit on the hiring line early each morning, engaging transient workers for the handy gangs. Any man was accepted who could walk up and ask for a job without falling down. Never before had we been called upon to hire such skilled virtuosos as stokers for handy-gang work, but we were called upon to hire them now.

The day foreman was wringing his hands and asking the Almighty if he was personally supposed to shovel this condemned coal, while there in a stolid, patient line were skilled men—García, Mendoza and others—waiting to be hired. We hired them, of course. There was nothing else to do.

Every day we had a line of resigning stokers, and another line of stokers seeking work. Our paper work became very complicated. At the Main Office they were jumping up and down. The procession of forms showing Juan García's resigning and being hired over and over again was too much for them. Sometimes Downtown had García on the payroll twice at the same time when someone down there was slow in entering a resignation. Our phone rang early and often.

Tolerantly and patiently we explained: "There's nothing we can do if a man wants to quit, and if there are stokers available when the plant needs stokers, we hire them."

Out of chaos, Downtown issued another order. I read it and whistled. Larry looked at it and said, "It is going to be very quiet around here."

The order read: "Hereafter, no employee who resigns may be rehired within a period of 30 days."

Juan García was due for another resignation, and when he came in we showed him the order and explained that standing in line the next day would do him no good if he resigned today. "Thirty days is a long time, Juan."

It was a grave matter and he took time to reflect on it. So did González, Mendoza, Ayala and Ortez. Ultimately, however, they were all back—and all resigned.

We did our best to dissuade them and we were sad about the parting. This time it was for keeps and they shook hands with us solemnly. It was very nice knowing us. Larry and I looked at each other when they were gone and we both knew that neither of us had been pulling for Downtown to win this duel. It was a blue day.

In the morning, however, they were all back in line. With the utmost gravity, Juan García informed me that he was a stoker looking for a job.

"No dice, Juan," I said. "Come back in thirty days. I warned you."

His eyes looked straight into mine without a flicker. "There is some mistake, Señor," he said. "I am Manuel Hernández. I work as the stoker in Pueblo, in Santa Fé, in many places."

I stared back at him, remembering the sick wife and the babies without medicine, the mother-in-law in the hospital, the many resignations and the rehirings. I knew that there was a gas plant in Pueblo, and that there wasn't any in Santa Fé; but who was I to argue with a man about his own name? A stoker is a stoker.

So I hired him. I hired González, too, who swore that his name was Carrera, and Ayala, who had shamelessly become Smith.

Three days later, the resigning started.

Within a week our payroll read like a history of Latin America. Everyone was on it: López and Obregón, Villa, Díaz, Batista, Gómez, and even San Martín and Bolívar. Finally Larry and I, growing weary of staring at familiar faces and writing unfamiliar names, went to the Superintendent and told him the whole story. He tried not to grin, and said, "Damned nonsense!"

The next day the orders were taken down. We called our most prominent stokers into the office and pointed to the board. No rules any more.

"The next time we hire you hombres," Larry said grim-ly, "come in under the names you like best, because that's the way you are going to stay on the books."

They looked at us and they looked at the board; then for the first time in the long duel, their teeth flashed white. "Sí Señores," they said.

And so it was.

A Fistful of Alamo Heroes

SYLVAN KARCHMER

My intention was to do a little writing this afternoon, but just listen to the noise! Every kid in this neighborhood is playing under my window, and you never heard such shouting. In another five minutes I'll have to give up. Maybe it's nicer to daydream and not try to work at all. . . . But one of these days I'm going to live in a fine Georgian house; it will be set in the middle of an immense lawn, and I'm going to have all the peace and quiet I need. Then . . . you watch me write. Now I'm not talking through my hat. Really I'm not. You see next Tuesday my first book will be released and I'm depending on it to be the start of something . . . big!

It won't be a Literary Guild selection or sell a million copies, though Mr. Robinson, the publisher's agent, wrote me that if I'll follow his suggestions in regard to the plotting of my next book, he doesn't have any doubt it'll make me some real money. Mr. Robinson should know. He's been scouting material for twenty-five years; he didn't discover Hemingway or Faulkner, to be sure, but he's pleased over the fact that two of his own "finds" have made more for his firm than either one of these so-called literary giants. In a way he "found" me. It was like this. I noticed in the paper that he was in town scouting material. That was three years ago, when after a spell in Italy, Southern France, and sixteen months in a PW camp in Ossheim, Germany, I was back. Before the war I'd worked at the Transcontinental Oil Company, where my job was to stamp *O.K. to Pay* on accounts payable invoices. I could process more invoices than anyone else in the department, but when I got back I wasn't interested in stamping invoices; I lagged behind the other stampers. This was bad enough, because it kept me from a sorely-needed raise, but what was worse I discovered I didn't care. Nevertheless, I might have gone on stamping *O.K. to Pay* on invoices the rest of my waking life except that one morning I chanced to read in the paper that an old army buddy of mine named De León from South Texas had been shot while he was driving home.

I got to thinking about De León and what he'd been through in the war and how funny it was that this had to be the way things ended for him, and first thing I knew I was determined to put down some of these reflections in what I told myself would be a novel. Now mind you, when I started, I didn't have any clear notion what I was up to. All I knew was that I wanted to write about these things; it helped clear up the confusion in my own mind and at the same time it permitted me to see De León a little better. He had always puzzled me.

When Mr. Robinson came to town searching for new talent, I had already completed three hundred pages of my book, and acting on a hunch of my wife, I took the MS. to him. While he idly glanced at it, tweaked his ear, asked me some questions about myself and leafed through the sheets, I had a sinking feeling inside me. What was I doing here? What business did I have even trying to write? Why wasn't I back at my desk stamping invoices? I guess I lived a thousand years in that moment until Mr. Robinson very casually said that when I finished the whole thing to send it to his office. Within a few weeks I mailed the MS. to him; and then after three months, when I was beginning to think they'd chucked the whole thing into the wastebasket, here comes a four-page letter from Mr. Robinson. His editor wanted the novel and would I sign the enclosed contract ... and then followed the four pages of projected changes. Oh boy, I thought, me, a nobody, a clerk for an oil company, a pfc in the army, and now an author! I skipped the four pages and wired my acceptance, and the next morning I did something I'd had in mind for a mighty long time: I told my boss I was quitting. I didn't even ask for a leave. I just quit outright. My wife and I figured we could live on our war bonds for six months and by that time my book would be out and we'd be on easy street.

After a day or two when I calmed down I studied Mr. Robinson's changes. My book was mostly about the war—what other theme did I have?—and this Mexican fellow from that border town in south Texas. I've said his name was De León but in the book he was called something else, which doesn't matter now because Mr. Robinson didn't like De León. . . .

In Naples De León got drunk every night just like any other GI, but that was when we first landed and he thought the fellows had forgotten he was not one of them but only a Mexican from a border town, where his people had never been accepted. Well he learned by degrees. He was a tall, thin fellow, skinny as a rail, with dark eyes and what in my book I called sensitive nostrils, and he was proud as a Spanish Don. At some insult he would draw himself up and there would be a contemptuous and angry look in his eyes and at other times he would be as timid as a child. In those days there was really much innocence about De León—something you don't often find in Americans. It was pathetic how hungry he was for friends. Once he started buddying around with a colored boy from a nearby service unit. That was in the early days. And then when we got to France De León found his pal—a lanky, taciturn guy from Nebraska, named John, who'd never seen a Mexican before. John taught him slang; how to deal with the French girls; and where to sell his cigarettes. De León was a fast learner; he even did John one better and fell for the I & E stuff they dished out to us; he learned to hate the Nazis, though down in that border town of his where he had been drafted, it wasn't the Nazis who had kept his people out of drug stores, off the buses, and segregated the boys and girls of his race in the classrooms of the public schools. De León was willing to learn anything if it meant acceptance. . . .

At Futa that day our company charged I saw him batter a German's skull to pulp. There was really no need; he could have used his bayonet as well. Afterwards I saw him go behind a tree. He stood with his eyes cast to the ground, his cheeks ashen, as if a sudden fever had come upon him. He was shaking all over. When he noticed me watching him, he straightened up and lighted a cigarette.

From the very start Mr. Robinson had objected to De

León and in no uncertain terms had advised me to relegate him to a subordinate place in the novel. Finally of course I yielded to his arguments, but last spring when I read proof on the book I was conscious for the first time of the injury I had done De León, for in the process of rewriting I had made him nothing more than a phony. So I took out the phony De León, borrowed in large part from the Mexicans of other writers I had read, and restored the original of my first draft—a timid, sensitive, confused fellow, trying to hold his own in two worlds and not succeeding in either. When Mr. Robinson got my corrected proofs he wrote me another of his friendly letters, pointing out the danger of changing proof and advising me that with each change I delayed the date of publication of the book. By now my wife and I were down to our last hundred bucks, so I decided not to fool around with De León any more. If Mr. Robinson decided he should be a minor character, well and good with me.
. . .

No doubt it was a wise decision, because Tuesday my book comes out. And, brother, it's going to mean a great deal in my life. Mr. Robinson is an old hand at these things. He's planned a slick publicity campaign. The idea is to sell fifteen thousand copies right here around Dallas. The National Book Store is giving me an autograph party on the 24th; that afternoon the book department of Loeb, Bach & Co. will be hosts for a similar event. At night there will be a formal dinner at the hotel, with the mayor presiding, and the next morning at ten I'll be at Chammon's Book Mart to do some more autographing. . . . There's also going to be a spread in all the Texas newspapers, with particular emphasis going to the East Texas dailies, because my novel in its final draft in large part is set in the azalea country. When Mr. Robinson first traveled through here last year, he fell in love with the countryside and said frankly he wouldn't rest until he had a novel written about it. Frankly I don't know how my novel came to be about the azalea country. I thought I was writing a war novel, but as Mr. Robinson explained, the market has been glutted with war books; people just won't read another one unless it has a romantic touch, whereas the azalea country is something new.

Well, if it means some money I'll be satisfied, though in the long run it's De León who'll suffer. I don't mind say-

ing it was tough giving up some of the incidents. For instance there was my account of the night we landed in
Southern France. The lieutenant in charge of our platoon,
a Yale boy about De León's age, and a little unsure of his
authority, didn't know how to carry out his written orders
that our platoon was to occupy the farm house on the hill.
He had to be sure that the surrounding field was clear of
mines. But who to send? The whole platoon waited in the
valley while he tried to make up his mind what to do. I
remember watching him crack his knuckles and wipe his
forehead with a brown handkerchief; it was very warm that
moonlight night back in August, 1944. Suddenly the lieutenant's eye lighted on De León's friend from Nebraska.
"You there," he called, and a sigh of relief went up from
the rest of us. Having once called his name, the lieutenant's voice grew bolder. "Yeap, you John Coles," he
said. John was so scared he could hardly move. "Me?" he
called, and his voice was something more than a whisper.
And then while we waited for John to get up the hill and
find the mines, which would make the path safe for the
rest of us, De León, holding his carbine in his hand, his
bedroll strapped to his back, his helmet askew on his
head, stepped forward. "I'll go," he volunteered, and as
the lieutenant, taken by surprise, stared mutely at him, he
insisted, "Please let me go."

Maybe he reasoned that being the only foreigner in our
outfit, he had to demonstrate his bravery, to show us he
wasn't afraid. Perhaps he was only thinking of sparing his
friend, John. But he, the stranger among us, shouldn't
have gone. And we, who remained silent and let him go
for us, should have spoken as one man against it. The hell
of it is that if he'd been killed, we wouldn't have minded.
It was only much later that I came to realize this.

That same night he found the well, where the water was
cold and clear and abundant. We couldn't get our fill of
drinking it; but in the morning we spied the dead Germans, lying in a neat row at the bottom of the well, their
green uniforms giving a murderous tint to the water. We
looked at them in revulsion and afterwards none of us
could touch our canteens, which the night before we had
been so eager to fill, and yet De León paid no attention to
our feelings. He filled his own canteen. "Good water," he
remarked. "Very good water," and when he drank there
was a shy, contemptuous smile on his face.

Mr. Robinson took this out of the book. Also much of

the business of the PW camp, though John managed to survive in some of the chapters; in fact under Mr. Robinson's guidance he became something of a major character. Actually the only thing I remember about him at the PW camp is that he tried on two different occasions to escape. The monotony was killing us. Only De León seemed to hold up. During the long winter nights, when we were caged up in our barracks, he taught us sad Mexican songs and told us stories of saints he had learned at convent school. If it hadn't been for him both John and I would have gone crazy. As it was the three of us held together, and then in May of that year when the Russians started to advance and the German guards abandoned the camp, we were free to return to the American lines; and then our difficulties began. John came down with pneumonia, and De León and I were confronted with the choice of staying with him and so falling into the hands of the Russians or taking out without him towards the Czech border. There was no question in De León's mind about deserting his friend, and no matter how hard I argued that neither of us could do John the least bit of good, he was determined to stay with him. Finally by sheerest chance we found a discarded German jeep with a tank full of gas. Now we could take John along. All day we drove towards the border, while John grew worse; he lay with his head on De León's knee babbling about Nebraska and the farm. He died about dusk, though I don't think De León realized it, because all the way into Prague I could hear him singing to John . . . those sad Mexican songs he'd taught us.

Mr. Robinson says the time for morbid war books is over. So all this came out of the book. Also the part about De León's illness, when the army doctors gave him up. Later he surprised them by getting well and begging to be sent back to combat duty. Up until the very end De León thought he had some personal quarrel with the Nazis. . . . In the novel it's John who recovers. There is a scene at the station back home when his wife runs down the ramp and cries darling and a sweet-faced lady, who'd lost her own son, wipes her eyes and begins to understand why. . . . You know the scene—you've seen it in the movies. I didn't add a thing. . . .

When the army finally relinquished De León, he was a hardened veteran. We were discharged the same day. I came back to the Transcontinental Oil Company and he returned to the little border town he had left four years ago, a shy, virginal boy, who wore a St. Christopher medallion around his neck. His war, it seemed, wasn't over. He got mixed up in the segregation squabble, worked to get the boys and girls of his people accepted in the public schools on an equal footing with the American children, failed, started again with petitions, letters to the press, protest meetings. I remember hearing him talk over the radio; he sounded angry and determined, and when he talked about fair play, I could feel myself cringe. It was hard to believe he was the same boy I had known in the army. Well anyway one night a gang of hoodlums ambushed him. The papers said there were sixteen bullet holes in his body. His death made the headlines, and in three days he was forgotten.

But what De León did after the war had no place in my book, for as Mr. Robinson said, the market has been glutted with books on segregation and racial discrimination.

And yet I ask you, how could I forget De León or my debt to him? I can still hear his laughter—gentle, effacing, slightly apologetic during those early days of basic training. . . . I can see his medallion swaying on his chest as he ran the obstacle course for the first time. I remember how desperately he tried to get drunk with the boys . . . and the interminable nights at Ossheim, when he regaled us with stories of angels and saints. I owe it to him to bring him back. After all if I want to write about De León, it's not for Mr. Robinson to say I can't.

If my wife sees this, she'll say I'm carping. All right, she'll fret, if you can't listen to Mr. Robinson, who obviously is familiar with the reading tastes of the public—and not only that, he's taken the trouble to help you—then go ahead and write your book, so that nobody will buy it and it'll only gather dust in the Bureau of Copyright in Washington; a number will be stamped on it, and it'll be filed away and that will be the end of De León and his dreams of angels and home. . . .

It's like this. Mr. Robinson didn't force me into this writing game. I'm free and over twenty-one. I can do what I damn please. But wait a minute . . . I'm married, and my wife and I are hoping the book will make it possible for us to start a family. We're hoping it will be soon.

In the meantime after next week we're going to Mexico, and there I plan to start in earnest on my second novel. Mr. Robinson is sure he can get an advance from the publishers for me. He's been telling me I ought to do a costume novel about the Alamo. I might even work in the Alamo heroes—Bowie, Fannin, Crockett. "You got a fistful of personalities," he said. "That material has never been touched. It's all yours." Mr. Robinson can be very emphatic when the occasion demands it. He feels that my military experience will help me in the descriptions of battles and campaigns. The thing for me to do while I'm in Mexico is pick up a little Spanish. You see in a way he is conceding me De León. Perhaps I can work him in with Bowie, Fannin, and think up a few seduction scenes and throw in a lost treasure . . . and the point is to do it artistically in three or four hundred pages. . . . Who knows, it might turn out to be a Literary Guild book.

Outside the kids are making one hell of a racket. You realize I live on a street without lawns and the only place these kids have to play is on the street. Poor kids. . . . My children, when they come, will have a lawn of their own; they'll live in a fine Georgian house with lots of rooms. . . . No sir, my kids won't have to play in the street!

The shouts grow louder. I've already put my book aside for the afternoon, and for a moment I napped. I saw the Germans in the well, their green uniforms coloring the sweet-tasting water. I saw De León's proud smile as he alone of the men in the platoon drank. I heard him singing to dead John the night we pulled into Prague. I listened again: his voice was coming over the radio, scolding us about fair play . . . while I sat working on a story set in the azalea country. . . .

Suddenly I'm up with a start. It's too hot to nap. I should be planning my new novel, the one about the Alamo boys. If only it'll make me some money! It's got to. . . . That's all there is to it. As for De León, I think maybe I can use him later on—perhaps in a long short story. There are magazines that pay fancy prices for stories. Mr. Robinson, I'm sure, knows which ones they are. . . .

El Patrón

JAMES K. BOWMAN

When he came within sight of the concrete tank at Four-Mile Well, Matthew Fennel saw that the cattle were gone. They usually lay in the long morning shade of the high tank, the Herefords rising to their foreknees and bawling, the more wary Brahmans shying away a safe distance into the desert. As he nudged the charcoal mare forward, he saw that the cattle troughs were half-filled with dry sand, as stark as untended flower boxes. Yet high overhead, the windmill cranked away in a breeze he could not feel on the ground.

Quickly he tied the horse and walked around the base of the big tank. On the west side he found the damp crack, and in the sand, the green hair he feared, a dozen blades that showed where tankfuls of water had seeped away into the blotting sand.

Slowly he climbed the rickety wooden ladder to the brim of the tank. It was empty, except for a small puddle below the supply pipe. He knew he should go back to the ranch for Chapo and some patching tar, but the old Mexican would pretend that he couldn't understand and it would mean dragging him.

If the boy, Jesús, were still here, Matthew thought, he could be sent out to fix it himself. But if he were here, the crack would have been spotted days ago. He wished he had not sent Jesús away, but it was a matter of getting rid of one Mexican rather than losing two to the immigration men. If Jesús had only been as content as Chapo,

172

he'd have stayed at the ranch. Matthew grunted and backed down, cursing.

At least he could plug the crack until he got back with the tar, and save that much water. His eyes ran over his saddle gear and his hands explored his pockets. He drew a rat's nest of string and cotton from his hip pocket. It shook out into a yard-square parachute.

"I might have known you'd find a way to show me your parachute, Kit," he muttered. "Good boy."

His eyes wrinkled into a smile as he saw himself telling Margaret—and the smile lingered as he climbed back to the rim of the tank.

He saw he would have to put the ladder down on the inside. Straddling the rim he hesitated for a moment, squinting at the white globe of the sun that pushed above the distant haze of dark mountains. Then he began, slowly, pulling the wooden frame up behind him. A nail jutting from one of the rungs caught. He tried to bend it over, but lacked leverage; he stood straight on the narrow wall, balancing, and jerked. The rusted head snapped. He felt himself falling and let go of the ladder. In slow motion it sidled to the ground and he tried to follow it. For a second he hung suspended, every muscle straining toward the outside of the tank. Then he knew he was going over backwards, on the inside. He grabbed at the edge, but was too late, and rough concrete grated his outstretched fingers.

He tried to turn in the air, but his left foot, bent inward, struck first. His toes and heel ground together under his weight. The hollow snap of the boot sole, breaking, hung in the tank after the soft crash of his body. His breath left his lungs in a single hoarse choke.

He lay a long time on his stomach, waiting for the pain in his foot to stop twisting and jumping. When the throb became steady, he rolled over from the waist up. He found he could move his left leg, but the effort left him faint. He looked around in the quick appraisal of one accustomed to meeting nature at its worst.

The tank was a grey cell, twenty feet across, its walls rising sheer and rough, shutting out all but the cloudless sky and the top of the windmill. The quiet was a vacuum in his ears.

Rays of the morning sun had just touched the rim of the west wall—a tiny arc that penetrated into the shadow like golden paint oozing down the inside of a grey can. The heat would feel good at first, soothing the pain-chills that lodged in the softness of his back. But then the concrete would absorb its share, and the fiery rays would bound and rebound from all angles. At midday there would be no shadow.

But he would surely hear Chapo's horse by afternoon. Chapo would come then, see the black mare tied, and after mulling over the fallen ladder, climb to the brim, and find him.

He sat up and bent forward, edging his hand slowly toward his left foot. The unornamented, tan Mexican boot, one that would have grown supple with age, was twisted into a grotesque knot that betrayed the foot within. There was a black split across the center of the sole. At one end of the break was a sticky, half-clotted trickle of blood.

He knew the boot must be cut away before the swelling came. The knife— He tried to get it from his tight pocket and winced. Finally he had it. He pulled open the blade. Be sure it's the leather, he thought, not the skin. Lucky Kit hadn't had his hands on the knife. . . .

The steel blade slid easily through the new leather. Cutting now, down past the ankle, he grew dizzy and knew he must finish in one long thrust. He braced himself and sliced along the side of the foot from the instep to the toe. The knife cut leather and skin, and the feeling was no different. He wanted to stop then, but he knew the boot must be pulled away. When the twisted foot was free, he saw there was no more to do. He fell back on the concrete to wait for Chapo and the sun.

The patch of light crept imperceptibly down the west wall and then seemed to spring across the floor.

It passed over the dust-soaked panama that lay near his head and lighted a face molded in two parts, young and old. The jaws were strong and tanned, with a coarse stubble of bleached grey whisker; the thin lips, dry and creased, gave an appearance of withered age; fine dark lines met at the corners of his brown, watery eyes. Above the grey brow a line divided the young and old. The forehead above the line was smooth, as milk-white as a baby's. Only a powdery veil of whiteness woven into his dark, thick hair betrayed this youthfulness of skin.

There was no sound except the occasional creak of the

windmill. Once, far away to the south, he heard the whistle of the Southern Pacific as it sped across the arid desert, in the lee of the Hornbacks, toward Tucson, Los Angeles, and San Francisco. Grinning fools, he thought, from the Alamo, and Houston, and New Orleans, lounging in their air-conditioned compartments, ignoring the landscape that has to be worked under the sun to feed their children. The train will pass Margaret and Kit on their way to El Paso. Kit will wave and want his mother to race, and they will lose. He listened for the whistle again, but it did not come.

Matthew Fennel tried to avoid the sun, but his legs would not move themselves. Chapo will come soon, if—and the thought was new and startling—if he would come at all. He had had no reason to put his hands on Chapo the day before. But sometimes they only understand what they can feel—as though only hearing through their skin.

The palomino was the only extra horse in the corral when Chapo had come in, riding the brown mare across the ranch yard. The mare's right front hoof was split and she was limping badly.

"Get down off that mare!" Matthew yelled from the porch.

The tall, stooped Mexican slid to the ground. He wore a buttonless blue shirt with a rip across the length of the back, and faded blue denim pants beneath a pair of grimy leather chaps. These same clothes, except for the chaps which he put on only when he rode, had been on him continually, even in sleep, since Matthew, three months before, had made him stand naked in the adobe shed and there sprayed him and cut his hair, Margaret Fennel meanwhile trying to wash away the crusted stench of his shirt and pants.

"Why didn't you lead her in? Look at that hoof!" He tried to be calm with the Mexican.

There was no answer. Chapo looked down at his feet, like a dog being punished.

Matthew's hand flashed out, grabbing the Mexican above the elbow and pulling him forward. Beneath the billow of blue sleeve his hand found only a narrow stick of warm flesh. His fingers encircled the arm and met and, as quickly, sprung open as if the arm had given off an electric shock. Matthew stepped back. "Do you want me to turn you in," he demanded, "and back to Chihuahua with you?"

"No, Patrón," Chapo whispered through clamped jaws. He turned and led the mare toward the corral.

"Take the palomino along the west fence," Matthew yelled at his back. "Patch that hole I showed you."

No answer.

The old Mexican took his time removing the saddle from the mare. The horse was nervous and turned in a circle when he tried to undo the cinch. He kicked at her hind legs. When the saddle, bridle, and sweaty blanket were off, he threw them over the corral fence, slapped the mare across her flank, and disappeared into his adobe shed.

Matthew waited on the porch, but the dust settled and there was no more movement in the corral.

He found Chapo on the straw mattress. His eyes were closed and his lips drawn tight.

"I told you to get the palomino!" He pulled the Mexican roughly to his feet.

"Devil horse!"

"Devil horse, hell!" Matthew was losing his temper and wanted to hit the sulky face. "Get on him and out of here or the uniforms will be here to take you across tonight."

Chapo stood still as though deciding which was worse, the immigration men or the palomino. Then he slowly strapped the chaps around his thin legs and walked listlessly back into the corral.

The palomino allowed himself to be caught and saddled; only his quivering nostrils gave away his fear. When he was ready, Chapo hesitated for an instant as though waiting for a reprieve, but none came and he climbed doggedly into the saddle.

The horse reared back, screaming, and dropped forward on stiff legs. Chapo kicked away the stirrups but stayed in the saddle. Without another kick or twist the palomino fell on his foreknees and then went into a roll. The Mexican threw himself clear.

"Devil horse!" he said when he got to his feet. Then he turned and hobbled to his shed, leaving Matthew to put away the horse and saddle.

The sun was now a white-hot ball rolling slowly and inevitably up and over the wall of the tank, until, he imagined, it would balance on the edge and then, with a final convulsion, tumble in on him, leaving a smoking cinder and blue fumes. He tried to maneuver his head into the shadow, but the sun was ahead of him now. His only protection was to place the panama over his eyes. If he took the sun now he would get the first shadow in the afternoon. He covered as much of his aching head as possible.

Chapo will come soon, he thought, bound to see Blackie tied and know where to look. Strict instructions to look for me always by afternoon. But Margaret and Kit in El Paso and can't tell him. And he can't tell time. Too dense to look for me. The wet spiks—they're the honest ones because they have to be honest, and cheap, and dense. Should have kept the kid, he thought. Jesús had brains.

"I'm taking Jesús back to the river tonight and putting him across," Matthew said to Margaret, when Kit had been put to bed.

"But Chapo's been so happy with him—why?"

"I caught him in town. Pretty soon he'll have himself and Chapo both picked up."

And that same night, Chapo had been talking to the young black-haired Jesús in the shed when Matthew came to take him away, the boy knowing he would go and the old Mexican smiling because he was about to solve a bad thing.

"He will stay here, Patrón. He will no longer go to the town. He will work with Chapo, very hard. Jesús is good—"

"Get a water bottle, Jesús. You have a long walk tonight," Matthew said.

When Jesús had gathered his belongings in a bag Chapo still could not realize that he was going. "Why do you fill your bag, boy? We have much work to do . . ."

"I will be in Chihuahua tomorrow," the boy said simply.

Chapo would not say good-by. He busied himself, examining the rusty stove where he boiled his tomatoes and onions. His head was turned when Matthew and the boy left.

The boy's shoulders heaved with quiet sobs and he could not speak when Matthew stopped the car in the darkness and pointed toward a muddy irrigation ditch that led through a field of cotton to the river. He ran quickly into the darkness without looking back and Matthew waited until the sound of his feet had died before he started the motor and drove away.

Yes, Jesús would have come looking, he thought.

Matthew Fennel now lay in a pit of flame. The shadow had disappeared entirely and the air seemed to contain a strange gas, thick and without odor. It clogged his throat and nostrils and pressed heavy against his brain. He could not shut his eyes tight enough to keep out the glare. To open them—his body jerked at the thought—and find a red velvet moonless night when there should be white day, blue sky, rustling cottonwood against a purple evening. Blackened lumps, sightless as broken bits of coal in northern snowmen—melting away into ice water.

He pictured Jesús climbing over the rim of the tank and dropping to his side, pouring cool canteen water on his burning tongue and over the broken foot. Chapo would not come now. He would come when Margaret got home from El Paso. He would be frightened by her frantic voice. He would search carefully, because she said, *"Con cuidad!"* in distinct Mexican Spanish that he understood and could not pretend to misunderstand.

Chapo would come at night when the fiery tank had died to an ember. Jesús would not come at all because he was in Mexico, because he was too smart.

When Chapo came he would have to be told what to do. He would not have to be told why he must do it because he would not need to know this and would not understand anyway.

A ragged Mexican had come walking across the desert from the south, three years before. He was alone, and old even then, and across his shoulder hung a burlap-covered water bottle. Matthew had stood in the corral and watched him as a plodding speck in the distance. He came into the corral, his black hair caked with blown dust.

"Chapo knows horses, and cattle, and the making of adobe brick," the Mexican said. "I will work hard, Patrón."

"For six months. Then I will pay you and take you to the river," Matthew said. He needed adobe bricks.

For six months of tomatoes and onions and two bags of coffee and a crisp alfalfa bed, Chapo had made many adobe bricks.

"Another six months and you will be paid and taken to the river." Matthew needed more adobe bricks.

Chapo had gone back, finally, to Chihuahua with his coins, and in a month he had returned.

"For six months . . ." Matthew hired him. For six months, and six months, and another bag of onions. Chapo knows horses, and cattle, and the making of adobe bricks, and he knows that after six months he will be paid and taken to the river, but still he does not know enough to come to Four-Mile Well unless he is told to come to Four-Mile Well.

The shadow came slowly across the concrete floor of the tank. It was sinister and felt its way over the hot concrete like a spider. Matthew had watched it come down the west wall. It did not come gay and triumphant like the morning sun. It came sneaking back, ashamed that it must be the messenger of night. Matthew watched it crawl toward him and he did not want it, because he knew he must have it. He did not even want the hoofbeats in the sand when he first heard them.

He did not want them then because it was too early and Chapo should not have known to come himself, and there was no one to tell him to come, and yet he had come.

The hoofbeats slowly circled the tank at a walk, a nervous, stomping walk, the palomino's walk. They stopped. Silence. Matthew lay, waiting. He did not speak or scream or even move. He only waited.

"Patrón," a voice whispered from beyond.

"Chapo," Matthew answered, and his voice trembled.

Again all was quiet.

A horse whinnied.

"Put the ladder up . . ." But already the two knobs of wood poked above the rim.

The ladder creaked as Chapo climbed. The familiar black sombrero with brown leather band came up, a silhouette against the sky. Grimy hair hid the ears and made the head appear large and rectangular. The face showed teeth but had no expression.

"Drop the ladder down inside," Matthew ordered, lifting his head slightly. "Did you bring water?"

But the dark face was no longer there, and as he strained to locate it he saw the two knobs of the ladder disappear. He heard it fall on the sand with a dry rattle of old wood.

"*Vámonos!*" Chapo's voice came loud above the sound of his hand on the charcoal mare's rump. Empty stirrups slapped against the black's ribs as she galloped away to the north, toward sweet piles of alfalfa and pleading voices that would mean nothing to her.

Matthew Fennel heard the hoofbeats of the palomino slowly fade southward and he felt the shadows of night begin to creep out from the blank walls of his tank.

The Wonderful Ice Cream Suit

RAY BRADBURY

It was summer twilight in the city, and out front of the
quiet-clicking pool hall three young Mexican-American
men breathed the warm air and looked around at the
world. Sometimes they talked and sometimes they said
nothing at all but watched the cars glide by like black
panthers on the hot asphalt or saw trolleys loom up like
thunderstorms, scatter lightning, and rumble away into
silence.

"Hey," sighed Martínez at last. He was the youngest,
the most sweetly sad of the three. "It's a swell night, huh?
Swell."

As he observed the world it moved very close and then
drifted away and then came close again. People, brushing
by, were suddenly across the street. Buildings five miles
away suddenly leaned over him. But most of the time
everything—people, cars, and buildings—stayed way out
on the edge of the world and could not be touched. On
this quiet warm summer evening Martínez's face was
cold.

"Nights like this you wish . . . lots of things."

"Wishing," said the second man, Villanazul, a man who
shouted books out loud in his room but spoke only in whispers on the street. "Wishing is the useless pastime of the
unemployed."

"Unemployed?" cried Vamenos, the unshaven. "Listen
to him! We got no jobs, no money!"

"So," said Martínez, "we got no friends."

"True." Villanazul gazed off toward the green plaza where the palm trees swayed in the soft night wind. "Do you know what I wish? I wish to go into that plaza and speak among the businessmen who gather there nights to talk big talk. But dressed as I am, poor as I am, who would listen? So, Martínez, we have each other. The friendship of the poor is real friendship. We—"

But now a handsome young Mexican with a fine thin mustache strolled by. And on each of his careless arms hung a laughing woman.

"Madre mía!" Martínez slapped his own brow. "How does that one rate *two* friends?"

"It's his nice new white summer suit." Vamenos chewed a black thumbnail. "He looks sharp."

Martínez leaned out to watch the three people moving away, and then at the tenement across the street, in one fourth-floor window of which, far above, a beautiful girl leaned out, her dark hair faintly stirred by the wind. She had been there forever, which was to say for six weeks. He had nodded, he had raised a hand, he had smiled, he had blinked rapidly, he had even bowed to her, on the street, in the hall when visiting friends, in the park, downtown. Even now, he put his hand up from his waist and moved his fingers. But all the lovely girl did was let the summer wind stir her dark hair. He did not exist. He was nothing.

"Madre mía!" He looked away and down the street where the man walked his two friends around a corner. "Oh, if just I had one suit, one! I wouldn't need money if I *looked* okay."

"I hesitate to suggest," said Villanazul, "that you see Gómez. But he's been talking some crazy talk for a month now about clothes. I keep on saying I'll be in on it to make him go away. That Gómez."

"Friend," said a quiet voice.

"Gómez!" Everyone turned to stare.

Smiling strangely, Gómez pulled forth an endless thin yellow ribbon which fluttered and swirled on the summer air.

"Gómez," said Martínez, "what are doing with that tape measure?"

Gómez beamed. "Measuring people's skeletons."

"Skeletons!"

"Hold on." Gómez squinted at Martínez. *"Caramba!* Where you *been* all my life! Let's try *you!"*

Martínez saw his arm seized and taped, his leg measured, his chest encircled.

"Hold still!" cried Gómez. "Arm—perfect. Leg—chest—*perfecto!* Now quick, the height! There! Yes! Five foot five! You're in! Shake!" Pumping Martínez's hand, he stopped suddenly. "Wait. You got ... ten bucks?"

"I have!" Vamenos waved some grimy bills. "Gómez, measure me!"

"All I got left in the world is nine dollars and ninety-two cents." Martínez searched his pockets. "That's enough for a new suit? Why?"

"Why? Because you got the right skeleton, that's why!"

"Señor Gómez, I don't hardly know you—"

"Know me? You're going to live with me! Come on!"

Gómez vanished into the poolroom. Martínez, escorted by the polite Villanazul, pushed by an eager Vamenos, found himself inside.

"Domínguez!" said Gómez.

Domínguez, at a wall telephone, winked at them. A woman's voice squeaked on the receiver.

"Manulo!" said Gómez.

Manulo, a wine bottle tilted bubbling to his mouth, turned.

Gómez pointed at Martínez.

"At last we found our fifth volunteer!"

Domínguez said, "I got a date, don't bother me—" and stopped. The receiver slipped from his fingers. His little black telephone book full of fine names and numbers went quickly back into his pocket. "Gómez, you—?"

"Yes, yes! Your money, now! *Ándale!*"

The woman's voice sizzled on the dangling phone.

Domínguez glanced at it uneasily.

Manulo considered the empty wine bottle in his hand and the liquor-store sign across the street.

Then very reluctantly both men laid ten dollars each on the green velvet pool table.

Villanazul, amazed, did likewise, as did Gómez, nudging Martínez. Martínez counted out his wrinkled bills and change. Gómez flourished the money like a royal flush.

"Fifty bucks! The suit costs sixty! All we need is ten bucks!"

"Wait," said Martínez. "Gómez, are we talking about *one* suit? *Uno?*"

"*Uno!*" Gómez raised a finger. "One wonderful white

ice cream summer suit! White, white as the August moon!"

"But who will own this one suit?"

"Me!" said Manulo.

"Me!" said Domínguez.

"Me!" said Villanazul.

"Me!" cried Gómez. "*And* you, Martínez. Men, let's show him. Line up!"

Villanazul, Manulo, Domínguez, and Gómez rushed to plant their backs against the poolroom wall.

"Martínez, you too, the other end, line up! Now, Vamenos, lay that billiard cue across our heads!"

"Sure, Gómez, sure!"

Martínez, in line, felt the cue tap his head and leaned out to see what was happening. "Ah!" he gasped.

The cue lay flat on all their heads, with no rise or fall, as Vamenos slid it along, grinning.

"We're all the same height!" said Martínez.

"The same!" Everyone laughed.

Gómez ran down the line, rustling the yellow tape measure here and there on the men so they laughed even more wildly.

"Sure!" he said. "It took a month, four weeks, mind you, to find four guys the same size and shape as me, a month of running around measuring. Sometimes I found guys with five-foot-five skeletons, sure, but all the meat on their bones was too much or not enough. Sometimes their bones were too long in the legs or too short in the arms. Boy, all the bones! I tell you! But now, five of us, same shoulders, chests, waists, arms, and as for weight? Men!"

Manulo, Domínguez, Villanazul, Gómez, and at last Martínez stepped onto the scales which flipped ink-stamped cards at them as Vamenos, still smiling wildly, fed pennies. Heart pounding, Martínez read the cards.

"One hundred thirty-five pounds . . . one thirty-six . . . one thirty-three . . . one thirty-four . . . one thirty-seven . . . a miracle!"

"No," said Villanazul simply, "Gómez."

They all smiled upon that genius who now circled them with his arms.

"Are we not fine?" he wondered. "All the same size, all the same dream—the suit. So each of us will look beautiful at least one night each week, eh?"

"I haven't looked beautiful in years," said Martínez. "The girls run away."

"They will run no more, they will freeze," said Gómez, "When they see you in the cool white summer ice cream suit."

"Gómez," said Villanazul, "just let me ask one thing."

"Of course, *compadre.*"

"When we get this nice new white ice cream summer suit, some night you're not going to put it on and walk down to the Greyhound bus in it and go live in El Paso for a year in it, are you?"

"Villanazul, Villanazul, how can you say that?"

"My eye sees and my tongue moves," said Villanazul. "How about the *Everybody Wins!* Punchboard Lotteries you ran and you kept running when nobody won? How about the United Chili Con Carne and Frijole Company you were going to organize and all that ever happened was the rent ran out on a two-by-four office?"

"The errors of a child now grown," said Gómez. "Enough! In this hot weather someone may buy the special suit that is made just for us that stands waiting in the window of SHUMWAY'S SUNSHINE SUITS! We have fifty dollars. Now we need just one more skeleton!"

Martínez saw the men peer around the pool hall. He looked where they looked. He felt his eyes hurry past Vamenos, then come reluctantly back to examine his dirty shirt, his huge nicotined fingers.

"Me!" Vamenos burst out at last. "My skeleton, measure it, it's great! Sure, my hands are big, and my arms, from digging ditches! But—"

Just then Martínez heard passing on the sidewalk outside that same terrible man with his two girls, all laughing together.

He saw anguish move like the shadow of a summer cloud on the faces of the other men in this poolroom.

Slowly Vamenos stepped onto the scales and dropped his penny. Eyes closed, he breathed a prayer.

"*Madre mía,* please . . ."

The machinery whirred; the card fell out. Vamenos opened his eyes.

"Look! One thirty-five pounds! Another miracle!"

The men stared at his right hand and the card, at his left hand and a soiled ten-dollar bill.

Gómez swayed. Sweating, he licked his lips. Then his hand shot out, seized the money.

"The clothing store! The suit! *Vamos!*"

Yelling, everyone ran from the poolroom.

The woman's voice was still squeaking on the abandoned telephone. Martínez, left behind, reached out and hung the voice up. In the silence he shook his head. *"Santos,* what a dream! Six men," he said, "one suit. What will come of this? Madness? Debauchery? Murder? But I go with God. Gómez, wait for me!"

Martínez was young. He ran fast.

Mr. Shumway, of SHUMWAY'S SUNSHINE SUITS, paused while adjusting a tie rack, aware of some subtle atmospheric change outside his establishment.

"Leo," he whispered to his assistant. "Look . . ."

Outside, one man, Gómez, strolled by, looking in. Two men, Manulo and Domínguez, hurried by, staring in. Three men, Villanazul, Martínez, and Vamenos, jostling shoulders, did the same.

"Leo." Mr. Shumway swallowed. "Call the police!"

Suddenly six men filled the doorway.

Martínez, crushed among them, his stomach slightly upset, his face feeling feverish, smiled so wildly at Leo that Leo let go the telephone.

"Hey," breathed Martínez, eyes wide. "There's a great suit over there!"

"No." Manulo touched a lapel. *"This* one!"

"There is only one suit in all the world!" said Gómez coldly. "Mr. Shumway, the ice cream white, size thirty-four, was in your window just an hour ago! It's gone! You didn't—"

"Sell it?" Mr. Shumway exhaled. "No, no. In the dressing room. It's still on the dummy."

Martínez did not know if he moved and moved the crowd or if the crowd moved and moved him. Suddenly they were all in motion. Mr. Shumway, running, tried to keep ahead of them.

"This way, gents. Now which of you . . . ?"

"All for one, one for all!" Martínez heard himself say, and laughed. "We'll all try it on!"

"All?" Mr. Shumway clutched at the booth curtain as if his shop were a steamship that had suddenly tilted in a great swell. He stared.

That's it, thought Martínez, look at our smiles. Now, look at the skeletons behind our smiles! Measure here, there, up, down, yes, do you *see?*

Mr. Shumway saw. He nodded. He shrugged.

"All!" He jerked the curtain. "There! Buy it, and I'll throw in the dummy free!"

Martínez peered quietly into the booth, his motion drawing the others to peer too.

The suit was there.

And it was white.

Martínez could not breathe. He did not want to. He did not need to. He was afraid his breath would melt the suit. It was enough, just looking.

But at last he took a great trembling breath and exhaled, whispering, *"Ay. Ay, caramba!"*

"It puts out my eyes," murmured Gómez.

"Mr. Shumway," Martínez heard Leo hissing. "Ain't it dangerous precedent, to sell it? I mean, what if everybody bought *one* suit for six people?"

"Leo," said Mr. Shumway, "you ever hear one single fifty-nine dollar suit make so many people happy at the same time before?"

"Angels' wings," murmured Martínez. "The wings of white angels."

Martínez felt Mr. Shumway peering over his shoulder into the booth. The pale glow filled his eyes.

"You know something, Leo?" he said in awe. "That's a *suit!*"

Gómez, shouting, whistling, ran up to the third-floor landing and turned to wave to the others, who staggered, laughed, stopped, and had to sit down on the steps below.

"Tonight!" cried Gómez. "Tonight you move in with me, eh? Save rent as well as clothes, eh? Sure! Martínez, you got the suit?"

"Have I?" Martínez lifted the white gift-wrapped box high. "From us to us! *Ay-hah!*"

"Vamenos, you got the dummy?"

"Here!"

Vamenos, chewing an old cigar, scattering sparks, slipped. The dummy, falling, toppled, turned over twice, and banged down the stairs.

"Vamenos! Dumb! Clumsy!"

They seized the dummy from him. Stricken, Vamenos looked about as if he'd lost something.

Manulo snapped his fingers. "Hey, Vamenos, we got to celebrate! Go borrow some wine!"

Vamenos plunged downstairs in a whirl of sparks.

The others moved into the room with the suit, leaving Martínez in the hall to study Gómez's face.

"Gómez, you look sick."

"I am," said Gómez. "For what have I done?" He
nodded to the shadows in the room working about the
dummy. "I pick Domínguez, a devil with the women. All
right. I pick Manulo, who drinks, yes, but who sings as
sweet as a girl, eh? Okay. Villanazul reads books. You,
you wash behind your ears. But then what do I do? Can I
wait? No! I got to buy that suit! So the last guy I pick is
a clumsy slob who has the right to wear *my* suit—" He
stopped, confused. "Who gets to wear *our* suit one night a
week, fall down in it, or not come in out of the rain in it!
Why, why, why did I *do* it!"

"Gómez," whispered Villanazul from the room. "The
suit is ready. Come see if it looks as good using *your* light
bulb."

Gómez and Martínez entered.

And there on the dummy in the center of the room was
the phosphorescent, the miraculously white-fired ghost
with the incredible lapels, the precise stitching, the neat
buttonholes. Standing with the white illumination of the
suit upon his cheeks, Martínez suddenly felt he was in
church. White! White! It was white as the whitest vanilla
ice cream, as the bottled milk in tenement halls at dawn.
White as a winter cloud all alone in the moonlit sky late
at night. Seeing it here in the warm summer-night room
made their breath almost show on the air. Shutting his
eyes, he could see it printed on his lids. He knew what
color his dreams would be this night.

"White . . ." murmured Villanazul. "White as the snow
on that mountain near our town in Mexico, which is
called the Sleeping Woman."

"Say that again," said Gómez.

Villanazul, proud yet humble, was glad to repeat his
tribute. " . . . white as the snow on the mountain called—"

"I'm back!"

Shocked, the men whirled to see Vamenos in the door,
wine bottles in each hand.

"A party! Here! Now tell us, who wears the suit first
tonight? Me?"

"It's too late!" said Gómez.

"Late! It's only nine-fifteen!"

"Late?" said everyone, bristling. "Late?"

Gómez edged away from these men who glared from
him to the suit to the open window.

Outside and below it was, after all, thought Martínez, a

fine Saturday night in a summer month and through the calm warm darkness the women drifted like flowers on a quiet stream. The men made a mournful sound.

"Gómez, a suggestion." Villanazul licked his pencil and drew a chart on a pad. "You wear the suit from nine-thirty to ten, Manulo till ten-thirty, Domínguez till eleven, myself till eleven-thirty, Martínez till midnight, and—"

"Why me *last?*" demanded Vamenos, scowling.

Martínez thought quickly and smiled. "After midnight is the *best* time, friend."

"Hey," said Vamenos, "that's right. I never thought of that. Okay."

Gómez sighed. "All right. A half hour each. But from now on, remember, we each wear the suit just one night a week. Sundays we draw straws for who wears the suit the extra night."

"Me!" laughed Vamenos. "I'm lucky!"

Gómez held onto Martínez, tight.

"Gómez," urged Martínez, "you first. Dress."

Gómez could not tear his eyes from that disreputable Vamenos. At last, impulsively, he yanked his shirt off over his head. "Ay-yeah!" he howled. "Ay-*yeee!*"

Whisper rustle . . . the clean shirt.

"Ah . . . !"

How clean the new clothes feel, thought Martínez, holding the coat ready. How clean they sound, how clean they smell!

Whisper . . . the pants . . . the tie, rustle . . . the suspenders. Whisper . . . now Martínez let loose the coat, which fell in place on flexing shoulders.

"*Olé!*"

Gómez turned like a matador in his wondrous suit-of-lights.

"*Olé*, Gómez, *olé!*"

Gómez bowed and went out the door.

Martínez fixed his eyes to his watch. At ten sharp he heard someone wandering about in the hall as if they had forgotten where to go. Martínez pulled the door open and looked out.

Gómez was there, heading for nowhere.

He looks sick, thought Martínez. No, stunned, shook up, surprised, many things.

"Gómez! This is the place!"

Gómez turned around and found his way through the door.

"Oh, friends, friends," he said. "Friends, what an experience! This suit! This suit!"

"Tell us, Gómez!" said Martínez.

"I can't, how can I say it!" He gazed at the heavens, arms spread, palms up.

"Tell us, Gómez!"

"I have no words, no words. You must see, yourself! Yes, you must see—" And here he lapsed into silence, shaking his head until at last he remembered they all stood watching him. "Who's next? Manulo?"

Manulo, stripped to his shorts, leapt forward.

"Ready!"

All laughed, shouted, whistled.

Manulo, ready, went out the door. He was gone twenty-nine minutes and thirty seconds. He came back holding to doorknobs, touching the wall, feeling his own elbows, putting the flat of his hand to his face.

"Oh, let me tell you," he said. *"Compadres,* I went to the bar, eh, to have a drink? But no, I did not go in the bar, do you hear? I did not drink. For as I walked I began to laugh and sing. Why, why? I listened to myself and asked this. Because. The suit made me feel better than wine ever did. The suit made me drunk, drunk! So I went to the *Guadalajara Refritería* instead and played the guitar and sang four songs, very high! The suit, ah, the suit!"

Domínguez, next to be dressed, moved out through the world, came back from the world.

The black telephone book! thought Martínez. He had it in his hands when he left! Now, he returns, hands empty! What? What?

"On the street," said Domínguez, seeing it all again, eyes wide, "on the street I walked, a woman cried, 'Domínguez, is that *you?*' Another said, 'Domínguez? No, Quetzalcoatl, the Great White God come from the East,' do you hear? And suddenly I didn't want to go with six women or eight, no. One, I thought. One! And to this one, who knows *what* I would say? 'Be mine!' Or 'Marry me!' *Caramba!* This suit is dangerous! But I did not care! I live, I live! Gómez, did it happen this way with you?"

Gómez, still dazed by the events of the evening, shook his head. "No, no talk. It's too much. Later. Villanazul. . . ?"

Villanazul moved shyly forward.

Villanazul went shyly out.

Villanazul came shyly home.

"Picture it," he said, not looking at them, looking at the floor, talking to the floor. "The Green Plaza, a group of elderly businessmen gathered under the stars and they are talking, nodding, talking. Now one of them whispers. All turn to stare. They move aside, they make a channel through which a white-hot light burns its way as through ice. At the center of the great light is this person. I take a deep breath. My stomach is jelly. My voice is very small, but it grows louder. And what do I say? I say, 'Friends. Do you know Carlyle's *Sartor Resartus?* In that book we find *his* Philosophy of Suits. . . .'"

And at last it was time for Martínez to let the suit float him out to haunt the darkness.

Four times he walked around the block. Four times he paused beneath the tenement porches, looking up at the window where the light was lit; a shadow moved, the beautiful girl was there, not there, away and gone, and on the fifth time there she was on the porch above, driven out by the summer heat, taking the cooler air. She glanced down. She made a gesture.

At first he thought she was waving to him. He felt like a white explosion that had riveted her attention. But she was not waving. Her hand gestured and the next moment a pair of dark-framed glasses sat upon her nose. She gazed at him.

Ah, ah, he thought, so that's it. So! Even the blind may see this suit! He smiled up at her. He did not have to wave. And at last she smiled back. She did not have to wave either. Then, because he did not know what else to do and he could not get rid of this smile that had fastened itself to his cheeks, he hurried, almost ran, around the corner, feeling her stare after him. When he looked back she had taken off her glasses and gazed now with the look of the nearsighted at what, at most, must be a moving blob of light in the great darkness here. Then for good measure he went around the block again, through a city so suddenly beautiful he wanted to yell, then laugh, then yell again.

Returning, he drifted, oblivious, eyes half closed, and seeing him in the door, the others saw not Martínez but themselves come home. In that moment, they sensed that something had happened to them all.

"You're late!" cried Vamenos, but stopped. The spell could not be broken.

"Somebody tell me," said Martínez. "Who am I?"

He moved in a slow circle through the room.

Yes, he thought, yes, it's the suit, yes, it had to do with the suit and them all together in that store on this fine Saturday night and then here, laughing and feeling more drunk without drinking as Manulo said himself, as the night ran and each slipped on the pants and held, toppling, to the others and, balanced, let the feeling get bigger and warmer and finer as each man departed and the next took his place in the suit until now here stood Martínez all splendid and white as one who gives orders and the world grows quiet and moves aside.

"Martínez, we borrowed three mirrors while you were gone. Look!"

The mirrors, set up as in the store, angled to reflect three Martínezes and the echoes and memories of those who had occupied this suit with him and known the bright world inside this thread and cloth. Now, in the shimmering mirror, Martínez saw the enormity of this thing they were living together and his eyes grew wet. The others blinked. Martínez touched the mirrors. They shifted. He saw a thousand, a million white-armored Martínezes march off into eternity, reflected, re-reflected, forever, indomitable, and unending.

He held the white coat out on the air. In a trance, the others did not at first recognize the dirty hand that reached to take the coat. Then:

"Vamenos!"

"Pig!"

"You didn't wash!" cried Gómez. "Or even shave, while you waited! *Compadres,* the bath!"

"The bath!" said everyone.

"No!" Vamenos flailed. "The night air! I'm dead!"

They hustled him yelling out and down the hall.

Now here stood Vamenos, unbelievable in white suit, beard shaved, hair combed, nails scrubbed.

His friends scowled darkly at him.

For was it not true, thought Martínez, that when Vamenos passed by, avalanches itched on mountaintops? If he walked under windows, people spat, dumped garbage, or worse. Tonight now, this night, he would stroll beneath ten thousand wide-opened windows, near balconies, past alleys. Suddenly the world absolutely sizzled with flies. And here was Vamenos, a fresh-frosted cake.

"You sure look keen in that suit, Vamenos," said Manulo sadly.

"Thanks." Vamenos twitched, trying to make his skeleton comfortable where all their skeletons had so recently been. In a small voice Vamenos said, "Can I go now?"

"Villanazul!" said Gómez. "Copy down these rules."

Villanazul licked his pencil.

"First," said Gómez, "don't fall down in that suit, Vamenos!"

"I won't."

"Don't lean against buildings in that suit."

"No buildings."

"Don't walk under trees with birds in them in that suit. Don't smoke. Don't drink—"

"Please," said Vamenos, "can I *sit down* in this suit?"

"When in doubt, take the pants off, fold them over a chair."

"Wish me luck," said Vamenos.

"Go with God, Vamenos."

He went out. He shut the door.

There was a ripping sound.

"Vamenos!" cried Martínez.

He whipped the door open.

Vamenos stood with two halves of a handkerchief torn in his hands, laughing.

"Rrrip! Look at your faces! Rrrip!" He tore the cloth again. "Oh, oh, your faces, your faces! Ha!"

Roaring, Vamenos slammed the door, leaving them stunned and alone.

Gómez put both hands on top of his head and turned away. "Stone me. Kill me. I have sold our souls to a demon!"

Villanazul dug in his pockets, took out a silver coin, and studied it for a long while.

"Here is my last fifty cents. Who else will help me buy back Vamenos' share of the suit?"

"It's no use." Manulo showed them ten cents. "We got only enough to buy the lapels and the buttonholes."

Gómez, at the open window, suddenly leaned out and yelled. "Vamenos! No!"

Below on the street, Vamenos, shocked, blew out a match and threw away an old cigar butt he had found somewhere. He made a strange gesture to all the men in the window above, then waved airily and sauntered on.

Somehow, the five men could not move away from the window. They were crushed together there.

"I bet he eats a hamburger in that suit," mused Villanazul. "I'm thinking of the mustard."

"Don't!" cried Gómez. "No, no!"

Manulo was suddenly at the door.

"I need a drink, bad."

"Manulo, there's wine here, that bottle on the floor—"

Manulo went out and shut the door.

A moment later Villanazul stretched with great exaggeration and strolled about the room.

"I think I'll walk down to the plaza, friends."

He was not gone a minute when Domínguez, waving his black book at the others, winked and turned the doorknob.

"Domínguez," said Gómez.

"Yes?"

"If you see Vamenos, by accident," said Gómez, "warn him away from Mickey Murrillo's Red Rooster Café. They got fights not only *on* TV but *out front* of the TV too."

"He wouldn't go into Murrillo's," said Domínguez. "That suit means too much to Vamenos. He wouldn't do anything to hurt it."

"He'd shoot his mother first," said Martínez.

"Sure he would."

Martínez and Gómez, alone, listened to Domínguez's footsteps hurry away down the stairs. They circled the undressed window dummy.

For a long while, biting his lips, Gómez stood at the window, looking out. He touched his shirt pocket twice, pulled his hand away, and then at last pulled something from the pocket. Without looking at it, he handed it to Martínez.

"Martínez, take this."

"What is it?"

Martínez looked at the piece of folded pink paper with print on it, with names and numbers. His eyes widened.

"A ticket on the bus to El Paso three weeks from now!"

Gómez nodded. He couldn't look at Martínez. He stared out into the summer night.

"Turn it in. Get the money," he said. "Buy us a nice

white panama hat and a pale blue tie to go with the white ice cream suit, Martínez. Do that."

"Gómez—"

"Shut up. Boy, is it hot in here! I need air."

"Gómez. I am touched. Gómez—"

But the door stood open. Gómez was gone.

Mickey Murrillo's Red Rooster Café and Cocktail Lounge was squashed between two big brick buildings and, being narrow, had to be deep. Outside, serpents of red and sulphur-green neon fizzed and snapped. Inside, dim shapes loomed and swam away to lose themselves in a swarming night sea.

Martínez, on tiptoe, peeked through a flaked place on the red-painted front window.

He felt a presence on his left, heard breathing on his right. He glanced in both directions.

"Manulo! Villanazul!"

"I decided I wasn't thirsty," said Manulo. "So I took a walk."

"I was just on my way to the plaza," said Villanazul, "and decided to go the long way around."

As if by agreement, the three men shut up now and turned together to peer on tiptoe through various flaked spots on the window.

A moment later, all three felt a new very warm presence behind them and heard still faster breathing.

"Is our white suit in there?" asked Gómez's voice.

"Gómez!" said everybody, surprised. "Hi!"

"Yes!" cried Domínguez, having just arrived to find his own peephole. "There's the suit! And, praise God, Vamenos is still *in* it!"

"I can't see!" Gómez squinted, shielding his eyes. "What's he *doing?*"

Martínez peered. Yes! There, way back in the shadows, was a big chunk of snow and the idiot smile of Vamenos winking above it, wreathed in smoke.

"He's smoking!" said Martínez.

"He's drinking!" said Domínguez.

"He's eating a taco!" reported Villanazul.

"A *juicy* taco!" added Manulo.

"No," said Gómez. "No, no, no. . . ."

"Ruby Escuadrillo's with him!"

"Let me see that!" Gómez pushed Martínez aside.

Yes, there was Ruby! Two hundred pounds of glittering

sequins and tight black satin on the hoof, her scarlet fingernails clutching Vamenos' shoulder. Her cowlike face, floured with powder, greasy with lipstick, hung over him!

"That hippo!" said Domínguez. "She's crushing the shoulder pads. Look, she's going to sit on his lap!"

"No, no, not with all that powder and lipstick!' said Gómez. "Manulo, inside! Grab that drink! Villanazul, the cigar, the taco! Domínguez, date Ruby Escuadrillo, get her away. *Ándale*, men!"

The three vanished, leaving Gómez and Martínez to stare, gasping, through the peephole.

"Manulo, he's got the drink, he's *drinking* it!"

"*Ay!* There's Villanazul, he's got the cigar, he's eating the taco!"

"Hey, Domínguez, he's got Ruby! What a *brave* one!"

A shadow bulked through Murrillo's front door, traveling fast.

"Gómez!" Martínez clutched Gómez's arm. "That was Ruby Escuadrillo's boy friend, Toro Ruíz. If he finds her with Vamenos, the ice cream suit will be covered with blood, *covered* with blood—"

"Don't make me nervous," said Gómez. "Quickly!"

Both ran. Inside they reached Vamenos just as Toro Ruíz grabbed about two feet of the lapels of that wonderful ice cream suit.

"Let go of Vamenos!" said Martínez.

"Let go that *suit!*" corrected Gómez.

Toro Ruíz, tap-dancing Vamenos, leered at these intruders.

Villanazul stepped up shyly.

Villanazul smiled. "Don't hit him. Hit me."

Toro Ruíz hit Villanazul smack on the nose.

Villanazul, holding his nose, tears stinging his eyes, wandered off.

Gómez grabbed one of Toro Ruíz's arms, Martínez the other.

"Drop him, let go, *cabrón, coyote, vaca!*"

Toro Ruíz twisted the ice cream suit material until all six men screamed in mortal agony. Grunting, sweating, Toro Ruíz dislodged as many as climbed on. He was winding up to hit Vamenos when Villanazul wandered back, eyes streaming.

"Don't hit him. Hit me!"

As Toro Ruíz hit Villanazul on the nose, a chair crashed on Toro's head.

"Ai!" said Gómez.

Toro Ruíz swayed, blinking, debating whether to fall. He began to drag Vamenos with him.

"Let go!" cried Gómez. "Let go!"

One by one, with great care, Toro Ruíz's banana-like fingers let loose of the suit. A moment later he was ruins at their feet.

"Compadres, this way!"

They ran Vamenos outside and set him down where he freed himself of their hands with injured dignity.

"Okay, okay. My time ain't up. I still got two minutes and, let's see—ten seconds."

"What!" said everybody.

"Vamenos," said Gómez, "you let a Guadalajara cow climb on you, you pick fights, you smoke, you drink, you eat tacos, and *now* you have the nerve to say your time ain't up?"

"I got two minutes and one second left!"

"Hey, Vamenos, you sure look sharp!" Distantly, a woman's voice called from across the street.

Vamenos smiled and buttoned the coat.

"It's Ramona Álvarez! Ramona, wait!" Vamenos stepped off the curb.

"Vamenos," pleaded Gómez. "What can you do in one minute and"—he checked his watch—"forty seconds!"

"Watch! Hey, Ramona!"

Vamenos loped.

"Vamenos, look out!"

Vamenos, surprised, whirled, saw a car, heard the shriek of brakes.

"No," said all five men on the sidewalk.

Martínez heard the impact and flinched. His head moved up. It looks like white laundry, he thought, flying through the air. His head came down.

Now he heard himself and each of the men make a different sound. Some swallowed too much air. Some let it out. Some choked. Some groaned. Some cried aloud for justice. Some covered their faces. Martínez felt his own fist pounding his heart in agony. He could not move his feet.

"I don't want to live," said Gómez quietly. "Kill me, someone."

Then shuffling, Martínez looked down and told his feet

to walk, stagger, follow one after the other. He collided
with other men. Now they were trying to run. They ran at
last and somehow crossed a street like a deep river
through which they could only wade, to look down at
Vamenos.

"Vamenos!" said Martínez. "You're alive!"

Strewn on his back, mouth open, eyes squeezed tight,
tight, Vamenos motioned his head back and forth, back
and forth, moaning.

"Tell me, tell me, oh, tell me, tell me."

"Tell you what, Vamenos?"

Vamenos clenched his fists, ground his teeth.

"The suit, what have I done to the suit, the suit, the
suit!"

The men crouched lower.

"Vamenos, it's . . . why, it's *okay!*"

"You lie!" said Vamenos. "It's torn, it must be, it must
be, it's torn, all around, *underneath?*"

"No." Martínez knelt and touched here and there.
"Vamenos, all around, underneath even, it's okay!"

Vamenos opened his eyes to let the tears run free at
last. "A miracle," he sobbed. "Praise the saints!" He
quieted at last. "The car?"

"Hit and run." Gómez suddenly remembered and glared
at the empty street. "It's good he didn't stop. We'd have——"

Everyone listened.

Distantly a siren wailed.

"Someone phoned for an ambulance."

"Quick!" said Vamenos, eyes rolling. "Set me up! Take
off our coat!"

"Vamenos——"

"Shut up, idiots!" cried Vamenos. "The coat, that's it!
Now, the pants, the pants, quick, quick, *peones!* Those
doctors! You seen movies? They rip the pants with razors
to get them off! They don't *care!* They're maniacs! Ah,
God, quick, quick!"

The siren screamed.

The men, panicking, all handled Vamenos at once.

"Right leg, *easy,* hurry, cows! Good! Left leg, now, left,
you hear, there, easy, *easy!* Ow, God! Quick! Martínez,
your pants, take them off!"

"What?" Martínez froze.

The siren shrieked.

"Fool!" wailed Vamenos. "All is lost! Your pants! Give
me!"

Martínez jerked at his belt buckle.

"Close in, make a circle!"

Dark pants, light pants flourished on the air.

"Quick, here comes the maniacs with the razors! Right leg on, left leg, *there!*"

"The zipper, cows, zip my zipper!" babbled Vamenos.

The siren died.

"Madre mía, yes, just in time! They arrive." Vamenos lay back down and shut his eyes. *"Gracias."*

Martínez turned, nonchalantly buckling on the white pants as the interns brushed past.

"Broken leg," said one intern as they moved Vamenos onto a stretcher.

"Compadres," said Vamenos, "don't be mad with me."

Gómez snorted. "Who's mad?"

In the ambulance, head tilted back, looking out at them upside down, Vamenos faltered.

"Compadres, when . . . when I come from the hospital . . . am I still in the bunch? You won't kick me out? Look, I'll give up smoking, keep away from Murrillo's, swear off women—"

"Vamenos," said Martínez gently, "don't promise nothing."

Vamenos, upside down, eyes brimming wet, saw Martínez there, all white now against the stars.

"Oh, Martínez, you sure look great in that suit. *Compadres,* don't he look *beautiful?"*

Villanazul climbed in beside Vamenos. The door slammed. The four remaining men watched the ambulance drive away.

Then, surrounded by his friends, inside the white suit, Martínez was carefully escorted back to the curb.

In the tenement, Martínez got out the cleaning fluid and the others stood around, telling him how to clean the suit and, later, how not to have the iron too hot, and how to work the lapels and the crease and all. When the suit was cleaned and pressed so it looked like a fresh gardenia just opened, they fitted it to the dummy.

"Two o'clock," murmured Villanazul. "I hope Vamenos sleeps well. When I left him at the hospital, he looked good."

Manulo cleared his throat. "Nobody else is going out with that suit tonight, huh?"

The others glared at him.

Manulo flushed. "I mean ... it's late. We're tired. Maybe no one will use the suit for forty-eight hours, huh? Give it a rest. Sure. Well. Where do we sleep?"

The night being still hot and the room unbearable, they carried the suit on its dummy out and down the hall. They brought with them also some pillows and blankets. They climbed the stairs toward the roof of the tenement. There, thought Martínez, is the cooler wind, and sleep.

On the way, they passed a dozen doors that stood open, people still perspiring and awake, playing cards, drinking pop, fanning themselves with movie magazines.

I wonder, thought Martínez. I wonder if— Yes!

On the fourth floor, a certain door stood open.

The beautiful girl looked up as the men passed. She wore glasses and when she saw Martínez she snatched them off and hid them under her book.

The others went on, not knowing they had lost Martínez, who seemed stuck fast in the open door.

For a long moment he could say nothing. Then he said:

"José Martínez."

And she said:

"Celia Obregón."

And then both said nothing.

He heard the men moving up on the tenement roof. He moved to follow.

She said quickly, "I saw you tonight!"

He came back.

"The suit," he said.

"The suit," she said, and paused. "But not the suit."

"Eh?" he said.

She lifted the book to show the glasses lying in her lap. She touched the glasses.

"I do not see well. You would think I would wear my glasses, but no. I walk around for years now, hiding them, seeing nothing. But tonight, even without the glasses, I see. A great whiteness passes below in the dark. So white! And I put on my glasses quickly!"

"The suit, as I said," said Martínez.

"The suit for a little moment, yes, but there is another whiteness above the suit."

"Another?"

"Your teeth! Oh, such white teeth, and so many!"

Martínez put his hand over his mouth.

"So happy, Mr. Martínez," she said. "I have not often seen such a happy face and such a smile."

"Ah," he said, not able to look at her, his face flushing now.

"So, you see," she said quietly, "the suit caught my eye, yes, the whiteness filled the night below. But the teeth were much whiter. Now, I have forgotten the suit."

Martínez flushed again. She, too, was overcome with what she had said. She put her glasses on her nose, and then took them off, nervously, and hid them again. She looked at her hands and at the door above his head.

"May I—" he said, at last.

"May you—"

"May I call for you," he asked, "when next the suit is mine to wear?"

"Why must you wait for the suit?" she said.

"I thought—"

"You do not need the suit," she said.

"But—"

"If it were just the suit," she said, "anyone would be fine in it. But no, I watched. I saw many men in that suit, all different, this night. So again I say, you do not need to wait for the suit."

"Madre mía, madre mía!" he cried happily. And then, quieter, "I will need the suit for a little while. A month, six months, a year. I am uncertain. I am fearful of many things. I am young."

"That is as it should be," she said.

"Good night, Miss—"

"Celia Obregón."

"Celia Obregón," he said, and was gone from the door.

The others were waiting on the roof of the tenement. Coming up through the trapdoor, Martínez saw they had placed the dummy and the suit in the center of the roof and put their blankets and pillows in a circle around it. Now they were lying down. Now a cooler night wind was blowing here, up in the sky.

Martínez stood alone by the white suit, smoothing the lapels, talking half to himself.

"Ay, *caramba*, what a night! Seems ten years since seven o'clock, when it all started and I had no friends. Two in the morning, I got all *kinds* of friends. . . ." He paused and thought, Celia Obregón, Celia Obregón. ". . . all kinds of friends," he went on. "I got a room, I got clothes. You tell *me*. You know what?" He looked around at the men lying on the rooftop, surrounding the dummy and himself. "It's funny. When I wear this suit, I know I will win at pool, like Gómez. A woman will look at me like Domínguez. I will be able to sing like Manulo, sweetly. I will talk fine politics like Villanazul. I'm strong as Vamenos. So? So tonight, I am more than Martínez. I am Gómez, Manulo, Domínguez, Villanazul, Vamenos. I am everyone. Ay ... ay ..." He stood a moment longer by this suit which could save all the ways they sat or stood or walked. This suit which could move fast and nervous like Gómez or slow and thoughfully like Villanazul or drift like Domínguez, who never touched ground, who always found a wind to take him somewhere. This suit which belonged to them but which also owned them all. This suit that was—what? A parade.

"Martínez," said Gómez. "You going to sleep?"

"Sure. I'm just thinking."

"What?"

"If we ever get rich," said Martínez softly, "it'll be kind of sad. Then we'll all have suits. And there won't be no more nights like tonight. It'll break up the old gang. It'll never be the same after that."

The men lay thinking of what had just been said.

"Yeah ... it'll never be the same ... after that."

Martínez lay down on his blanket. In darkness, with the others, he faced the middle of the roof and the dummy, which was the center of their lives.

And their eyes were bright, shining, and good to see in the dark as the neon lights from nearby buildings flicked on, flicked off, flicked on, flicked off, revealing and then vanishing, revealing and then vanishing, their wonderful white vanilla ice cream summer suit.

Mr. Iscariot

RICHARD G. BROWN

At 2 A.M. in the black dark night Mario Alejandro de Valera y Guerrero rolled nonchalantly up the white-powdered driveway to the white powder-covered '61 deluxe robin-egg-blue Caddy, that he would have walked up to nonchalantly but bulky chest-torso on squat little body-legs made him roll instead of walk and as he rolled, nonchalantly, deceptively rolling in the black dark he squinted cunningly at the dark house. He was not afraid of Big John Sánchez.

He had been waiting the two hours pulling at the white port hidden in the bushes across the road. Waiting for the house of Big John Sánchez to quiet; Big John's Caddy he was snatching. Repossessing, technically. Big John a "leetle beet" behind in payments to Credit Finance Ink (like he-wasn't-gonna-pay-what-ya-gonna-do-about-it). But it was a difficult snatch. Impossible they said. And then asked him to do it. For three months then coming by Big John's house, here, a mile across the border what they called skunk hollow casing this snatch. And only tonight for the first time in three months was the Caddy not parked way up in front of the garage, with the chain on it, and the big truck in back tied to the chain so it was impossible to get out but now instead halfway out in the white-powdered drive yet still right beside the ominous quiet-dark house of Big John Sánchez. Who was the local chicano gangster who had the smuggling, prostitution and pornography of this border town sewed up in his chicano pocket with a reputation of *el desarmado* but mostly because of the 'marican magnum he'd somehow got hold of, as he walked across the white-powdered drive, and he was not afraid of Big John Sánchez. He did not want to die. But he was decidedly not afraid of Big John. Nor of the magnum.

It was only the other . . .

He took the first key of the fifty on the ring bunch he'd held in his hand, tight, all the way up so it would not sound and carefully, very quietly, tried it to the doorlock. The dog immediately started barking and he walked nonchalantly back across the road and sat down with the white port bottle. He looked up at the black night and wished it was dawn and drank the white port. Credit Finance Ink was a job, he thought but bitterly, the first bitter thought he'd had all night and so it was a job even though he only snatched a couple times a month. And all chicano's cars he thought.

The dog had quieted and he got up, padded across the white-powdered drive in the dark with the second of the fifty-key-ring bunch and he was not afraid of Big John Sánchez still. Nor his guns, nor his rifles, nor his knives, nor his Tarzanes then thought again of the recurring dream, his mother with no clothes and looking like a *homo* and him wakening just before he could ask why, the second key did not work and the dog started barking and he walked nonchalantly back to the white port.

While waiting the light came on once in the house and a voice yelled at the dog and the light went out.

It was she who had wanted to go to Los Angeles fifteen years ago where his father had died trying to be a CHICANO SUCCESS in Los Angeles and finally from where he and the mother returned to the border town with Chana, fourteen years old, from the anglo wife he'd married while in the navy who chipped on him and he'd beaten up and taken the girl back with them.

After fifteen minutes he got up to the dark silence again to try the third key thinking if it's fifty it'll be all night he should've got the right one at the office instead of using his whole master fifty-key-ring set except he did not like to go to the office. *They* would see him.

On the fourth key he thought the dog would not bark and he could try the fifth but at the last minute the dog barked and he had to go back for another fifteen minutes but the fifth key did work and it was time and he ripped open the door dived for the ignition roared three fast times, first, loud as he could get his foot smacking the accelerator and revvied out of the white-powdered drive, roaring let the door fly shut as he geared forward and away picking up speed to 60 in eight seconds with a cold engine thinking it was a big good motor for that in the black dark.

He was heading home, after he'd crossed without trouble feeling warm wheeling the big robin-egg-blue Caddy that wheeled so marvelously easy that he was jealous of Big John Sánchez for that, but taking the back streets because he did not want to be seen waiting, reminding himself to get another white port bottle to the gate where he'd forgotten Credit Finance Ink was closed, the gate would not be unlocked until six-thirty, knowing now the one hour at the most he could expect before Big John would have the Tarzanes out. So he headed home, too shrewd to leave the car on the street but almost out of town remembered the white port, turned when he was almost out of town, almost home and came back in using the side alley that paralleled the main street, feeling the good warm easy power of the big Caddy wheel in his lap.

Three houses away, in back, just around the back alley corner he rolled in dead motor without lights between the high view-shutting sumacs and widow Tomás' garage side, got out and walked, rollingly peaceful down the alley around to the liquora beside the cantina that fronted the main street. It was here while he was standing in front of the liquora entrance that he saw the first Tarzane torpedoing wide open the main street leaving dust funneling behind in the dark, him standing for a moment, placidly watching for a second hardly even curious before he turned and went in to get his white port which was of more serious business—because he had to decide whether to get a small or a large bottle; the small would not last until dawn unless he was exceptionally frugal but the large would make him drunk. But he did not have money for a large bottle as he watched the owner speculatively; he would not get paid for the snatch until the end of the month. And the owner was in a bad mood so he did not mention the end of the month and finally got a small bottle. Then he had only come out when the second torpedo came barreling after the first easy to recognize by the 'marican fins, chrome, duals, off-color-luminescent-chartreuses-and-fuchsias and he rolled

back to the Caddy that at least had taste (gave grudgingly
Big John that) and threw the white port in the seat and had
an idea and padded back down the alley to the street, the
first torpedo returning in front of his funnel which would
have made him think of keystone-cop movies except he
was no longer interested and he went into the cantina.

There was little business. The old man at the end, and
González sitting . . .

"Mario, my friend," Roberto González opened his
arms. "A drink señor bartender for my best friend."

"Hiya Bob," he grinned. *"Como'sta?"*

"Ah, what chickencrut luck. They—"

Several chicanos came in. Hey, Mario, you working yet?
Catch me, man, grins, laughs. Hear the U.S. Testing Station open for jobs. Ah-choorguy, I theenk I try *mañana*,
laughs, they pass down the bar.

"Maybe I'll go out there tomorrow," Bob González said.
"Want to go?"

"Choorguy," Mario grinned gently. They laughed.

"Ah, what chickencrut luck," Bob swore. "They come
took my Rosita's new kitchen set."

"Who?"

"Credit Finance. Cabrones. I can't go home, she—
Stove, washing machine, everything. For two lousy payments!"

Mario looked away.

"They find out I was working part time 'cross the
border. How the hell they find out?"

Down at the end the old man was hitting a string.
Mario took his drink, moved off "see ya Bob." He did not
look back.

"They get your stuff?" a chicano called to Bob.

"How the hell they find out?" Bob swore.

"They find out. Somehow they know because last time I
work, man, they—"

"There is a Judas," somebody said loudly. "A Judas
. . ."

Viejito Don Marquez pulled his soft grey goatee hair
before each time someone else tossed off their snifter of
tequila or wine. Out of the corner of his eye he followed
Mario's advance like an ancient turkey buzzard.

Salute Mario Alejandro," and then settled the old guitar
behind him. "How is your family?"

"My father is not well," Mario grinned.

The old man ignored the witticism.

"Not very well at all," Mario repeated.

"I knew your father when he had *cojones*."

"You never knew him after he left for Los Angeles."

"No, I never saw him after that but I knew your father before, when he had *cojones*. Before he married Chana Cristobal Samienego."

"He never married Samienego. He went to jail in Samienego." Mario knocked off the remainder of the snifter clean.

The old man shifted his guitar in front. "He was not a warrior like your grandfather. Like the Guerreros. But he never worked for anybody just the same."

"There is no middle class in Mexico," Mario said.

"No, there is no middle class and you must either work for a grandee or you must be a grandee. But your father never worked for anybody. He traveled on the oceans or he went for long trips. If what I hear is true he once owned a cattle ranch in Argentina. Even the warriors worked for somebody else."

"A conquistador?"

"No, a conquistador conquers for somebody else. Although he also is very lonely."

"Would you like a drink, old man? I would be very pleased if you would accept a drink in my honor."

"I would be most honored Mario Alejandro."

"Señor bartender. Please. A drink of your best tequila for my good friend Viejito Don Marquez."

The bartender glowered at them but made no move.

"Come, señor bartender. Is it not a point of respect and friendship that I should offer to buy the very best friend of my father a small drink?"

The bartender finally came over. "Come off that, Mario. You know he's cut off. Doc said one more drink his ticker'll explode like a bomb. Just lay off," he grumbled sourly as he left.

"Yes," Mario said earnestly. "It is true. That last heart attack was a very bad one, Viejito Don Marquez."

The old man sighed and pulled at his goatee hair. "Perhaps you could, ah, obtain certain substance at the liquora next door?"

Mario speculated. He had three cents left in his pocket. Most certainly not enough for a large bottle.

"Why, old man, why is the Gumuchil on top of the hill in back of the town growing there? So far north?"

"I do not know. Nobody knows."

"I heard my father say it is an underground spring."

"Nobody knows," the old man repeated fingering the glossy guitar neck.

"Somebody knows," Mario said.

"I do not know," the old man said.

"Who knows?"

The old man replied in very formal Spanish. "Why do the young always expect impossible answers from the old when the only answer is time. Which is the one answer the old do not have. Oh, yes, they say it. They say it to boredom but both know they do not mean it."

"What was my father like before he became emasculated?" Mario asked in Spanish.

Viejito Don Marquez softly fingered some strings and did not answer. Mario smiled sweetly. He did not believe the old man would speak again. He acted like that sometimes.

"Emasculated," Viejito Don Marquez said slowly. "Yes. For the sake of this new modern thing that is very strange and of which I do not understand."

"What is that, old man?"

Viejito Don Marquez shrugged.

"Security?" Mario asked.

The old man shrugged.

In back of them the news of Big John's car had exploded in the room. Who did thees? when did thees thing happen? incredulous! disbelief! Por Diáz, that poor hombre that took eet! A Tarzane had come in, looked evilly around and tramped out again. Mario was bored. It was only the Gumuchil tree that he could not get out of his mind.

"Perhaps I could get a bottle," Mario said kindly. "But unfortunately, it is terrible. I have no money."

"I have money," the old man said very simply. But quickly.

"But your heart, por Diáz . . ."

"An old man has not much," Viejito Don Marquez sighed. "He has not love nor family nor servants. Nor work. Perhaps a bottle is better than a heart? You think so?"

"Perhaps. If two bottles are better than two hearts, then."

"Of course," the old man smiled.

Mario went back out into the dark night, onto the comic opera stage again which was very funny now and he wondered why he was not amused before when clearly it was so very ridiculously funny. Up one street, down another, zing, wham, whoosh, torpedos to the right of you, torpedos to the left of you . . .

Placidly, letting the Gumuchil tree sink back into the darkness of his subconscious, he went into the liquora with the old man's grimy wrinkle-hidden bill thinking the crazy bastard will kill himself, but he'd get it somewhere, and met him back in the darkness behind the liquora to give him his bottle, the greedy old bastard, he thought angrily, and nipping at the white port slowly, placidly wheeled the big robin-egg-blue Caddy out of town by the alley that paralled the main street . . .

"Go away!"

"I wanna come in," he kicked the door.

"Get out! Go away!"

He kicked the door again, louder.

"What do you want? Go away!"

"It is no more important that you are a mother to let me in," he screamed in Spanish.

"Why don't you get a job?" his mother screamed back. "I work hard all day. I feed you and your daughter. I tired and sleep little you banging all night this door."

"Let me in you blank old woman." He kicked the door again.

"Go away. My back is sore, my legs ache from working hard all day. I go to sleep now."

"Let me in you dirty old woman. My bed is in there on which I want to sleep. In order to keep me out of my bed you think you have a perfect right?"

"Why don't you get a job and be a decent man? All you do is drink," she screamed.

"Let me in you black mammyjammer." He kicked the door until his feet hurt and he stopped.

"Drunk! Every night drunk. Go away! You will not come in my house on my dear dead husband's name!"

"Oh, you dirty old black mammyjammer," he yelled. He kicked the door but his foot was too painful and he started beating with his fists.

"I will now call the police," his mother threatened.

"*Mierda* on you," he yelled.

"Oh, *el monstruo!*" she yelled. "*El monstruo!*"

Finally his fists also hurt and he stopped beating on the door altogether. The sudden black silence twisted at him inside.

"Where is Chana?" his mother scolded him. "Why she no come home tonight. Fourteen years old."

"Whatdya mean, not home? Where is she?"

"She no come home I told you," she screamed. "Go away! Go find your daughter."

"Where is she?" he roared.

"How do I know? She never tell me anything. Every night all this week she stay out almost all night. Why you no get a job? Take care of your own family."

He did not say anything. He did not know Chana had been staying out so late. Or so often.

"I'm tired, my back aches. Go away! Get your daughter and find a job. Goodnight!"

"You black mammyjammer," he yelled half indifferently. "Where is she?" He kicked the door again. Not hard because his foot hurt.

"My legs are aching standing here all night. Go away! Goodnight!"

"Well, to hell with you," he screamed. *"Chinga a tu madre!"*

"Oh, *el monstruo*. EL MONSTRUO INFAME!!"

He walked away and then came back and beat and kicked on the door again. "On your grave when you die I will *cagar* and *mear* on your grave," he yelled. And then had to trudge back again completely across the long crop field in back of the house to get to the Caddy he'd hidden there. He actually didn't know how he made it and he was so exhausted and out of breath that he had to lean on the car to get his breath back before he could even open the door and get the white port.

On the hilltop above the town with the rare Gumuchil tree growing where he came and parked waiting for the dawn was a place he had come many times. It was really because of the Gumuchil he thought such a very strange wonder for this semi-arid border town in the north but also from here on the hilltop on a dark clear night he could look down across the lights of the town, deep across beyond that into the heart of the Sierras and big Mexico beyond (Méjico is masculine he thought), and sometimes if he did not drink white port until he passed out he could see the dawn rising clear and very golden and beautiful lighting up the face of this golden homeland across where he and his father had come so many years before. When he was too small to even remember.

But the Gumuchil with the impossible-to-climb thorns studding out at every branch fork, yet very large branches grown for a shade tree on the central plateau and Mexico City where there was adequate rainfall but so rare for up here that no one knew why. A spring under the hill, he thought (also thinking although he couldn't remember the gender for Gumuchil, the word tree, *árbol,* is masculine) because the sucker needed such a *fantastic* amount of water and he wished the sucking dawn would come.

He wondered if the Tarzanes were still down below, leaving their broads for this long a time which was a very long time for a Tarzane, even for the robin-egg-blue Caddy of Big John Sánchez and was glad he had also the large bottle with him instead of just the one little half quart already dead and wondered how the old man was getting along ...

Boredom, leaning back bulky-torsoed, deep into the matching blue cushions, thoughts. An idle idea, curiosity, hah! As though the car of Big John Sánchez had suddenly become a personal thing, he started rummaging around, in the glove compartment, behind the sunshades, under the seat, climbing over the back (searching for private treasure, ha!), back in front, feeling very personal, inhibited personal, like searching with your hand in another man's pocket, finally finding something under the floor mat beneath the front seat. A white envelope with photographs, giggling hilariously at his cleverness recognizing with delight the rooms of the house, the beds, even the broads, even some of the Tarzanes (laughing because these were Big John's exports for norteamericanos) and of course the positions and seeing Chana suddenly in the fifth and sixth shot.

He laid the photographs carefully on the front seat, very surprised that he felt no anger at Chana whom he loved above anyone, really no anger at all although of course he was no longer chuckling at his own cleverness and wished more desperately now as he looked out the window eastward much more desperately now for the dawn to come.

But then he could even smile sadly thinking my dear-own-beloved-more-than-anyone-Chana had returned more than he and she not even full blood he thought wondering-ly. And all this still with the sad smile realizing, completing this whole picture-story, what he had done to his own self-strings. But not to her.

But to the tree, he thought looking northward to the great giant eucalyptus-like Gumuchil that covered the car like an eagle. It is the tree and the tree he thought sucking the white port. The tree. Yet there is a tree of Buddha he remembered called the Bo tree. And there is a tree of knowledge, also a tree of knowledge of good and evil, and a tree of life. A tree of porphyry, a tree of heaven, a tree of the sun, a trembling tree and a Tyburn tree. There is also up the tree, he thought. But not the Gumuchil because you can never climb the Gumuchil.

Them . . .

He opened the car door and stepped out hoping against hope to see the dawn he was so desperate for now looking off to the Sierras and the east beyond that mountain range across the face of which the red golden would come and not seeing it. He thought it must be dawn time yet he could not drive into town before that and he got out to *see!*

But out in the cool blackness of the hilltop it was as black as the coffin tomb of a womb . . . not even the light before the dawn and he realized not with scaredness but with sickness of the night darkness and he would not even look at the lights of the town. He clambered up on the fender of the robin-egg-blue Caddy and balancing himself bulky-torso-clumsy but one hand holding the white port up onto the roof of Big John's car searching the face of the faraway Sierras for that gold, thought he saw it but could not find it again. If only he was tall enough, him already stretching tiptoes on the car roof, just high enough to see over the Sierras to the broad central plateau in whose nestling, comforting apex was Mexico City. He clambered down awkwardly and opened the trunk of Big John's car looking until he found what he wanted and carried the rope back up to the roof and threw the end over the large bottom branch of the Gumuchil who he thought he'd cheat after all, wanting to get up in its branches which were unclimbable but knowing *the rare Gumuchil could see . . .* catching the rope end, securing the navy hitch, drawing it up and fastening the noose knowing all along it was not true, you could not cheat the Gumuchil.

He took the last long drink of the white port he'd at least outfoxed that sly one thinking last of all that Chana was right and he was wrong before he put the noose over his head and stepped off Big John's robin-egg-blue Caddy, swinging, jerking, thinking, twisting ... *He had to do it, he had to go with that. Yes, obviously. He did it, so it had to be ...*

Sánchez and the Víbora
A New Mexican Tale

ROBERT GRANAT

Now a *víbora*, in case you didn't know, means a rattlesnake. But that doesn't come in till later on. Right now be concerned with *cabrón*, a curse for which there is no really adequate English equivalent. At least not the way Perfecto M. Sánchez just used it as he saw the rosebud tear off the crepe-paper wreath he was extricating from the ancient dome-lidded trunk of his forefathers. He didn't wonder it tore, so entangled was it in the intestinal mess of belts, reins, ropes, socks, and mousetraps he stored there. His *cabrón* was anger at the inevitable.

He reached back among the guts of the trunk, fumbled about with his old speckled hand, so horny with adobe and callous it looked soled by a cobbler, found the rose inside a worn-out boot, went to the kitchen table, cleared a work space with a swift sweep of his forearm, spilt a little flour into an empty sardine can, and made paste with his spit and forefinger.

The rose restored, he held up the wreath, cleaned the dust from it with several vigorous gusts from his lungs, spruced it up a little here and there, and looped it over the doorknob so as not to forget it. A little faded, *quizás*, but after a day in the sun they all faded anyway. "Two for $1.29—Special." The taste of last year's bargain rose like a burp in his mind and he resavored it. The first he'd laid on *la vieja's* grave last Memorial Day. This one he'd place there now on the way to the *rancho*. Maybe he should have bought a half-dozen wreaths at that price. But who knows? He gave an upwards El Greco-like glance. He was eighty-four years old himself.

It was still very early. He'd beaten the sun up so as to avoid the rush out to the cemetery and then continue on to the *rancho*—seven acres under the ditch three miles west of here—where he and his *peón*, doña Agneda, were three-quarters through hoeing the chili. In the first luminous stain of dawn he'd made his fire, relieved the goat of its milk, which he mixed with the blue corn he'd grown, toasted and ground, to make his *atole*, fried up a potato with chili and a few scraps of mutton, heated up last night's coffee and dunked into it one of the tortillas Agneda made for him on commission. Now he felt ready to go. Got everything? Hoes? Buckets? Lunch? Alarm clock? Glasses? Instead of feeling to determine if his glasses were on, he gave a quick stare at the section of wall where hung the painting of San Ysidro with his oxen and next to it himself with his *vieja*, in the blueish-brownish photo from back in their wedding clothes and bodies. He looked—the glasses were on. The Saint and his *bueyes*, the old woman and himself, were all clearer than the other way, and cracked through the middle from the time he stepped on the lenses.

He looped the wreath over his shoulder and flung open the door. The dog, who was sleeping on the stoop, made way with a yelp. Don Perfecto walked first to the well, and as he drew his two buckets of water he looked at the sky. Flawlessly clear and transparent. The edges were already being licked by a flaming pink. Today was going to be a *sanamagán*, hot as the *infierno*. Not that it bothered him. Eighty years of sun had taken all the water out of him. He sweat no longer; he was hard and dry, partially mummified while yet alive. Just so long as it didn't rain. If they didn't get that first hoeing done with today, you wouldn't be able to find the *matas* of chili in all the weeds. Even now he had to call Agneda over from time to time to point out which from which. His two buckets full, he walked over to his truck, a huge banged-up black-and-blue Model A, which stood on a little hill behind the corrals waiting for him. Every morning before starting off for the *rancho* he had to water the truck, just as he had formerly had to water the team till the *caballo* died and the mare, by herself, was too fast, too *bailadora*, for him to keep up with. The truck's radiator had cracked a few winters ago and now it held water just long enough to reach the *rancho* before it boiled out. As he poured the two buckets into it now he wondered what was going to be wrong with the truck today. Like himself the truck suffered from a variety of minor ailments which appeared and disappeared. Usually it merely refused to go. So he would raise the hood on its hinges of bailing wire—"Mexican rawhide" the *gringos* called it—and make his ritual movements underneath among the connections, screws, wires, and plugs with the solemnity of a Navajo shaman. Invariably, if he manipulated long enough, the truck would start. But it took patience, sometimes half a day. Occasionally, of course, it got really sick, and then the only thing he could do was let it rest, don't force it to work that day. But that usually happened in winter.

He threw all the day's materials—alarm clock, hoes, buckets, jar of coffee, cans of sardines, two tortillas as large as cowpats, a shovel, a heavy iron tow chain (only this last need be remembered)—onto the bed of the truck. Then he opened the door, lay the wreath on the pants (the upholstery of the seat had of course worn away years ago and he had clothed the naked springs with a dozen pairs of old pants, of which he'd naturally accumulated a fine supply during the last seventy years or so). He next removed the stone that blocked the front wheel and as the truck began to roll down the slope, leapt aboard like a desert rodent and threw it into gear. The iron bulk roared with a fierce protesting groan—"No-no-oh-no!"—and it did not start. It shuddered to an anticlimactic stop on level ground. Perfecto Sánchez sat for a moment without moving on his pile of pants.

"*Cabrón!*" Except for his morning prayers, which were hardly uttered, this pair of *cabrones* were his only utterances of the day. He peered over at the instrument panel, out of habit mostly, since the last dial, the ammeter, had got stuck on -30 at least five years ago. He was about to go out and insert a stick into the gas tank when he noticed that the ignition switch was off. He'd forgotten to turn it on.

"*Cabrón!*"

This third *cabrón* of the morning was sworn in a slightly milder tone, for now he was calling himself one.

He slid off the pants and stepped-stood on the starter.

"Uuuh ... uuuh ... uhhh ..." The motor convulsed thrice with a deathbed moan and it died. The battery was something like the radiator. It held juice for ten hours exactly.

Dismounting, Sánchez disinterred the crank from under the pants, and began to crank the motor by hand. He did it with the intimate anger one uses with domestic animals, one's children, and at times one's wife. It was like disentangling the mare's legs from a mess of barbed wire.

The truck started up abruptly, with a strange sound, inappropriate to a manufactured product somehow, a sequence of wheezes. With a small tight smile he climbed back up into the now violently shaking truck, adjusted the pants beneath him so as to command a better view over the steering wheel, and bent so far forward that his black felt hat almost touched the windshield. The world was well-centered between two cracks now, the horizontal one from his glasses and the vertical one from where the rock had hit the windshield; they intersected like the crosshairs on a gunsight and the old man studied them with the intensity of a sharpshooter.

The *rancho* lay three miles down the dirt road and *la vieja* lay in the old graveyard halfway there—very convenient. The truck gathered speed, bounced over the cattle-guard, and clattered down the hard adobe ruts like a horsewagon. The fire of the sun was just breaking out over the Truchas Peaks. Jackrabbits still loped along the road returning from their nightly raid on the alfalfa fields and on some run-over rodent a raven couple was feasting. They did not fly off as the truck clattered past, but only hopped sufficiently aside to watch it go by in safety. It would not have seemed out of the way to hear them croak, *"Buenos días, don Perfecto* ... and how'd you wake up this morning?" or to see him tip his crow-black hat to them. But Sánchez studied his crosshairs, gripped his steering wheel, listened to each cough of each cylinder, and absorbed each jolt of the road. Before him the cemetery was already rocking inward on his sights, and behind him rose a huge cloud of pink-tan dust.

Nobody was there yet. They were still at Mass. He himself never went to Memorial Day Mass. Between work and Mass, work came first. Mass on Sunday. What with all these masses all the time for every little thing, if a man went to them all he'd eat weeds.

As he was about to pull up in front of the cemetery, he found out what was wrong with the truck today. No *brecas*. He plunged the brake pedal to the floor again

and again. The truck rolled on unaffected. Thinking he
might have made some mistake, he tried all the pedals,
clutch, accelerator, starter. Nothing. No *brecas* whatso-
ever.

"*Sanamagán!*" he swore. This was a stronger curse than
cabrón, viler still for being in English.

The *campo santo* was bouncing away. He thought
quickly: should he switch off the key and stop the truck
that way? No, he might not be able to get it started again.
It would take half a mile to stop. Agneda must be waiting
at the *rancho*. He was paying her by the hour. . . .

"*La voluntad de Dios*," he thought with a whisper. "An
act of God." And who was he to put *his* will above God's?
He crossed himself, glanced quickly at his wife's receding
grave in the rear-view mirror, silently vowed to lay the
wreath on her wooden cross on the way back home—
what's a few hours to the dead?—and stepped on the
accelerator. . . .

Doña Agneda Herrera was standing by the swinging
gate of Sánchez's *rancho*—a mere seven acres of irrigated
land—exchanging a few words across the barbed-wire
fence with don Sotero Olivas, who was harnessing up his
horse preparatory to giving his corn the first cultivation of
the season. Doña Agneda was a square, solid woman,
almost pure Pueblo, with a handsome square adobe-
brown face and a shape as square and solid as a block
quarried for a pyramid to Quetzalcoatl. Well, not quite
square; she was graced with a pair of great breasts from
which thirteen babies had sucked, and amply, of the
strength of life, and these she kept cinched tightly inside a
heavy canvas brassiere whose strong straps showed
through her thin, flour-sack dress. But this bosom spoke
not just of femininity but of power. When she got angry,
for instance, her hand would clutch at these same straps,
as if she wore a Mexican bandoleer with grenades she
wouldn't hesitate to yank forth and hurl at her foe. When
sickness, birth, death, catastrophe struck, she stood as a
rock among the weaker souls. She could work as hard as a
man, ten or twelve hours in the sun. And yet small reptiles
of any kind, snakes, toads, *guajalotes* (mud puppies)
would send her screaming like a little girl. A beautiful
combination of femininity and strength, like the great pink
breasty mountains of New Mexico.

But at the moment she was angry—at Perfecto

Sánchez—and had been giving it to him, via Sotero Olivas. She had not minced words, used a few, in fact, that
we have already heard this morning.

"Ah no, Señora, we should not judge him; God will take
care of that. Who knows, maybe we are worse than he
is." Don Sotero adjusted the lines on his skinny droop-
lipped horse. He was old too, though not as old as
Sánchez, a spare man whose frail and pale appearance
belied all his years of sun and hail and sheep. He had no
reason to be charitable to Perfecto Sánchez. His neighbor
had blatantly cheated him many times. Once, while he was
away sheepherding in Utah, Sánchez had shifted the entire
boundary fence, forty cedar logs, over ten feet on the
pretense of "straightening it out." They had not exchanged
a word in the eight years since. But the farthest Sotero
Olivas had gone to judge his neighbor was to say on
occasion, *"Este hombre es muy duro,* he's a hard man."

Agneda had just been explaining-complaining to him,
her hand tugging at her brassiere-strap all the while, how
Sánchez had cheated her on her wages the last time she
worked as his *peón* by allowing the alarm clock he always
set on the truck hood to run down then having to "estimate" the hours. . . . "Estimate!"

"Yes, you are right, don Sotero; we should not judge
Señor Sánchez. God will judge him . . . but still, anyway,
es un cabrón!"

The second person this morning to refer thus to Perfecto M. Sánchez.

"Here he comes," Sotero Olivas said, clicking up his
horse so as not to be present.

"Yes, here he comes," Agneda sighed, scratching her
shoulder under the strap. She watched the truck come
crawling across the dry pink plain, a large black horsefly
that has lost its wings. It rounded the corner and clattered
in toward the gate, pursued by a great jet trail of pink
dust. "He's coming fast," Agneda said aloud. She had no
need of privacy. What she said she said aloud; what she
thought even, she thought aloud. If she was not incessantly
talking it was because she didn't waste too much of life
saying or thinking things. *"Very* fast," she said again,
moving toward the gate. She squinted at the truck and
made out the driver in a frenzy of excitement, arms
waving, head bobbing in and out of the window, shouting
at her.

"El portón! Ábrelo, pronto, por Dios!"

"Open the gate?" Agneda said. "Something is not right." With the litheness of youth she sprang to the gate, slipped off its wire loop fastener, and with a tremendous heave sent it swinging wide just as the clattering mass of vehicle roared through. She watched it head for the log bridge over the ditch, sail off into the farther air like a skier on a jump, fall with an awful crash back to earth, roll on and on, careening wildly, until finally it described a wide arc and came to a halt in the middle of the wheat field. The door opened and Señor Sánchez climbed out like an astronaut from a capsule. He wasted no time but immediately began unloading the hoes and the buckets from the truck bed.

He was just setting the alarm clock on the hood when Agneda got there.

"*Válgame Dios, Señor Sánchez*—Good God, what happened?"

"*Brecas fregadas*," he said. "Brakes are shot. You use the one with the short handle." He handed her the hoe.

Halfway through the afternoon it began to rain. It had to, the heat had become insufferable. Sánchez and his *peón* had hoed all day, exchanging only ten words between them—"*Qué calor*," spoken five times. Agneda as usual sweat vastly; her body shone like the earth under a cloudburst. Arroyos ran down the slopes of her face, over the hillocks of her collarbones and disappeared in a torrent down the canyon of her chest. Sánchez perspired not a drop. If anything he dried, twisted. Like an elongation of his hoe he chopped, chopped, chopped. Beyond the fence Sotero Olivas and his horse plodded back and forth between the rows of young corn, pausing now and then to catch their breaths or empty their bladders.

And suddenly into the white-hot sky, rising out of the Jémez beyond Española, a huge brown-black cloud flew eastward, blotting out the sun like the devil's cloak. It began to rain, great fat splats of it that turned into hailstones and made the fields white for a minute until they melted and the rain decided on a steady downpour.

Sánchez did not even glance up. Agneda glanced up, saw that Sánchez did not glance up, glanced back down and went on hoeing. But within twenty minutes the earth in front of them had become a gummy muck that could be worked into nothing but adobes.

"*Vamos*," growled Sánchez, suddenly and sullenly. The two unweeded rows might now be a total loss, but whom could you blame? Nobody. Again, the will of God. Yet he couldn't suppress a vague intuition that Agneda was somehow responsible, as if she had turned his chili patch into a claypit with all her damn female sweating.

"Water is falling," Agneda said blandly, readjusting her brassiere from where it had shifted forward during a day of stooping.

Sánchez did not deign to reply. The mare had a bigger brain than this one, he thought.

But when he reached the truck his attitude reversed itself in a hurry. Intimations of disaster made him flee psychologically to her shelter. "Look ... look what happened! ... *Ay, que sanamagán!*"

The truck had chosen to halt in the long narrow depression the plow had left down the center of the wheatfield as it spiraled inward, throwing the soil outward. That depression was now a long narrow pond.

"Oh," said Agneda Herrera. She watched as Señor Sánchez, like a watersnipe, lifted one leg high, took a cautious step forward into the puddle, and sank up to his knee. Cursing, he waded slowly toward the truck, pulling his boots with a loud gulp from the sucking mud with each step. He then pulled himself wearily up into the cab like a man rescued from the sea.

He had merely to touch the starter when the motor started up briskly. He shifted the gears, the wheels went round and the truck began to move—downward, into the mud.

"No, no, Señor Sánchez!" He climbed out on the runningboard, gave one pained look aft and saw the woman was right. He sat back down on the pile of pants, stared through the windshield and began to meditate.

Through his cross-sights just then passed Sotero Olivas, leading his horse back up to the corral. As if his own thought were arriving from outside his head, he heard Agneda's voice.

"Don Sotero's team, Señor Sánchez. He could pull you out, no?"

"Sure, but he wouldn't do it. He doesn't like me ... a small man, full of vengeance, a little deranged, it seems to me. ..."

"No, he's a Christian, He'll pull you."

Sánchez shook his head. "No, not me he wouldn't." But maybe, maybe he would ... for money. Money talks, as the *gringos* said. But how much money? If Olivas asked more than a *peso*, the hell with it. He'd just leave the truck here and walk—no, couldn't do that, the thieving neighbors would strip it bare. Well, he'd stay here and sleep the night in the truck.

His willingness to refuse help was a bargaining point, a source of strength. *"Bueno*, you go ask him if he'll give us a pull. We'll see if he's a Christian."

"Me, Señor Sánchez? You want me to ask?"

"Sure you, who else? Don't worry, I'm keeping account of the hours. It's easier work to talk than to hoe, no? And I'm paying you the same wages for both ... anyhow, you and him are great buddies."

Agneda went sloshing off through the wheat. She hailed Olivas, who stopped the horse. Both looked at him, and beyond this Perfecto Sánchez could not bear to watch. His eyes fell downward, on the wreath. He patted it gingerly with his hard brown fingers, just as he used to caress *la vieja* when she was on the point of losing her temper with him. Or the mare. ...

When he saw the team approaching, Sánchez felt a sudden need to be busy. He leapt out of the cab, raised the hood and began to tinker, one eye cocked outward. Then, when they were upon him, he banged the hood shut and wiped his hands ceremoniously on his pants.

"Buenas tardes," Sotero said, the first words in eight years.

"Buenas tardes."

"A lot of water, no?"

Sánchez did not answer. Same mentality as the woman. Exactly.

"You got a chain?" he asked. He was all business. Like a *gringo*.

"No."

"Then I'll use mine." He waded to the back of the truck and dug out the heavy tow chain he had thrown in there this morning. The heavy hook on one end he fastened to the truck's front axle and the heavy hook of the other to the drawbar of the team Sotero was backing into position. Then he climbed back up on the pants.

"Bueno," he called out. The team strained forward, and with unforeseen obedience the truck followed docilely behind. Sánchez's smile was self-contained, like a monarch in a royal coach.

"How much I owe you, neighbor?" he asked Olivas—

though not looking at him directly—when the team had pulled him to solid ground. He was busy gathering up the tow chain to throw back onto the truck.

"That's all right."

Though he did not show it in any other way, this reply startled Perfecto Sánchez enough to toss the tow chain a little too hard; it slid quietly off the other side of the bed but he was so preoccupied at the return of his kissed-goodbye dollar that he failed to notice.

"Come on, the laborer is worth his hire . . . here, here's *dos reales*." He held out a quarter.

"No, that's all right."

Sánchez smiled. "I like your attitude, don Sotero. We neighbors have to help each other out, eh?"

"*Bueno* . . . and Agneda, here's a *peso*," Sánchez said when Olivas had gone, "I'm a little short. Had to buy this wreath for the old lady. I'll pay you the first of the month."

"What lies!" murmured Agneda Herrera with no particular emotion, it being merely the thought that followed his statement. Sánchez, busy adjusting the choke, did not hear her.

He drove home in a happy mood, remembered to shift into neutral five hundred yards before the graveyard, so that the truck stopped not ten paces from *la vieja*, to whom he paid his Memorial Day respects, thinking, "See, you have a dry fresh one, at least. . . ."

Happily he milked the goat, fed the pig, gathered the eggs, lit his fire, shared his beans and *posole* with the dog, and even read a few lines about Scribes and Pharisees before dropping off to sleep; happily he dreamed he was aloft, floating among the clouds on a pair of strong white wings.

Happily he got up, did the morning chores, readjusted the brakes, got the truck running. But then everything joyful in him went suddenly black, as if hit by an October frost. The tow chain. The tow chain was gone!

He tried to remember all the details concerning the tow chain yesterday. Sotero Olivas' smiling face kept insinuating itself into his mind.

At the *rancho* his neighbor greeted him for the first time in eight years, as if yesterday's incident had meant peace had come. But Sánchez only muttered sourly in return, peering at him through his cracked lenses, trying to read the guilt in Sotero's face. But it betrayed nothing.

"Listen, you didn't by any chance happen to see my chain, eh?"

"Your chain, don Perfecto?"

"Yes, my chain. The one we used yesterday."

"The one we used yesterday? No, why, did you lose it?"

Lose it? thought Perfecto M. Sánchez. Thinks he's fooling me. No wonder he wouldn't take the quarter . . . hypocrite . . . Pharisee. . . .

A hundred mornings passed and it was seven A.M. on the sixth of September, and Perfecto M. Sánchez had reached that stage of his morning routine where he was ministering to the truck. This morning it was suffering from a slight case of *chorte*—automotive terms were always English words (the Conquistadores were not motorized) marinated in Spanish. It must be a *chorte* there being no spark, but it couldn't be the battery. The battery was new, not two weeks old. Its predecessor had been doing all right, keeping its current for seven hours or so, when one morning Sánchez had yawned too long, run off the road, hitting a rock with a jolt that lifted his head to and practically through the fabric roof, that ripped the hood right off its bailing-wire hinges and sent the battery on its suicidal leap, after which it evinced not the smallest spark of life. So he had had to buy a new secondhand battery from Rafael Quintana, the mechanic, for four *pesos*. It couldn't be the battery.

After half an hour of *monkeyando* with the wires, he began to lose hope. For a change of pace he checked the oil. The rod showed no oil. He poured in a dozen gulps of heavy oil from a two-gallon can, half of which gulped onto the fan, generator, plugs, and elsewhere.

Then he returned to the ignition system, approaching the motor from the opposite side this time. Maybe it was the starter. A good part of the time shorts had some intimate relation to the starter. He picked up a fist-sized piece of lava rock and began to tap the starter. Two taps and the motor began to chug. He straightened up with a smile which immediately was coated with a warm viscous bath of motor oil.

"*Chite!*" he swore, squeegeeing himself off as best he could with his forefingers. He was blinded. His glasses were filmed with grease. By feel he wired the hood shut, climbed into the truck and wiped the glasses on the pants, redistributing the oil on the lenses. Then he remembered the radiator must be about empty, he'd been fooling with the ignition so long. So he climbed back down, took off his opaque glasses, lay them on the pants, returned to the well, drew water, and refilled the radiator.

As he sat down once more with a sigh behind the steering wheel, he was conscious of a delicate crunching beneath his backside.

All this to explain why Perfecto M. Sánchez drove to his *rancho* on the sixth of September without his glasses. That he was a menace to life and limb there was no doubt, but at that hour and on that road there were few lives and limbs and what few there were got out of the way in time. The truck itself did most of the steering, the road to the *rancho* having impregnated itself into the very iron, rubber, and wood of its being. The only mishap came at the end when it grazed the gate post and tore away a section of fender that served no function anyway.

Sánchez climbed down and began to feel the truck bed for the roll of burlap sacks and the alarm clock. He jumped somewhat to hear the voice of Agneda Herrera very close to his ear.

"*Buenos días de Dios, Señor Sánchez.* Where are your glasses?"

"*Fregados,*" he grunted. "Shot."

"And you drove here without your glasses, don Perfecto?"

He did not deign to respond. "Here, take these sacks," he said. She was once more working as his *peón.* The chili had begun to color now and they were spending the days before the frost gathering all the pods that showed even a touch of red to store till they could tie them into five-foot-long *ristras* to take to Santa Fe or up to Colorado to peddle or barter.

They worked the morning in silence, Sánchez bent over at an even more acute angle than usual, his nose among the leaves, in order to see better which chilis to pick. After a pleasant lunch of tortillas, pinto beans, and coffee, together with tomatoes and cucumbers picked from the garden, the old man was walking through the wheat field towards a clump of wild plum bushes in search of some necessary privacy. The wheat had been harvested last week by Rafael's combine, and Sánchez, as he walked through the stubble, was wondering whether it would be worth the work salvaging the stalks that the machine had missed now and then.

Suddenly, in the grass ahead of him, he saw the largest rattlesnake he had ever seen in his life, and he had seen many. A red one, coiled up, at least four inches thick and six feet long. Its flat wide ugly head seemed about to strike.

Sánchez froze. Then he imperceptibly rotated his head to one side and back over his shoulder projected a strangely modulated voice, a kind of shouted whisper.

"Agneda! *Ven pa' 'ca!* Quick! Bring the hoe, the big one! Hurry! Run!"

Emergency registered in Agneda. She thrust aside the jar of cold coffee she was drinking, jumped to her feet, grabbed the hoe, and ran towards the old man like an infantryman on the attack. When she was close Sánchez stifled her to a halt with a frenzied motion of his fingers.

"What is it, Señor Sánchez?"

"Shut up. Be quiet. You don't have a pistol on you?"

"A pistol?"

"Shut up. Hand me the hoe! Quick! Don't move."

"What is it?" Agneda whispered, trying to make out what it was Sánchez had in the grass in front of him.

"*Una víbora,*" he hissed. "Big as the *infierno.*"

Almost in transparency a process now took place in Agneda's head. The word *víbora* went into her ear like a little red light, looped quickly around the semicircular canal, boarded the appropriate nerve, and rode to her brain. The little red light touched off a large red light that flared brilliantly. "UNA VÍBORA!" As she thought the word, of course she said it, that is, screamed it.

Despite the vast difference in size, her reaction to the rattlesnake was identical to a kangaroo rat's. But she did not altogether lose her head; from twenty feet farther back she begged Sánchez to save his life too.

"Run, run, don Perfecto. For the love of God, run!"

"Woman: shut up!" Cautiously raising the hoe, he took a slow step forward.

He could see the snake clearly now, bright red, with diamond-shaped loops along its length, its flat head, ugly and merciless, fixing him with its beady stare.

With all his strength he brought the hoe down. His aim was true: the blade struck the snake right behind its bulging poison glands, hard enough to sever the head from the body. A stunning blow—for Sánchez. The crack of steel on steel seemed to yank his arms once and for all out of their sockets. But he recovered himself swiftly and raising the hoe again, bent cautiously forward.

That was too hard for a snake, not even bone would clank like that. He inched forward, reached out slowly and touched the reptile gingerly with the blade of the hoe. It clinked. It was metal. He picked it up and examined it. It was heavy. The chain, his tow chain, red with the rust of one hundred days. *"Qué sanamagán!"*

"What is it?" Agneda whispered, keeping her distance.

"The chain, I found my chain," Sánchez said, walking over to the truck and depositing the rusty links carefully on the bed.

The following day, the seventh of September, Perfecto Sánchez went with Rafael Quintana to Santa Fe to get new glasses. But on the eighth he arrived bright and early at his *rancho* with a brand new vision of the world.

Sotero Olivas heard his neighbor's truck rattle to a halt across the fence from where he stood in his boots giving his garden its last irrigation of the season. He immediately turned and began to shovel mud, to dam up a furrow he'd had already dammed up once.

"Buenos días, don Sotero, how'd you wake up this morning?"

Sotero Olivas turned and looked up at Perfecto Sánchez, his mouth slightly agape. The old face beneath the black felt hat was alight with a winking grin, neighborliness itself.

"Irrigating, eh? Sure a pretty garden you've got there, neighbor."

"Qué hombre tan raro," Sotero thought. He nodded cautiously.

"Buenos días de Dios, Señor Sánchez," he said.

To Endure

ROBERT GRANAT

Who speaks of conquering? To endure is everything.—
Rilke.

I just come home from school when Anastasio die.
"Queeeh!" he say, and that was all.

Right away I go to the picture Mama cut from the
calendar where Jesus is pulling open his chest for to show
us his beautiful heart and I cross myself. Then I go tell
everybody—Daddy, Franque (that is Francisco, my
brother) and Arcelia (that is Arcelia, my sister). And we
all begin to cry for the old man but really we was pretty
happy. We like Anastasio OK but he take too long to
die.

Anastasio was the uncle of my mother and he live with
us since I can remember. But he been sick three months
and he take all the kitchen for himself, because Mama
didn't want for none of us to sleep in the room with
Anastasio when he was sick, so Franque and me and
Arcelia all got to sleep together in one bed in the other
room with Daddy and Mama in another bed and Ubaldo
in the basket. And one thing, I sure don't like to sleep
with nobody else in the bed, especially Franque and Arcelia, and that was the real reason I was pretty happy when
Anastasio die. He make too many people sleep in one
place.

Mama and the other ladies put the wedding suit of
Anastasio on him and we put him on the long bench
Carlos Trujillo loan us and after supper everybody come
to make the *velorio* and we cry and sing *alabados* and

228

drink coffee and eat bizcochitos. Arcelia got to go to bed all by herself but I stay up all night, I think.

Next morning we didn't go to school on account Anastasio was dead. Carlos Trujillo and Daddy and Franque and me take the tarpaulin off the pickup and we make I guess you call it a tent right outside the window and we carry Anastasio on the bench and put him under so Mama can fix the kitchen and look out to see if Anastasio OK.

"He gonna be cold out here," Arcelia say. She don't know nothing; she only six.

"Está muerto," I tell her. "He's dead. He don't feel nothing."

Mama and Mrs. Trujillo and my Aunt Manuelita and Arcelia and Ubaldo was going to stay home and take care of everything because all the men—me and Franque and Daddy and Carlos Trujillo—got to take the pickup to Sandoval to buy a box to bury Anastasio with. Sandoval is the biggest town in Madera County, about a hundred miles from Piñoncito and I never been there but Franque been two times with Daddy. I help Franque kick the mud off the pickup and put in water ... was cold, almost winter, and we let out the water every night so it don't freeze and bust the motor. I put on my clean levis, I was always saving for something like this, and I was happy I didn't have no school today and was going to Sandoval.

Then Arcelia—big cry-baby—start to cry she want to go with us, and she make me cry too because I didn't want no girls with us, especially Arcelia. But Mama say why not, and Daddy get mad and say "Shut your mouth or ain't nobody going to go." So Arcelia get in and she stick her tongue at me and I was going to hit her only everybody was there and I couldn't. So Daddy and Franque and Carlos Trujillo get inside and Franque drive. Arcelia and me ride in the back with the rope and the chains and the shovel and the boards for if we get stuck. She stand in one corner and me in the other one.

Is about forty-five miles to the black-top road the other side Mesa Quemada. The farther I ever go before was to Peña's Cash Store in Rio Seco where my cousin live. But Franque didn't stop. He keep right on going. The roads was pretty bad. The grader ain't been through and some places got pretty lot of mud. But we didn't get stuck. Franque, he's fifteen. He's a pretty good driver.

Then I fall asleep. I was trying not to but I couldn't help it. To sit all night with Anastasio make me too tired.

And I was ashamed too, because I ain't no kid like Arcelia. I already have eleven years.

I feel Arcelia shake me. *"Pendejo, pendejo, levántate!"*

I shake my head fast. *" 'Onde 'stamos?"* I say. "Where are we?"

"Sandoval, *tonto!"* she say.

"Don't call me no *tonto,* you monkey!" I say, that's *chongo* in Mexican. But I was ashamed anyway to be sleeping when we got to Sandoval.

We was already at the funeral company. Daddy get out. "We going inside to buy the box for Anastasio. You want to come with us or wait out here?"

I want to come and see the funeral company, and Arcelia do too, but Daddy say no, she too little, she got to wait outside in the pickup.

"Varoz Brothers Mortuary" I say when I read the big sign they got there. I can read pretty good English, better than Franque and better than Daddy too. Inside was Mr. Varoz. I think he was going to be Americano but he was Spanish like us, only got Anglo clothes with a tie on. He talk in Mexican with Daddy and Carlos Trujillo and they tell him Anastasio die and they want a nice box to bury him with. So Mr. Varoz take us in the back where they keep the boxes. "Ah *qué!"* . . . how many they got there! Big ones, brown ones, black ones, all colors, shiny like a new car. They even got little white ones for little kids. They got enough boxes to put everybody in Piñoncito, I think.

"What kind you want?" say Mr. Varoz.

"Well, we want a pretty good one," say Daddy, "maybe the Welfare going to help pay."

Mr. Varoz pick a nice box, grey color like the pickup, only shiny with gold things to carry it with. I tell Franque maybe was too big for Anastasio but Franque say no, Anastasio going to fit good inside. Mr. Varoz call some other men—maybe they was his brothers—and everybody carry the box out and put it on the pickup. I help. Ah *qué!* was heavy, more heavy than Anastasio on Carlos Trujillo's bench.

"Arcelia, get out the way!" I say and we throw the box in back of the pickup. Franque and Carlos Trujillo tie it on with the rope.

"That rope going to hold OK?" say Mr. Varoz in English and he push it with his hands. "I guess it's OK if you take it easy."

"Está bien," Daddy say. My Daddy know only few words in English, maybe twenty.

Daddy and Carlos Trujillo got to buy some things and so we drive back to where the stores was. We all get inside the pickup because was not far. "Nice man, that Varoz," say Carlos Trujillo. Daddy say yes, only make him pay twenty dollars down-payment.

Franque park in front of a bar and he go in there for a drink with Daddy and Carlos Trujillo. Daddy give me fifty cents and say for me and Arcelia to buy something. I go in a store and get some change and I keep thirty cents and give Arcelia twenty cents. That was fair. She only six and don't know what is money. For me I buy two comic books and two Milky Way. Milky Way only cost a nickel in Sandoval. Arcelia look at everything and don't know what she want, so I take her out the store. "OK, you ain't going to get nothing," I say, "and Daddy going to get mad we taking so long."

We was almost back at the pickup and then Arcelia start yelling. "That . . . *eso quiero* . . . I want that!"

I look and seen she was pointing her finger at something in the window of a store. Inside the window was shoes and stockings and ribbons and levis and things like that. "What you want?" I tell her. I was wishing Daddy let me go with him and not stay with Arcelia. She don't know nothing. "You make everything always bad," I tell her.

But she was yelling and everybody in the street was starting to look at me like I was hitting her.

"Qué quieres?" I say again, "What you want?"

"The dress," she say, "I want that dress!"

I look and seen what she want was a white dress like girls wear for First Communion.

"Arcelia—*pendeja!*—you think the man going to give you that dress for twenty cents?"

"Sí, sí, ese quiero, lo quiero!" she yell. So I take her inside the store so she will shut her mouth.

"How much cost the white dress in the window?" I say to the man. He was Americano.

"Three eighty-nine," he say, "you got the money?"

"See, *tonta!* Cost more than three dollars!" I say, but Arcelia keep crying so I pull her outside again, "Is not my fault," I tell the Americano. "She don't understand nothing."

Daddy and Carlos Trujillo and Franque was coming out

of the bar. They smell like whisky. They look at Arcelia crying.

"What's the matter with Arcelia? You hit her?" Daddy say.

"No, I didn't do nothing. She want to buy that dress, cost three dollars." I was feeling mad and bad and was starting to cry too because I didn't do nothing bad.

"What dress?" say Carlos Trujillo.

"The white one in the window."

"It's a dress for First Communion."

"Arcelia's too little for that dress," Daddy say. *"Vamos,* is getting dark. Franque, you feel OK to drive?"

"Yah," say Franque and he open his mouth like when you tired. I know he was tired like me from the *velorio,* and Daddy let him drink whisky, too.

Arcelia and me get in the back of the pickup with the box of Anastasio. It made like a little wall for us, because was getting pretty cold. Arcelia was still crying in the corner and I feel bad too. Poor kid, she didn't know what is three dollars.

"Anyway, you still got twenty cents. I don't got nothing," I say to her. "Tomorrow you can buy two Milky Way at Mr. Bond." Mr. Bond cost ten cents for a Milky Way.

But Arcelia was still crying. Better for her to stay home.

"Here." I break one of my Milky Way in half and I give the biggest one to her. She didn't say nothing but she take it.

Hiii-jolá, was cold! I stand up and look at the road. Franque was going pretty fast. We pass a big trailer truck. I think almost he was going to hit it. "Take it easy, Franque, take it easy," I hear Carlos Trujillo say inside.

I sit down again. I seen Arcelia was sleeping under the blanket Mama give her to keep warm, behind the box of Anastasio. Was like a hole there where the wind can't come in. I make myself little and put my nose inside my shirt so I feel warm and I was ashamed because again I fall asleep.

Hijo, was terrible! When that happen was dark. I was sleeping so I didn't know what it was. But was terrible. Everything come in one minute. Daddy yell "Franque! Franque!" and then was a big noise and the pickup hit something and something hit me and then everything stop. I didn't know nothing till was finished. But was terrible, I tell you that much.

Then I hear Daddy yell in the front. "*Tonto! Imbécil! Animal!*" and I hear he was hitting Franque. Franque jump out with his hands on his head and making a noise like a dog when somebody kick him.

Then Daddy come out with Carlos Trujillo.

"Abrán! Arcelia! *Qué pasó!* You OK? You not hurt?"

"I'm OK, Daddy," I say. But then they turn on the flashlight and everybody see was sure terrible thing that happen. Was the box of Anastasio.

When the pickup hit, the rope break and the box come on us, and was sure big. Now I feel it. Was on my leg.

"Abrán! Where's Arcelia?"

"She was sleeping."

"*Apúrense,* quick, pull away the box!" Carlos Trujillo say. They pull it off my leg. I get up. It hurt, but not too bad. "I'm OK, Daddy," I say.

But nobody listen to me. They was all looking at Arcelia. Carlos turn the light on her.

"*Ay Dios!* No! Arcelia, Arcelia! *Hijita mía!*" Daddy was saying. He try to wake her up.

"Don't shake her, . . . that's bad," say Carlos Trujillo. Carlos is pretty smart. His mother is the *médica,* and she knows about sick people and babies. Poor Franque, he just stand there shaking and crying and like eating his lips.

"Maybe she just knock out, Daddy," I say.

"Look, her mouth!" Daddy say.

"No, is just Milky Way," I say.

Carlos wipe her mouth with his handkerchief. It was candy, except a little bit on the corner. That was blood, only not much, like when you cut your lip. Carlos pick up Arcelia. "May be bad," he say, "we got to go back and see the doctor."

Carlos tell Franque to go see how was the truck. But Franque seem like he can't move so I go. I seen we run into a place where they cut out the hill to make the road. Not rock, just sand. The front of the pickup look pretty bad, but the tires was OK and the lights was still on.

The motor start OK and Carlos get the pickup back on the road and drive back to Sandoval. Daddy was holding Arcelia wrapped up in the blanket. I hear him talking to Arcelia but she didn't say nothing to him. Franque and me ride in the back with the box of Anastasio, and we didn't say nothing either.

Only got two doctors in Madera County and my teacher say it's not enough for all those thousand people. The doctor's house was full of people waiting when we get there. The lady who work for the doctor didn't understand Mexican so good, so I tell her in English what happen with Franque and the pickup and the box of Anastasio. She look scared.

"Es malo? Qué tiene mi hijita?" Daddy say in Mexican.

"My Daddy want to know if it's bad," I tell the lady in English.

The lady say she don't know, she not the nurse, only secretary, and the doctor is out on "emergency call" but he was coming right back.

I tell this to my Daddy but he didn't understand what was an emergency call so he sit down with Arcelia and try to make her speak. Was funny. Was some ladies there sitting holding little babies like Ubaldo, and Daddy with his levis and black leather jacket was sitting holding Arcelia. No, was terrible. Daddy was crying and I like it better when he is mad.

We wait and wait and the doctor was still on emergency call. Then Carlos Trujillo bend down and put his ear on Arcelia's chest and feel her neck.

"Está muerta, tu hijita," he say to Daddy, "your little girl is dead."

Carlos Trujillo was driving very slow and careful and it take a long time to get back to Piñoncito. But this time I didn't fall asleep. I wasn't tired. I was thinking.

Poor Franque, he was crying in the back of the pickup with me. He tell me he was going to run away to the Army, but he was too young and Daddy need him to take care the sheep. Carlos Trujillo was sure nice to him. He tell Franque was not his fault. They let him drink whisky and he was tired from the *velorio*. It was wrong to let him drive.

And was sure nice what Carlos do for Arcelia too. He go back to the store and buy the white First Communion dress Arcelia want with his own three dollars.

And Mr. Varoz from the funeral company sure was nice too. He didn't believe it till he seen Arcelia. Then he give Daddy a big *abrazo*, that means like a kiss, and he tell us to wait in the front room. In a little while he bring Arcelia back in a little white box special for children. He make her look pretty, all clean and with her hair brushed and he put the white dress on her. Inside the box was soft like a sheep only more white and shiny. The dress was too big for her but Mr. Varoz fix it so she look like a fairy in the second-grade reader. And he didn't cost us nothing for it.

But when we get past Peña's Cash Store in Rio Seco I think only one thing. What was we going to tell Mama? And I think everybody was thinking that like me.

Mama was sitting with Ubaldo when we come in. She got her dress open and Ubaldo was sucking his milk. "It's late," she say and she go to put beans and coffee on the fire. Everybody stand there waiting.

"'Onde 'stá la Arcelia?" she say and I seen her eyes get big. Then Carlos Trujillo come and grab her tight and tell her. Mama make a terrible scream like a goat when you going to cut his neck. Worse than that. I was scared and I run outside to the pickup. I call to Franque but he was gone. I wait and I was shivering because was cold. I hear Mama crying worse than everybody together at the *velorio* for Anastasio. And I hear Ubaldo screaming too because he didn't get no more milk. Then everything was quiet.

Mama come to the door. "Abrán, hurry, eat your supper," she say and I come. I want to kiss Mama but I was scared. The beans was in the plates. Mama sit down in the corner under the picture of the Virgin next to the one of Jesus opening his chest to show us his beautiful heart. She was talking to the Virgin.

"*Ay María Santísima . . . Madre Purísima de Dios . . . óyeme-óyeme . . . perdí mi hijita, mi hijita perdí . . . Ay . . . Ay . . . Ay . . . Ay . . . Ay . . .*"

And underneath she hold Ubaldo up so he could suck his milk.

Dilemma, Mi Amigo

GEORGE SEALE

Mrs. Martínez arrived on the early afternoon bus. She found a Spanish-speaking porter in the depot, and he directed her to the section of town called "Little Mexico." She lugged the rope-bound cardboard box of belongings which she had brought from Mazatlán, and walked in the hot sun until she reached the area. It took her an hour to get there; tired and perspiring, she placed the cardboard box at the edge of a sandy street and sat down to rest.

An old man came by pushing a junk cart. Mrs. Martínez stopped him to inquire of her friend Mrs. Ríos. The old man knew of several Mrs. Ríos's and to which was the *señora* referring? The Mrs. Ríos from Mazatlán, *señora?* The old man removed his sombrero and mopped his forehead on his sleeve. A number of boys playing baseball in a nearby lot saw them, suspended their game, and crowded around the inquisitive stranger. Mrs. Valdez put down her washing and crossed the street. Gloria García, leafing through *Photoplay* in her mother's kitchen, closed the magazine and joined the group. Jesús Pererra was aroused from his siesta, and Mrs. Rodríguez passed by on her way to confession. Alfonso Dávila left his yard work; Pancho Sánchez' dog raced by chasing one of the Adames' chickens; the Benavides' dog and several strays joined in pursuit. The chicken flew over Mrs. Santos' fence and the dogs barked and howled wildly.

The group in the street could not agree on the identity of Mrs. Martínez' friend. They considered the fat Mrs. Ríos

who lived in back of Medina's Grocery & Market, and
the skinny Mrs. Ríos who married Angel Garza and
moved to California. Some said there were no Mrs. Ríos's
from Mazatlán in Little Mexico, and others said they
weren't sure which Mrs. Ríos from Mazatlán the *señora*
was looking for. Finally it was decided to employ the process of elimination, and Mrs. Valdez led Mrs. Martínez off
on an escorted tour of the homes of the various Mrs. Ríos's
in Little Mexico.

A few calls disclosed the Mrs. Ríos from Mazatlán, and
she and Mrs. Martínez embraced joyfully. Mrs. Ríos
insisted that Mrs. Martínez was to stay in her home, and
with a touching expression of appreciation, Mrs. Martínez
accepted. She was shown to a room, and Mrs. Ríos helped
her take her belongings from the cardboard box. After she
was unpacked, Mrs. Martínez set about helping her friend
prepare the evening meal, and a month later you couldn't
tell if Mrs. Martínez was a native of Old Mexico or Little
Mexico: she was at home.

The news of Mrs. Martínez arrival spread through
Little Mexico like water spilled from a bucket. Everyone
heard it, and its general effect might best be stated by
quoting Mrs. Ramírez who said, "We want to meet the
new lady who has come from Mazatlán to live with Papa
and Mama Ríos near the plaza." And so there was a
pilgrimage to the house of Papa and Mama Ríos near the
plaza. Father Paulos came by to pay his respects, and Mr.
and Mrs. Guzmán invited Papa and Mama Ríos and Mrs.
Martínez to see Jorge Negrete at Teatro Pan Americano.
Rosa Herrera dropped in and asked of friends in
Mazatlán, and at the Sunday concert in the plaza Mrs.
Martínez was introduced to Alicia Velásquez, who has a
botica, and Tony Prado, who runs a shoe repair shop, and
Mary Luna, who wraps packages in one of the stores
downtown. José Costilla, who owns a grocery store,
brought his wife and family for a visit, and so did Pablo
Mendoza, who delivers telegrams for Western Union, and
Ferdinand Rayado, who pushes a junk cart, and Juan
López, who sells candy from a little stand on the plaza,
and Raúl Camarata, who grows marijuana in his back
yard and sells it to the Santos boys. One of the last to drop
by was Alfredo, and Mrs. Martínez wished he'd come
sooner, because of all she met, she liked Alfredo best.

Alfredo had no regular job. Rather, he was a man of
many jobs. Primarily he did yard work, and it was said

that he was one of the finest at pruning hedges and spading gardens. He was also a good cook, and sometimes in the community they would slaughter a goat and bring it to Alfredo for preparation. These were momentous occasions and always took place in the spring, during fiesta, or on *Cinco de Mayo*, when no one worked, not even those who were regularly employed. Alfredo was also a carpenter of some repute; or rather, a dependable handyman, and sometimes he found employment on construction jobs, helping full-fledged carpenters erect new buildings in the booming suburbs that were encircling the town. Alfredo had had many jobs. He had been a bus boy and a dishwasher and a window washer and a janitor and a hot tamale peddler and a shoeshine boy and an elevator operator. But mostly, he had been a yard man.

Because he was self-employed and did not suffer the confinement of a steady job, it was possible for Alfredo to court Mrs. Martínez in a wonderfully carefree and exciting manner. He would call at the Ríos's house in the early morning and escort her to mass; or he would call late in the afternoon and take her for a stroll around the plaza. He came by at noon and thrilled her with his tamales, or in mid-morning, and helped her with her gardening. On warm nights they would sit on the Ríos's porch, and Alfredo would pay the *mariachi* to serenade. After a while, in the thinking of Little Mexico, it wasn't "Alfredo" or "Mrs. Martínez," but "Alfredo and Mrs. Martínez." They were seen together constantly, in the morning, in the afternoon, at night; at the dances on Saturday, and in the plaza on Sunday. Alfredo was enamored of Mrs. Martínez, and Mrs. Martínez was enamored, not only of Alfredo, who was *muy simpático*, but of her new-found life, of which she said, *Ay, Señor—Los Estados Unidos! Qué bonito, qué grande, qué magnífico!*

Alfredo had a house on a corner lot not far from Papa and Mama Ríos. It wasn't anything pretentious: just one room without a bath or running water, but it was all Alfredo's, and he was proud of it. He had worked and saved for years to buy this house, and he paid a lawyer downtown to check the title papers and make sure everything was in order and that no one could take it away from him. Actually, it was nothing more than a shack, beaten and worn from seasons of cold and heat and wind and sand, and except for the door there wasn't a drop of paint on it. For some reason the door was painted yellow. Why

Alfredo would paint the door and none of the rest of the house had always puzzled his neighbors, but that was Alfredo's affair, and they were sure that he was quite pleased with it. In any event it would have been rude for them to suggest that anything was wrong with the house, so they smiled and said that sometimes it was healthy for a man to give vent to his whims.

Alfredo had lived in this house a long time, and he found it exactly to his liking. In the center of the house he had placed his wood stove, and its chimney ran straight up to the ceiling. His bed was against the east wall, and between the bed and the stove was a huge barber chair which he delighted in adjusting to various heights and angles, and which he always used for his siesta. In the summer, he kept both doors open, and there was always a pleasant north-south breeze. In winter, sealed up, the house was snug and cozy. There were no windows.

Alfredo's natural wish was to bring Mrs. Martínez to this house as his wife. But he was reluctant to propose. In the first place, he was content with their relationship as it stood. In the second place, he loved his house and was quite satisfied with his bachelor life. Why should he take the chance of destroying his happiness? He pondered for months, but could reach only one conclusion: if he did not ask Mrs. Martínez to come to his house as his wife, it was possible that some other bachelor in Little Mexico would charm her away from him. He decided that it would be better to marry at the risk of losing his peace of mind than to gamble on maintaining the status quo when so desirable a prize as Mrs. Martínez was at stake.

In the fall Father Paulos conducted the wedding ceremony of Alfredo and Mrs. Martínez. It was a memorable night. All of Little Mexico was there, and wine and music and happiness made the reception Papa and Mama Ríos held for the newlyweds a great success. Alfredo was bashful as an adolescent, and felt awkward with his shirt collar buttoned, but Mrs. Martínez, with the worldliness of experience, was masterful. After all the guests had gone, and Alfredo had the last of the wine, he helped Mrs. Martínez put her things in the cardboard box, and they walked down the street to their home. Papa and Mama Ríos, overcome with emotion, watched them leave.

"They will be very happy," sniffed Papa, and he reached for his handkerchief to wipe a big tear that rolled down his cheek as he spoke.

"Sí," Mama moaned, *"Muy contento."* Not having Papa's restraint, she sobbed freely as the last shadow of Alfredo and Mrs. Martínez was lost in the darkness.

Mrs. Martínez became Alfredo's wife in all but one respect: Little Mexico refused to drop its designation of her as Mrs. Martínez. She was "Alfredo's wife"; "Alfredo's wife, Mrs. Martínez"; or just plain "Mrs. Martínez," and so she would always be. Alfredo did not object to this. After all, he philosophized, it was only a matter of form, and it seemed a little unreasonable to expect one to disregard a name that had been used for years. It would be like changing "Alfredo" to "Pedro," and just as pointless. Besides, Alfredo was too pleased with his new domestic life to complain.

Mrs. Martínez was energetic and worked every hour except siesta. The first thing she did was move the furniture out and clean the house. She scrubbed the floor and walls and dusted each piece carefully before she moved it back. She took great pains to place it exactly where it had been put by Alfredo.

Then she repaired his wardrobe. He had worn shirts and trousers for years without regard to holes or worn seams. All his socks were out at the toes and heels and his union suits were ragged. She patched his *pantalones* and shirts and darned his socks and neatly mended his drawers. Then she washed and pressed all the clothes and stacked them in orderly fashion in one corner of the house.

After that, she planted a vegetable garden and nursed it to productivity. This provided tomatoes and cabbage and turnips and okra and onions and put vitality in Alfredo's diet of biscuit and beans. She knew how to prepare food in a variety of ways, and her candy, especially, was superb. Breakfast, dinner, and supper were always hot and waiting for Alfredo. He relearned the joy of eating, and looked forward to each meal with fervent anticipation as he recalled the thrill of the preceding one. He was amazed by the wonders his wife performed with food. Alfredo reflected after supper each night that his marriage had been, indeed, an act of great proportion.

Alfredo had not worked as much as he should have during their courtship, and it became increasingly necessary for him to spend time away from home. This displeased Mrs. Martínez. She missed Alfredo's company and was afraid he would work too hard. She decided to obtain employment till Alfredo's bank roll was replenished, and then quit. After that they could live in the manner that suited them. She was handicapped by the language barrier, however; trying to find work, she was uniformly rejected because her knowledge of English was so poor. Finally she hit on a good idea: be self-employed, like Alfredo. The thing grew in her mind. She could make enough money to fill the gap in Alfredo's savings in no time.

She went down to the scrap pile and found some lumber and made a little tray which she hung over her neck with a cord. She put handles on each side so it would be easy to carry, and painted it red. Then she was set, but she didn't tell Alfredo her plans. She wanted to make a little wad and surprise him with it.

The first time Alfredo left on an all-day job, she hurried to the stove and made pralines. The thing excited her. Juan López had supported a family for twenty years by selling candy on the plaza in Little Mexico, and everyone knew that her candy was superior to Juan's. Besides, she would not work in Little Mexico. She would go downtown, where home-made Mexican candy was a rarity, and sell to an appreciative public at an advanced price over Juan's. She arranged the candy neatly in the tray and walked up the hill toward town.

It took a while to catch on. She had never done any work of this type, and she was uncertain at first. She was conscious of the language barrier, and people asked things about the candy she could not explain. But she was not content to stand on corners and let customers come to her. She approached people with a genuine smile and extended the tray for their examination. Her gestures and expressions were comical, but they were also sincere, and even though no one understood her, everyone trusted her and it was a pleasure to buy the candy because her *gracias's* were so heartfelt and effusive.

She began to stock her tray with *charamusca* and *lechequemada* and every day she would take a little more to town with her. She started going into the office buildings, and made friends in each of them. She established regular customers, and fixed routes, and people in the buildings could tell the time of day by Mrs. Martínez' arrivals and departures.

When he learned of her success, Alfredo was very proud. The two of them sat on the steps of their home

one night several months after Mrs. Martínez had established her trade. The *mariachi* played in the distance, and
Alfredo was filled with romance. He took Mrs. Martínez'
hand and thanked her for coming into his life and told her
she was a wife of whom a man could be proud. She told
him he was a deserving husband and said that any contribution she could make towards his happiness would be
but a trifling compared to the magnanimity of his soul.
Their thoughts turned to Mexico, and Alfredo talked of
nights in Monterrey, and listened while his wife told him of
Mazatlán. They were very proud and happy and con-
tented. A *mariachi* passed and Alfredo hailed them to
serenade. He sent one of the group for wine, and they
listened to the *mariachi* and drank the wine and talked of
Mexico and each other.

Alfredo overslept the next day, so Mrs. Martínez had
to scramble to make candy and get to town. She was late,
and her customers chided her about it, saying she over
cerveza-ed the night before. Mrs. Martínez took it good-
naturedly, and made excited denials. She was in good
spirits. The elevator in the State Building stopped to let her
off, and she padded down the hall to one of the large
offices. She giggled at the thought of Alfredo the night
before.

Suddenly, three men stepped in front of her and blocked
the way. One of them flashed a badge.

"You're under arrest," he said.

A man stood on each side of her and they towed her
back to the elevator. The third man stayed behind, and
when they were downstairs he shook hands with the other
two.

"That's her," he said. "Been coming here for
months."

"We'll put a stop to it," said the man on Mrs. Martínez' right.

A squad car pulled up to the curb and the two men
motioned for Mrs. Martínez to get in. Then they sat on
the back seat beside her. The driver wore a uniform, and
he talked a lot.

"Whatcha got?" he asked.

"Just a peddler," the man on Mrs. Martínez' left answered.

"Since when do plainclothesmen go after peddlers?"
said the driver.

"Ain't that a note?" the detective, Shafter, replied. "This is one of Runnels' projects."

The other detective, Runnels, promptly explained. "The guy who runs that building's a buddy of mine," he said, shifting his weight and crossing his legs.

Mrs. Martínez remained quite still. She hadn't any idea why she was there, but she respected lawful authority and knew it was all right. She offered the men a praline.

"Want a piece of spic candy?" Runnels asked, responding to the gesture.

"I'd as soon eat earwax," Shafter replied, and the man in front laughed.

Mrs. Martínez put the praline back in her tray and didn't move again until they signaled for her to. They had gone down a ramp into the jail basement and were now stopped at a section reserved for police cars with prisoners. A tunnellike gallery led to the admitting office on their left. The men conducted Mrs. Martínez down the passageway until they came to the grimy outer door. They opened it and stepped through it one at a time. Mrs. Martínez found herself in a compact, low-ceilinged room with yellowing walls and a stained concrete floor. Ahead of her was an elevator, and a man leaned against its door in squalid resignation. One side of the room was partitioned off by a sturdy wire net, and a uniformed officer occupied a desk behind it. The man looked up with clerical boredom when they entered.

"Got a peddler for you to book," Runnels told him.

"O.K.," the uniformed clerk said, taking a file card from his desk. "What's your name?" he asked.

Mrs. Martínez told him.

"How do you spell it?" the man said.

She repeated her name.

"Spell it," the officer commanded.

Mrs. Martínez did not understand. *"Perdóneme?"* she said. *"Qué quiere?"*

"What's she saying?" the clerk in uniform wanted to know.

"You got me," Shafter said.

"If that's a name, she must be Hindu instead of spic," the man behind the cage wisecracked.

"Maybe we better check on her," said Runnels.

"Yeah, I think we had," Shafter agreed.

The detectives guided Mrs. Martínez to a door across the room from the cage and directed her to go through it.

They walked down another dungeonlike hall and came to a small room with a lower ceiling than the one in which they had been. The room was furnished with a small table and straight chairs. Shafter sat backwards across a chair and Runnels leaned against the wall. Neither of them had removed his hat.

They went through the questions over and over again. Mrs. Martínez' answers were lively and animated, but if it hadn't been for the no's and O.K.'s every word she said would have been lost on the men. Nor could she understand what they said. She was receptive and cooperative and paid careful attention, but it wasn't any use. She sighed and shook her head perplexedly.

"No entiendo," she said.

Shafter got up from the chair, exasperated.

"I can't make any sense out of it," he said.

"I don't think we're going to," Runnels added.

Mrs. Martínez watched them anxiously.

"We'd better call Nemo," said Shafter.

"Yeah," said Runnels, "I think you're right."

They took Mrs. Martínez by the arm and led her back to the entrance pen. The man behind the cage lit a cigarette.

"Any luck?" he asked, in a cloud of smoke.

"Nothing but jabber," said Shafter. "I don't know why all these rich bastards wanta go to Mexico."

"I don't either," Runnels appended.

They looked at Mrs. Martínez.

"We're gonna take her upstairs and call Nemo," said Shafter. "You can get the dope from him."

"O.K.," the man behind the cage said; "hadn't I better put that tray in the property room?"

"Yeah," said Runnels, and he reached to take the candy tray from Mrs. Martínez.

Mrs. Martínez' deference to law and order did not outweigh her native instinct to remain secure in her person and property. She turned backwards as Shafter reached for the cord around her neck, and when she did, Runnels grabbed for her arms.

"Watch her," said the man behind the cage, and he put out his cigarette to come around and help.

"C'mon, gimme that tray and let's go upstairs like a good girl," said Shafter, but Mrs. Martínez kicked him in the shins and clawed Runnels' face. The candy spilled out of the tray and broke into a hundred pieces on the floor.

Shafter grabbed the cord and pulled and Mrs. Martínez
screamed for them to let the tray alone, and kicked and
clawed and gouged and bit and twisted to get away from
them. Runnels tightened his grip on her arms and the man
who had been behind the cage grabbed the other side of
the cord and pulled with Shafter. Blood trickled down
Runnels' face and his stomach ached where she had el-
bowed him. He let go of her arms and hugged her chest.
She bit at his hands and threw her head back violently to
keep Shafter and the other man from removing the cord.
Runnels tightened his hold until she couldn't breathe, and
then Shafter and the man who was behind the cage pulled
the cord over her head. The man took the tray and went
back to the cage.

They got on the elevator and Shafter told Mrs. Martínez
to shut up yelling.

"She's a tiger," said Runnels.

"Nemo'll take care of her," said Shafter.

"I wouldn't trade jobs with him," said Runnels.

The elevator stopped and they got out. Lucille was
waiting for them and they turned Mrs. Martínez over to
her.

"You can have her," said Shafter.

"What's the matter, boys?" Lucille asked. "Can'tcha take
it?" She smiled with sinister glee.

"I hope she goes after you," said Runnels, wiping the
blood off his cheek.

Lucille sank a bearlike claw into Mrs. Martínez and
Shafter and Runnels left to call Nemo.

"C'mon, baby," Lucille said, as she steered Mrs. Martínez down the corridor to a windowless room that was dim
and putrid, and shoved her through the door.

"See you later," said Lucille.

Mrs. Martínez was stunned. A girl walked up and
looked her over.

"Got a cigarette?" she asked.

Mrs. Martínez looked at her. *"Cigarillo?"* she said.

"Hey girls, come look—we got a wet spic," said the
girl.

The others in the room crowded around.

"Still dripping," said one.

"Whatta you reckon they got on her?" asked another.

"She damned sure wasn't hustling," one of them quipped.

"Does she smoke?" someone asked.

"I just asked her, but she says she don't savvy," said the first.

"Let's frisk her," suggested one of them. "Maybe she's got 'em hid."

They pawed over her.

"Aw, she ain't got any," said a boney one. "Just another spic."

"Fat mama, ain't she?" one of them observed as they walked away.

Mrs. Martínez went over and sat down. She was nervous and uneasy, and frightened and helpless and couldn't understand it. Things had been illusory. After a while she leaned against the wall to rest.

Alfredo left his job early that day and went to his home in Little Mexico for siesta. He washed his hands and face and twirled the ends of his *mustachio* lightly. Then he took off his belt and loosened his shoes and got in the barber chair. He raised it to various levels before he was pleased, and he experimented with horizontal angles for some time until he found one that was restful. It was a pleasant day, and the doors were partly open. Alfredo floated into a sleep of healthy dreams.

When he awakened it was nightfall and Mrs. Martínez was not at home. He got out of the barber chair and stretched. Then he went to the door and looked up the street to see if she was coming. He couldn't imagine what was detaining her. She had never been late, but there must be a valid reason for the delay, he assured himself, and decided to prepare supper and have a surprise for her when she arrived. He started the fire and made dough and put biscuits in the oven. Then he poured water over the beans and put them on the stove to heat. He got the frying pan and dropped little chunks of beef in hot grease. Then he put the coffee on. While he was doing this he looked out the door intermittently. Then he went and sat on the steps of the house and kept his eyes on the street. When the biscuits were done and the beans were warm and the meat was sizzling in the pan and the coffee was boiling, Mrs. Martínez had still not come home.

Alfredo took the meal from the stove and set it over the irons so it would not get cold. Then he put on his sombrero and buckled his belt and tied his shoelaces and left to look for his wife. He went to Medina's Grocery and Alicia Velásquez' *botica,* and across the plaza and over to the Mission. He asked everyone he saw. No one had seen her. He went Papa and Mama Ríos's, and to the Guzmán's, and to José Costilla's store. He went by Teatro Pan Americano, and back by his house to see if she had come. He went up and down the streets of Little Mexico, to the homes of all his friends, to every store and cafe. She was nowhere to be found. Finally he went back to the Mission and sought the advice of Father Paulos.

Father Paulos was consoling and assured Alfredo that no evil had befallen his wife. He suggested that Alfredo return to his house and wait patiently for her to return. Alfredo protested and said that his wife was very punctual and dependable and that something ominous had undoubtedly occurred. Father Paulos laughed at his speculations.

"You are a man of great imagination," the priest said, in flowing Spanish; "you are also a man in love." With a wink, he added that Alfredo's was merely lover's fancy. "Go home and eat your meal and await your wife's pleasure," he said. "She is well. If anything were wrong, you would have been notified."

But Alfredo was not to be swayed. He insisted that his wife had fallen prey to mischief, and Father Paulos finally compromised the issue by going home with Alfredo to keep him company. When they arrived at the house, the meal was still warm, and Father Paulos made Alfredo eat. Then they sat on the steps together and smoked while they waited for Mrs. Martínez to return. The *mariachi* was playing in the distance.

As the night progressed, Father Paulos' confidence waned. He suggested that they return to his mission and telephone the authorities. He informed Alfredo that the City Police Department maintained a Missing Persons Bureau which was cooperative and vastly helpful in situations such as his. Alfredo was never a man of resolution, even in youth, and that night, under the strain, he was completely without independent judgment. Anything Father Paulos recommended was accepted by Alfredo without question. They went to the rectory and called the Missing Persons Bureau. The man who answered the phone took Mrs. Martínez' name and address and Father Paulos' telephone number. They would advise if they got a line on her, he said, and told Father Paulos to call the jail to see if she was there. Father Paulos thought this was a silly suggestion, and scoffed at the idea, but it would only take a minute, and it was well to rule out the possibility. Alfredo agreed. He remembered the New Year's Eve when the policeman had arrested him for being Drunk and Disorderly. He had merely shot firecrackers from the door of his home, and stood in the street with a bottle of tequila yelling *Viva Méjico*. He did not understand the reasons for his incarceration, and he had had a mortal fear of policemen and jails ever since.

The night man was behind the cage when the telephone rang in the jail office. He answered it and heard Father Paulos on the other end of the wire ask for Mrs. Martínez. The man told Father Paulos to wait while he checked the records. He set the receiver down and witlessly thumbed through the cards until he came to one with a Mexican name on it and a notation from the man who had indexed it that the name probably was not correct because the prisoner's speech was unintelligible. He removed it from the file, bovinelike, and mulled over it while his square-wheeled mind lumbered to a conclusion. Finally he picked up the phone.

"We got one up here that cain't speak English," he said.

"What does she look like?" asked Father Paulos.

"I don't know," he said.

"May we see her?" Father Paulos inquired.

"Naw," said the man, "visitin' ain't allowed in the City Jail."

Father Paulos hesitated for a moment. "What is she being held for?" he finally asked.

"Peddling," said the jailer.

"I see," said Father Paulos, and the man hung up the receiver.

Father Paulos turned to Alfredo.

"We don't know for sure, of course, but it would seem that she is being held in the City Jail," he said.

Alfredo asked what for, and Father told him, and Alfredo didn't understand, so he asked how long she was going to be there, and Father Paulos told him he couldn't tell. Alfredo wondered if there wasn't something he could do, and Father Paulos said there was not at the moment. He said it would be best to go home to bed and begin in the morning. Alfredo wanted to do something then, but Father Paulos dissuaded him.

"Let's rest on it, and tomorrow we will consult a lawyer," he said.

Alfredo knew a lawyer because he had hired one when

he purchased his house, and Father Paulos said they would go to see him. Alfredo reluctantly went home. But he was awake at dawn.

They were waiting when the lawyer came to his office the next day. He agreed to investigate, and showed them chairs in his reception room and reëntered his office and closed the door. After a considerable interval he came out and motioned them in.

"That's her all right," he said.

Alfredo breathed easier. At least she's safe, he thought.

"What's she being held for?" asked Father Paulos.

"She was peddling candy in a building without consent of the owner," said the lawyer. "There's an ordinance against it," he added, "and the judge fined her twenty bucks."

"Won't she be released if the fine is paid?" asked Father Paulos.

Alfredo was bright-eyed. "I got twenty dollars," he said, smiling broadly.

"Normally yes," said the lawyer, "but they have a 'hold' on her for the Immigration Bureau. They think she's a wetback because they can't understand what she says."

"I'm sure she's not a wetback," said Father Paulos.

"Well, if she's got a visa everything'll be all right," said the lawyer. "I just talked with the head man over there, and he's going to see her this morning. If he clears her, we can pay the fine and it'll be O.K.," he shrugged. "But if he don't, we'll have to run a writ and make bond and fight deportation, and if she's a wetback there's nothing to fight. She's going back to Mexico."

Alfredo shuddered.

"There no need to spend any money right now, though," he continued. "Let's wait'll we hear from Nemo, and then we'll know where we stand."

Father Paulos and Alfredo went back to the rectory to await the lawyer's call. Alfredo thought of his wife in jail and felt very depressed. Father Paulos was reassuring.

"Everything will be all right," he told Alfredo. "Do not worry."

Alfredo worried the whole time, and when the telephone rang he jumped with anticipation. Alfredo watched Father Paulos' face as he talked on the phone. He could not read the expression. It was blank and inscrutable. The priest put down the receiver and told Alfredo to get his hat. The lawyer wanted them in his office.

The lawyer did not mince words when they returned. "Your wife's a wetback," he said to Alfredo.

Father Paulos consoled him as the lawyer went on: "Nemo tells me she don't know it herself. Some guy came through Mazatlán and said he had immigration visas which the American government was letting him sell. She fell for it."

Alfredo was heartsick as the lawyer went on. "She got past the border some way," he said. "The immigration man must have been drunk. Anyhow, you know the rest."

"Does this mean she'll be deported?" asked Father Paulos.

"Yep," replied the lawyer, "and if she's deported, she'll never get back. But if she leaves voluntarily, she can immediately apply for permanent entry. She'll have to be sponsored, which means that someone in America will take care of her. Alfredo can do that. He's a property owner and a hard worker. I can prepare the affidavits and I think she'll be granted a visa without any trouble. Then she can come back for good."

Alfredo smiled.

"Nemo says he'll let her out of jail on personal recognizance if she agrees to leave. This'll save making bond and contesting a suit that can't be won. She won't have to go for a coupla weeks, and I'll fix the papers for her to take with her."

The lawyer waited for their reaction.

"I guess it is the only thing to do," said Alfredo helplessly. He had confidence in the lawyer, but distress showed in his speech, and his accent was heavier than usual. Father Paulos patted him on the back.

"It is best," he said. "She will only be gone for a short time."

"But she might not get a visa," Alfredo cried.

"That's a chance you'll have to take," said the lawyer.

"She will get one, because you are able to take care of her," said Father Paulos. "Can we get her out of jail?" he then asked.

"You'll have to pay the peddling fine," said the lawyer, "and they'll release her to Nemo."

"Let's do that," said Father Paulos.

They left the lawyer's office and went to the jail. The man who had been behind the cage when Mrs. Martínez was first brought in greeted them with a defiant look. The lawyer walked up to the cage and told him he wanted to pay Mrs. Martínez' fine and get her out.

"I ain't so sure about that," said the man behind the cage.

"Why not?" asked the lawyer.

"Nemo's got something to say about it," said the man behind the cage.

"I've already talked to Nemo," said the lawyer.

The man looked disappointed. "All I know's what's written down," he said fretfully, "and if Nemo's got a 'hold' on her, it's gotta stick till he takes it off."

The lawyer looked at the man behind the cage with disgust. "May I borrow your telephone?" he asked solicitously, and bowed.

The man behind the cage grunted and the lawyer called Nemo. Nemo told the man to release Mrs. Martínez to the lawyer.

"Well, I hope you know what you're doing," the man said to Nemo. Then he hung up the phone and turned on the speaker system. He did not look up after his conversation with Nemo. In a while the lawyer and Father Paulos and Alfredo heard Lucille's voice.

"Send that Mexican down," the man told her.

"You guys safely hid?" she asked.

The man snapped off the machine. Alfredo and Father Paulos and the lawyer stood there and waited silently.

Lucille ambled down the hall, whistling. The keys on her belt clattered and clinked sharply in the narrow corridor. She was massive, with legs and arms of stone and paws for hands. She looked ludicrous in a dress. She also looked forbidding. She came to the cage and unlocked the door.

"O.K., baby," said Lucille, "let's go."

Mrs. Martínez was against the wall, petrified.

Lucille motioned for her.

"She wants to stay, Lucille," someone snickered.

"Aw, Lucille, don't take her away," a girl cackled.

"Hey, Fat Fatima, where you going?" someone shouted.

They laughed and yelled and crowded around Mrs. Martínez.

"Watch her waddle," one said.

"Does José like that?" another asked, patting her hips.

"Don't swallow any punkin' seeds," still another one said, and they all roared.

Lucille stood patiently in the door. "That's the girl," she said. "Come along."

Mrs. Martínez plodded up and Lucille wrapped a paw around her arm. Then she closed and locked the door.

"So long, girls," said Lucille, and she started whistling again. Mrs. Martínez padded along obediently. They got on the elevator and it started down with a great hum. It jerked to a halt and the attendant wearily opened the door. Lucille released Mrs. Martínez and gave her a little send-off. "See you again, baby," said Lucille.

Mrs. Martínez lit up when she saw Alfredo standing there, and they embraced hysterically. There was crying and sobbing and wailing. The man behind the cage threw down his pencil and looked menacing.

"Let's get out of here," said the lawyer, and he showed them through the door and over to the Immigration Bureau.

Nemo explained the situation fully to Mrs. Martínez. She was bewildered, and couldn't understand that the visa she bought in Mazatlán was a fake. She looked at Alfredo with tormented eyes and he held her hands and tried to be encouraging. After a while, she agreed to follow the lawyer's recommendations, everything was straightened out with Nemo, and he released her on personal recognizance with ten days to leave the country.

Her last day was Sunday, and the bus station became Little Mexico. Papa and Mama Ríos were there, and so were Mr. and Mrs. Guzmán, and the Ramírez' and the Santos' and the Valdez' and the Medinas' and the Mendozas' and the Prados' and the José Costillas' and the Camaratas'. Lupe Pérez couldn't leave her children at home, so she brought them with her, all six, the smallest still nursing. They mingled with Juan López' little ones and played hide-and-seek in the depot with the Ordóñez' children. Mary Luna and Alfonso Dávila were there with Nina Encinal and Ricardo Gómez. Father Paulos milled through the group, and the lawyer came down at the last minute to bring some additional papers. Mrs. Martínez stood with Alfredo in the center of her friends. She had discarded her *reboza,* and was wearing a flowered straw hat that tilted on her head. The chatter was clamorous as the time of departure drew near. Mrs. Martínez' eyes watered as she hugged Mama Ríos, and she cried out when Father Paulos held her, and she broke completely when the loud speaker called her bus and Alfredo put his arms around her.

He clasped her to his breast and they kissed and wept and moaned convulsively. Then he picked up the cardboard box and handed it to her and she entered the door. She took a seat by the window and they could see her plainly as the driver started the motor and drove from the station. She leaned out and waved, and held her hat against the wind.

Alfredo stood motionless till the bus was out of sight. Then he left with Father Paulos and went to his home in Little Mexico. He hung his sombrero on the wall and unbuttoned his collar and pulled off his shoes and loosened his trousers and got in the barber chair. He adjusted until it hit a high position that was nearly horizontal. Then he stretched his toes across the foot rest and looked at the ceiling. Waiting would be dreadful. He took a bus schedule from his pocket and studied it carefully before he put it back. Then he closed his eyes and leaned against the head rest of the barber chair to think. It would cost very little to go to Mazatlán, but the sacrifice would be great. He hoped he wouldn't have to do it.

Sánchez

RICHARD DOKEY

That summer the son of Juan Sánchez went to work for the Flotill Cannery in Stockton. Juan drove with him to the valley in the old Ford.

While they drove, the boy, whose name was Jesús, told him of the greatness of the cannery, of the great aluminum buildings, the marvelous machines, and the belts of cans that never stopped running. He told him of the building on one side of the road where the cans were made and how the cans ran in a metal tube across the road to the cannery. He described the food machines, the sanitary precautions. He laughed when he spoke of the labeling. His voice was serious about the money.

When they got to Stockton, Jesús directed him to the central district of town, the skidrow where the boy was to live while he worked for the Flotill. It was a cheap hotel on Center Street. The room smelled. There was a table with one chair. The floor was stained like the floor of a public urinal and the bed was soiled, as were the walls. There were no drapes on the windows. A pall spread out from the single light bulb overhead that was worked with a length of grimy string.

"I will not stay much in the room," Jesús said, seeing his father's face. "It is only for sleep. I will be working overtime too. There is also the entertainment."

Jesús led him from the room and they went out into the street. Next to the hotel there was a vacant lot where a building had stood. The hole which was left had that

254

recent, peculiar look of uprootedness. There were the remains of the foundation, the broken flooring, and the cracked bricks of tired red to which the gray blotches of mortar clung like dried phlegm. But the ground had not yet taken on the opaqueness of wear that the air and sun give it. It gleamed dully in the light and held to itself where it had been torn, as earth does behind a plow. Juan studied the hole for a time; then they walked up Center Street to Main, passing other empty lots, and then moved east toward Hunter Street. At the corner of Hunter and Main a wrecking crew was at work. An iron ball was suspended from the end of a cable and a tall machine swung the ball up and back and then whipped it forward against the building. The ball was very thick-looking, and when it struck the wall the building trembled, spurted dust, and seemed to cringe inward. The vertical lines of the building had gone awry. Juan shook each time the iron struck the wall.

"They are tearing down the old buildings," Jesús explained. "Redevelopment," he pronounced. "Even my building is to go someday."

Juan looked at his son. "And what of the men?" he asked. "Where do the men go when there are no buildings?"

Jesús, who was a head taller than his father, looked down at him and then shrugged in that Mexican way, the head descending and cocking while the shoulders rise as though on puppet strings. "*Quién sabe?*"

"And the large building there?" Juan said, looking across the rows of parked cars in Hunter Square. "The one whose roof rubs the sky. Of what significance?"

"That is the new courthouse," Jesús said.

"There are no curtains on the windows."

"They do not put curtains on such windows," Jesús explained.

"No," Juan sighed, "that is true."

They walked north on Hunter past the new Bank of America and entered an old building. They stood to one side of the entrance. Jesús smiled proudly and inhaled the stale air.

"This is the entertainment," he said.

Juan looked about. A bar was at his immediate left and a bald man in a soiled apron stood behind it. Beyond the bar there were many thick-wooded tables covered with green material. Men crouched over them and cone-shaped lights hung low from the ceiling casting broadening cones of light downward upon the men and tables. Smoke drifted and rolled in the light and pursued the men when they moved quickly. There was the breaking noise of balls striking together, the hard wooden rattle of the cues in the racks upon the wall, the hum slither of the scoring disks along the loose wires overhead, the explosive cursing of the men. The room was warm and dirty. Juan shook his head.

"I have become proficient at the game," Jesús said.

"This is the entertainment," Juan said, still moving his head.

Jesús turned and walked outside. Juan followed. The boy pointed across the parked cars past the courthouse to a marquee on Main Street. "There are also motion pictures," Jesús said.

Juan had seen one movie as a young man working in the fields near Fresno. He had understood no English then. He sat with his friends in the leather seats that had gum under the arms and watched the images move upon the white canvas. The images were dressed in expensive clothes. There was laughing and dancing. One of the men did kissing with two very beautiful women, taking turns with each when the other was absent. This had embarrassed Juan, the embracing and unhesitating submission of the women with so many unfamiliar people to watch. Juan loved his wife, was very tender and gentle with her before she died. He never went to another motion picture, even after he had learned English, and this kept him from the Spanish films as well.

"We will go to the cannery now," Jesús said, taking his father's arm. "I will show you the machines."

Juan permitted himself to be led away, and they moved back past the bank to where the men were destroying the building. A ragged hole, like a wound, had been opened in the wall. Juan stopped and watched. The iron ball came forward tearing at the hole, enlarging it, exposing the empty interior space that had once been a room. The floor of the room teetered at a precarious angle. The wood was splintered and very dry in the noon light.

"I do not think I will go to the cannery," Juan said.

The boy looked at his father like a child who has made a toy out of string and bottle caps only to have it ignored.

"But it is honorable work," Jesús said, suspecting his father. "And it pays well."

"Honor," Juan said. "Honor is a serious matter. It is not a question of honor. You are a man now. All that is needed is a room and a job at the Flotill. Your father is tired, that is all."

"You are disappointed," Jesús said, hanging his head.

"No," Juan said. "I am beyond disappointment. You are my son. Now you have a place in the world. You have the Flotill."

Nothing more was said, and they walked to the car. Juan got in behind the wheel. Jesús stood beside the door, his arms at his sides, the fingers spread. Juan looked up at him. The boy's eyes were big.

"You are my son," Juan said, "and I love you. Do not have disappointment. I am not of the Flotill. Seeing the machines would make it worse. You understand, niño?"

"Sí, Papa," Jesús said. He put a hand on his father's shoulder.

"It is a strange world, niñito," Juan said.

"I will earn money. I will buy a red car and visit you. All in Twin Pines will be envious of the son of Sánchez, and they will say that Juan Sánchez has a son of purpose."

"Of course, Jesús mío," Juan said. He bent and placed his lips against the boy's hand. "I will look for the bright car. I will write regardless." He smiled, showing yellowed teeth. "Goodbye, querido," he said. He started the car, raced the engine once too high, and drove off up the street.

When Juan Sánchez returned to Twin Pines, he drove the old Ford to the top of Bear Mountain and pushed it over. He then proceeded systematically to burn all that was of importance to him, all that was of nostalgic value, and all else that meant nothing in itself, like the extra chest of drawers he had kept after his wife's death, the small table in the bedroom, and the faded mahogany stand in which he kept his pipe and tobacco and which sat next to the stuffed chair in the front room. He broke all the dishes, cups, plates, discarded all the cooking and eating utensils in the same way. The fire rose in the blue wind carrying dust wafers of ash in quick, breathless spirals and then released them in a panoply of diluted smoke, from which they drifted and spun and fell like burnt snow. The forks, knives, and spoons became very black with a flaky crust of oxidized metal. Then Juan burned his clothing, all that was unnecessary, and the smoke dampened and took on a thick smell. Finally he threw his wife's rosary into the flames. It was a cheap one, made of wood, and disappeared immediately. He went into his house then and lay down on the bed. He went to sleep.

When he woke, it was dark and cool. He stepped outside, urinated, and then returned, shutting the door. The darkness was like a mammoth held breath, and he felt very awake listening to the beating of his heart. He would not be able to sleep now, and so he lay awake thinking.

He thought of his village in Mexico, the baked white clay of the small houses spread like little forts against the stillness of the bare mountains, the men with their great wide hats, their wide, white pants, and their naked, brown-skinned feet, splayed against the fine dust of the road. He saw the village cistern and the women all so big and slow, always with child, enervated by the earth and the unbearable sun, the enervation passing into their very wombs like the heat from the yellow sun so that the wombs themselves bred quiet acceptance, slow, silent blood. The men walked bent as though carrying the air or sky, slept against the buildings in the shade like old dogs, ate dry, hot food that dried them inside and seemed to bake the moisture from the flesh, so that the men and women while still young had faces like eroded fields and fingers like stringy, empty stream beds. It was a hard land. It took the life of his father and mother before he was twelve and the life of his aunt, with whom he then lived, before he was sixteen.

When he was seventeen he went to Mexicali because he had heard much of America and the money to be obtained there. They took him in a truck with other men to work in the fields around Bakersfield, then in the fields near Fresno. On his return to Mexicali he met La Belleza, as he came to call her: loveliness. He married her when he was nineteen and she only fifteen. The following year she had a baby girl. It was stillborn and the birth almost killed her, for the doctor said the passage was oversmall. The doctor cautioned him (warned him, really) La Belleza could not have children and live, and he went outside into the moonlight and wept.

He had heard much of the loveliness of the Sierra Nevada above what was called the Mother Lode, and because he feared the land, believed almost that it possessed the power to kill him—as it had killed his mother and father, his aunt, was, in fact, slowly killing so many of his people—he wanted to run away from it to the high white cold of the California mountains, where he believed his heart would grow, his blood run and, perhaps, the passage of La Belleza might open. Two years later he was taken in the trucks to Stockton in the San Joaquin Valley to pick tomatoes and he saw the Sierra Nevada above the Mother Lode.

It was from a distance, of course, and in the summer, so that there was no snow. But when he returned he told La Belleza about the blueness of the mountains in the warm, still dawn, the extension of them, the aristocracy of their unmoving height, and that they were only fifty miles away from where he had stood.

He worked very hard now and saved his money. He took La Belleza back to his village, where he owned the white clay house of his father. It was cheaper to live there while he waited, fearing the sun, the dust, and the dry, airless silence, for the money to accumulate. That fall La Belleza became pregnant again by an accident of passion and the pregnancy was very difficult. In the fifth month the doctor—who was an atheist—said that the baby would have to be taken or else the mother would die. The village priest, a very loud, dramatic man—an educated man who took pleasure in striking a pose—proclaimed the wrath of God in the face of such sacrilege. It was the child who must live, the priest cried. The pregnancy must go on. There was the immortal soul of the child to consider. But Juan decided for the atheist doctor, who did take the child. La Belleza lost much blood. At one point her heart had stopped beating. When the child was torn from its mother and Juan saw that it was a boy, he ran out of the clay house of his father and up the dusty road straight into a hideous red moon. He cursed the earth, the sky. He cursed his village, himself, the soulless indifference of the burnt mountains. He cursed God.

Juan was very afraid now, and though it cost more money he had himself tied by the atheist doctor so that he could never again put the life of La Belleza in danger, for the next time, he knew with certainty, would kill her.

The following summer he went again on the trucks to

the San Joaquin Valley. The mountains were still there,
high and blue in the quiet dawn, turned to a milky pastel by
the heat swirls and haze of midday. Sometimes at night he
stepped outside the shacks in which the men were housed
and faced the darkness. It was tragic to be so close to what
you wanted, he would think, and be unable to possess it. So
strong was the feeling in him, particularly during the hot,
windless evenings, that he sometimes went with the other
men into Stockton, where he stood on the street corners
of skidrow and talked, though he did not get drunk on
cheap wine or go to the whores, as did the other men.
Nor did he fight.

They rode in old tilted trucks covered with canvas and
sat on rude benches staring out over the slats of the tail
gate. The white glare of headlights crawled up and lay
upon them, waiting to pass. They stared over the
whiteness. When the lights swept out and by, the glass of
the side windows shone. Behind the windows sometimes
there would be the ghost flash of an upturned face, before
the darkness clamped shut. Also, if one of the men had a
relative who lived in the area, there was the opportunity
to ride in a car.

He had done so once. He had watched the headlights of
the car pale then whiten the back of one of the trucks. He
saw the faces of the men turned outward and the looks on
the faces that seemed to float upon the whiteness of the
light. The men sat forward, arms on knees, and looked
over the glare into the darkness. After that he always rode
in the trucks.

When he returned to his village after that season's
harvest, he knew they could wait no longer. He purchased
a dress of silk for La Belleza and in a secondhand store
bought an American suit for himself. He had worked
hard, sold his father's house, saved all his money, and on a
bright day in early September they crossed the border
at Mexicali and caught the Greyhound for Fresno.

Juan got up from his bed to go outside. He stood looking up at the stars. The stars were pinned to the darkness,
uttering little flickering cries of light, and as always he was
moved by the nearness and profusion of their agony. His
mother had told him the stars were a kind of purgatory in
which souls burned in cold, silent repentance. He had
wondered after her death if the earth too were not a star
burning in loneliness, and he could never look at them

later without thinking this and believing that the earth must be the brightest of all stars. He walked over to the remains of the fire. A dull heat came from the ashes and a column of limp smoke rose and then bent against the night wind. He studied the ashes for a time and then looked over the tall pine shapes to the southern sky. It was there all right. He could feel the dry char of its heat, that deeper, dryer burning. He imagined it, of course. But it was there nevertheless. He went back into the cabin and lay down, but now his thoughts were only of La Belleza and the beautiful Sierra Nevada.

From Fresno all the way up the long valley to Stockton they had been full with pride and expectation. They had purchased oranges and chocolate bars and they ate them laughing. The other people on the bus looked at them, shook their heads, and slept or read magazines. He and La Belleza gazed out the window at the land.

In Stockton they were helped by a man named Eugenio Méndez. Juan had met him while picking tomatoes in the delta. Eugenio had eight children and a very fat but very kind and tolerant wife named Anilla. He helped them find a cheap room off Center Street, where they stayed while determining their next course of action. Eugenio had access to a car, and it was he who drove them finally to the mountains.

It was a day like no other day in his life: to be sitting in the car with La Belleza, to be in this moving car with his Belleza heading straight toward the high, lovely mountains. The car traveled from the flatness of the valley into the rolling brown swells of the foothills, where hundreds of deciduous and evergreen oaks grew, their puffball shapes like still pictures of exploding holiday rockets, only green, but spreading up and out and then around and down in nearly perfect canopies. At Jackson the road turned and began an immediate, constant climb upward.

It was as though his dream about it had materialized. He had never seen so many trees, great with dignity: pines that had bark gray twisted and stringy like hemp; others whose bark resembled dry, flat ginger cookies fastened with black glue about a drum, and others whose bark pulled easily away; and those called redwoods, standing stiff and tall, amber-hued with straight rolls of bark as thick as his fist, flinging out high above great arms of green. And the earth, rich red, as though the blood of scores of Indians had just flowed there and dried. Dark patches of shadow

stunned with light, blue flowers, orange flowers, birds,
even deer. They saw them all on that first day.

"*Adónde vamos?*" Eugenio had asked. "Where are we
going?"

"*Bellísima,*" Juan replied. "Into much loveliness."

They did not reach Twin Pines that day. But on their
return a week later they inquired in Jackson about the
opportunity of buying land or a house in the mountains.
The man, though surprised, told them of the sawmill town
of Twin Pines, where there were houses for sale.

Their continued luck on that day precipitated the feeling in Juan that it was indeed the materialization of a
dream. He had been able in all those years to save two
thousand dollars and a man had a small shack for sale at
the far edge of town. He looked carefully at Juan, at La
Belleza and Eugenio and said, "One thousand dollars,"
believing they could never begin to possess such a sum.
When Juan handed him the money, the man was so struck
that he made out a bill of sale. Juan Sánchez and his wife
had their home in the Sierra.

When Juan saw the cabin close up, he knew the man
had stolen their money. It was small, the roof slanted to
one side, the door would not close evenly. The cabin was
gradually falling downhill. But it was theirs and he could,
with work, repair it. Hurriedly they drove back to Jackson, rented a truck, bought some cheap furniture and
hauled it back to the cabin. When they had moved in,
Juan brought forth a bottle of whiskey and for the first
time in his life proceeded to get truly drunk.

Juan was very happy with La Belleza. She accepted his
philosophy completely, understood his need, made it her
own. In spite of the people of the town, they created a
peculiar kind of joy. And anyway Juan had knowledge
about the people.

Twin Pines had been founded, he learned, by one Benjamin Carter, who lived with his daughter in a magnificent
house on the hill overlooking town. This Benjamin Carter
was a very wealthy man. He had come to the mountains
thirty years before to save his marriage, for he had been
poor once and loved when he was poor, but then he grew
very rich because of oil discovered on his father's Ohio
farm and he went away to the city and became incapable
of love in the pursuit of money and power. When he at
last married the woman whom he had loved, a barrier had
grown between them, for Ben Carter had changed but the

woman had not. Then the woman became ill and Ben
Carter promised her he would take her West, all the way
West away from the city so that it could be as it had been
in the beginning of their love. But the woman was with
child. And so Ben Carter rushed to the California mountains, bought a thousand acres of land, and hurried to
build his house before the rain and snows came. He hired
many men and the house was completed, except for the
interior work and the furnishings. All that winter men he
had hired worked in the snow to finish the house while
Ben Carter waited with his wife in the city. When it was
early spring they set out for California, Ben Carter, his
wife, and the doctor, who strongly advised against the
rough train trip and the still rougher climb by horse and
wagon from Jackson to the house. But the woman wanted
the child born properly, so they went. The baby came the
evening of their arrival at the house, and the woman died
all night having it. It was this Ben Carter who lived with
that daughter now in the great house on the hill, possess-
ing her to the point, it was said about his madness, that he
had murdered a young man who had shown interest in
her.

Juan learned all this from a Mexican servant who had
worked at the great house from the beginning, and when
he told the story to La Belleza she wept because of its
sadness. It was a tragedy of love, she explained, and
Juan—soaring to the heights of his imagination—believed
that the town, all one hundred souls, had somehow been
infected with the tragedy, as they were touched by the
shadow of the house itself, which crept directly up the
highway each night when the sun set. This was why they
left dead chickens and fish on the porch of the cabin or
dumped garbage into the yard. He believed he understood
something profound and so did nothing about these incidents, which, after all, might have been the pranks of boys.
He did not want the infection to touch him, nor the deeper
infection of their prejudice because he was Mexican. He
was not indifferent. He was simply too much in love with
La Belleza and the Sierra Nevada. Finally the incidents stopped.

Now the life of Juan Sánchez entered its most beautiful
time. When the first snows fell he became delirious, running through the pines, shouting, rolling on the ground,
catching the flakes in his open mouth, bringing them in his
cupped hands to rub in the hair of La Belleza, who stood

in the doorway of their cabin laughing at him. He danced, made up a song about snowflakes falling on a desert and then a prayer which he addressed to the Virgin of Snowflakes. That night while the snow fluttered like wings against the bedroom window, he celebrated the coming of the whiteness with La Belleza.

He understood that first year in the mountains that love was an enlargement of himself, that it enabled him to be somehow more than he had ever been before, as though certain pores of his senses had only just been opened. Whereas before he had desired the Sierra Nevada for its beauty and contrast to his harsh fatherland, now he came to acquire a love for it, and he loved it as he loved La Belleza; he loved it as a woman. Also in that year he came to realize that there was a fear or dread about such love. It was more a feeling than anything else, something which reached thought now and then, particularly in those last moments before sleep. It was an absolutely minor thing. The primary knowledge was of the manner in which this love seemed to assimilate everything, rejecting all that would not yield. This love was a kind of blindness.

That summer Juan left La Belleza at times to pick the crops of the San Joaquin Valley. He had become good friends with the servant of the big house and this man had access to the owner's car, which he always drove down the mountain in a reckless but confident manner. After that summer Juan planned also to buy a car, not out of material desire, but simply because he believed this man would one day kill himself, and also because he did not wish to be dependent.

He worked in the walnuts near the town of Linden and again in the tomatoes of the rich delta. He wanted very much to have La Belleza with him, but that would have meant more money and a hotel room in the skidrow, and that was impossible because of the pimps and whores, the drunks and criminals and the general despair, which the police always tapped at periodic intervals, as one does a vat of fermenting wine. The skidrow was a place his love could not assimilate, but he could not ignore it because so many of his people were lost there. He stayed in the labor camps, which were also bad because of what the men did with themselves, but they were tolerable. He worked hard and as often as he could and gazed at the mountains, which he could always see clearly in the morning light.

When tomato season was over he returned to La Belleza.

Though the town would never accept them as equals, it came that summer to tolerate their presence. La Belleza made straw baskets which she sold to the townspeople and which were desired for their beauty and intricacy of design. Juan carved animals, a skill he had acquired from his father, and these were also sold. The activity succeeded so well that Juan took a box of their things to Jackson, where they were readily purchased. The following spring he was able to buy the Ford.

Juan acquired another understanding that second year in the mountains. It was, he believed, that love, his love, was the single greatness of which he was capable, the thing which ennobled him and gave him honor. Love, he became convinced, was his only ability, the one success he had accomplished in a world of insignificance. It was a simple thing, after all, made so painfully simple each time he went to the valley to work with his face toward the ground, every time he saw the men in the fields and listened to their talk and watched them drive off to the skidrow at night. After he had acquired this knowledge, the nights he had to spend away from La Belleza were occupied by a new kind of loneliness, as though a part of his body had been separated from the whole. He began also to understand something more of the fear or dread that seemed to trail behind love.

It happened late in the sixth year of their marriage. It was impossible, of course, and he spent many hours at the fire in their cabin telling La Belleza of the impossibility, for the doctor had assured him that all had been well tied. He had conducted himself on the basis of that assumption. But doctors can be wrong. Doctors can make mistakes. La Belleza was with child.

For the first five months the pregnancy was not difficult, and he came almost to believe that indeed the passage of La Belleza would open. He prayed to God. He prayed to the earth and sky. He prayed to the soul of his mother. But after the fifth month the true sickness began and he discarded prayer completely in favor of blasphemy. There was no God and never could be God in the face of such sickness, such unbelievable human sickness. Even when he had her removed to the hospital in Stockton, the doctors could not stop it, but it continued so terribly that he believed that La Belleza carried sickness itself in her womb.

After seven months the doctors decided to take the child. They brought La Belleza into a room with lights and instruments, they worked on her for a long time and she died there under the lights with the doctors cursing and perspiring above the large wound of her pain. They did not tell him of the child, which they had cleaned and placed in an incubator, until the next day. That night he sat in the Ford and tried to see it all, but he could only remember the eyes of La Belleza in the vortex of pain. They were of an almost eerie calmness. They had possessed calmness, as one possesses the truth. Toward morning he slumped sideways on the seat and went to sleep.

So he put her body away in the red earth of the town cemetery beyond the cabin. The pines came together overhead and in the heat of midday a shadow sprinkled with spires of light lay upon the ground so that the earth was cool and clean to smell. He did not even think of taking her back to Mexico, since, from the very beginning, she had always been part of that dream he had dreamed. Now she would be always in the Sierra Nevada, with the orange and blue flowers, the quiet, deep whiteness of winter, and all that he ever was or could be was with her.

But he did not think these last thoughts then, as he did now. He had simply performed them out of instinct for their necessity, as he had performed the years of labor while waiting for the infant Jesús to grow to manhood. Jesús. Why had he named the boy Jesús? That, perhaps, had been instinct too. He had stayed after La Belleza's death for the boy, to be with him until manhood, to show him the loveliness of the Sierra Nevada, to instruct him toward true manhood. But Jesús. Ah, Jesús. Jesús the American. Jesús of the Flotill. Jesús understood nothing. Jesús, he believed, was forever lost to knowledge. That day with Jesús had been his own liberation.

For a truth had come upon him after the years of waiting, the ultimate truth that he understood only because La Belleza had passed through his life. Love was beauty, La Belleza and the Sierra Nevada, a kind of created or made thing. But there was another kind of love, a very profound, embracing love that he had felt of late blowing across the mountains, from the south and that, he knew now, had always been there from the beginning of his life, disguised in the sun and wind. In this love there was blood and earth and, yes, even God, some kind of god, at least the power of a god. This love wanted him for its own. He understood it, that it had permitted him to have La Belleza and that without it there could have been no Belleza.

Juan placed an arm over his eyes and turned to face the wall. The old bed sighed. An image went off in his head and he remembered vividly the lovely body of La Belleza. In that instant the sound that loving had produced with the bed was alive in him like a forgotten melody, and his body seemed to swell and press against the ceiling. It was particularly cruel because it was so sudden, so intense, and came from so deep within him that he knew it must all still be alive somewhere, and that was the cruelest part of all. He wept softly and held the arm across his eyes.

In the dark morning the people of the town were awakened by the blaze of fire that was the house of Juan Sánchez. Believing that he had perished in the flames, several of the townspeople placed a marker next to the grave of his wife with his name on it. But, of course, on that score they were mistaken. Juan Sánchez had simply gone home.

THE MEXICAN-AMERICAN VIEW:

Señor Garza

MARIO SUÁREZ

Many consider Garza's Barber Shop as not truly in El Hoyo because it is on Congress Street and therefore downtown. Señor Garza, its proprietor, cashier, janitor, and Saint Francis, philosophizes that since it is situated in that part of the street where the land decidedly slopes, it is in El Hoyo. Who would question it? Who contributes to every cause for which a solicitor comes in with a long face and a longer relation of sadness? Who is the easiest touch for all the drunks who have to buy their daily cures? For loafers who go to look for jobs and never find them? For bullfighters on the wrong side of the border? For boxers still amateurs though punchy? For barbers without barber shops? And for the endless line of moochers who drop in to borrow anything from two bits to two dollars? Naturally, Garza.

Garza's Barber Shop is more than razors, scissors, and hair. It is where men, disgruntled at the vice of the rest of the world, come to air their views. It is where they come to get things off their chests along with the hair off their heads and beard off their faces. Garza's Barber Shop is where everybody sooner or later goes or should. This does not mean that there are no other barber shops in El Hoyo. There are. But none of them seem quite to capture the atmosphere that Garza's does. If it were not downtown it would probably have a little fighting rooster tied to a stake by the front door. If it were not rented to Señor Garza only it would perhaps smell of sherry wine all day. To Garza's Barber Shop goes all that is good and bad. The

lawbreakers come in to rub elbows with the sheriff's deputies. And toward all Garza is the same. When zoot suiters
come in for a very slight trim, Garza, who is very versa-
tile, puts on a bit of zoot talk and hep-cats with the
zootiest of them. When the boys that are not zoot suiters
come in, he becomes, for the purpose of accommodating
his clientele, just as big a snob as their individual personalities require. When necessity calls for a change in his
character Garza can assume the proportions of a Greek, a
Chinaman, a gypsy, a republican, a democrat, or if only
his close friends are in the shop, plain Garza.

Perhaps Garza's pet philosophy is that a man should not
work too hard. Garza tries not to. His day begins according to the humor of his wife. When Garza drives up
late, conditions are perhaps good. When Garza drives up
early, all is perhaps not well. Garza's Barber Shop has
been known, accordingly, to stay closed for a week. It has
also been known to open before the sun comes up and to
remain open for three consecutive days. But on normal
days and with conditions so-so, Garza comes about eight
in the morning. After opening, he pulls up the green
venetian blinds. He brings out two green ash cans containing the hair cut the preceding day and puts them on the
edge of the sidewalk. After this he goes to a little back
room in the back of the shop, brings out a long crank, and
lowers the red awning that keeps out the morning sun.
Lily-boy, the fat barber who through time and diligence
occupies chair number two, is usually late. This does not
mean that Lily-boy is lazy, but he is married and there are
rumors, which he promptly denies, that state he is hen-
pecked. Rodríguez, barber number three, usually fails to
show up for five out of six workdays.

On ordinary mornings Garza sits in the shoeshine stand
because it is closest to the window and nods at the pretty
girls going to work and to the ugly ones, too. He works on
an occasional customer. He goes to Sally and Sam's for a
cup of coffee, and on returning continues to sit. At noon
Garza takes off his small apron, folds it, hangs it on the
arm of his chair, and after combing his hair goes to La
Estrella to eat and flirt with the waitresses who, for
reasons that even they cannot understand, have taken him
into their confidence. They are well aware of his marital
standing; but Garza has black wavy hair and a picaresque
charm that sends them to the kitchen giggling. After
eating his usual meal of beans, rice, tortilla, and coffee, he

bids all the girls good-bye and goes back to his barber
shop. The afternoons are spent in much the same manner
as the mornings except that on such days as Saturday,
there is such a rush of business that Garza very often
seeks some excuse to go away from his own business and
goes for the afternoon to Nogales in Mexico or downstairs
to the Tecolote Club to drink beer.

On most days, by five-thirty everybody has usually been
in the shop for friendly reasons, commercial reasons, and
even spiritual reasons. Loco-Chu, whose lack of brains
everybody understands, has gone by and insulted the customers. Take-It-Easy, whose liquor-saturated brain everybody respects, has either made nasty signs at everybody or
has come in to quote the words and poems of the immortal Antonio Plaza. Cuco has come from his job at
Feldman's Furniture Store to converse of the beauty of
Mexico and the comfort of the United States. Procuna has
come in, and being a university student with more absences than the rest of his class put together, has very
politely explained his need for two dollars until the check
comes in. Chonito has shined shoes and danced a dozen or
so boogie pieces. There have been arguments. Fortunes
made and lost. Women loved. The great Cuate Cuete has
come in to talk of the glory and grandeur of zoot suitism in
Los Angeles. Old customers due about that day have
come. Also new ones who had to be told that all the
loafers who seemingly live in Garza's Barber Shop were
not waiting for haircuts. Then the venetian blinds are let
down. The red awning is cranked up. The door is latched
on the inside although it is continually opened on request
for friends, and the remaining customers are attended to
and let out.

Inside, Garza opens his little National Cash Register,
counts the day's money, and puts it away. He opens his
small writing desk and adds and subtracts for a little while
in his green record book. Meanwhile Chonito grudgingly
sweeps and says very nasty words. Lily-boy phones his
wife to tell her that he is about to start home and that he
will not be waylaid by friends and that he will not arrive
drunk. Rodríguez relates to everybody in the shop that
when he was a young man getting tired was not like him.
The friends who have already dropped in wait until the
beer is spoken for and then Chonito is sent for it. When
it is brought in and distributed everything is talked about.
Lastly, women are thoroughly insulted although their

necessity is emphasized. Garza, being a man of experience and one known to say what he feels when he feels it, recalls the ditty he heard while still in the cradle and says, "To women neither all your love nor all your money." The friends, drinking Garza's beer, agree.

Not always has Señor Garza enjoyed the place of distinction if not of material achievement that he enjoys among his friends today. In his thirty-five years his life has gone through transition after transition, conquest after conquest, setback after setback. But now Señor Garza is one of those to whom most refer, whether for reasons of friendship, indebtedness, or of having never read Plato and Aristotle, as an oracle pouring out his worldly knowledge during and between the course of his haircuts.

Garza was born in El Hoyo, the second of seven Garzas. He was born with so much hair that perhaps this is what later prompted him to be a barber. At five he almost burned the house down while playing with matches. At ten he was still waiting for his older brother to outgrow his clothes so that they could be handed down to him. Garza had the desire to learn, but even before he found out about school Garza had already attained a fair knowledge of everything. Especially the knowledge of want. Finally, his older brother got a new pair of overalls and Garza got his clothes. On going to school he immediately claimed having gone to school in Mexico so Garza was tried out in the 3B. In the 4A his long legs fitted under the desk, so he had to begin his education there. In the 5B he fell in love with the teacher and was promptly promoted to avert a scandal. When Garza was sixteen and had managed to get to the eighth grade, school suddenly became a mass of equations, blocks, lines, angles, foreign names, and headaches. At seventeen it might have driven him to insanity so Garza wisely cut his schooling short at sixteen.

On leaving school Garza tried various enterprises. He became a delivery boy for a drug store. He became a stock room clerk for a shoe store. But of all enterprises the one he found most profitable was that of shearing dogs. He advertised his business and it flourished until it became very obvious that his house and brothers were getting quite flea ridden. Garza had to give it up. The following year he was overcome with the tales of vast riches in California. Not that there was gold, but there were grapes to be picked. He went to California. But of that trip he has more than once said that the tallness of the Californian garbage cans made him come back twenty pounds lighter and without hair under his armpits. Garza then tried the CCC camp. But it turned out that there were too many bosses with muscles that looked like golf balls whom Garza thought it best not to have much to do with. Garza was already one that could keep everybody laughing all day long, but this prevented almost everybody from working. At night when most boys at camp were either listening to the juke box in the canteen, or listening to the playing of sad guitars, Garza trimmed heads at fifteen cents. After three months of piling rocks, carrying logs, and of getting fed up with his bosses' perpetual desires of making him work, Garza came back to the city with the money he had saved cutting hair and through a series of deals was allowed a barber's chair in a going establishment.

In a few years Garza came to be a barber of prominence. He had grown to love the idle conversation that is typical of barber shops, the mere idle gossip that often speaks of broken homes and forsaken women in need of friends. These Garza has always sought and in his way has done his best to put in higher spirits. Even after his marriage he continued to receive anonymous after anonymous phone call. He came to know the bigtime operators and their brand of filthy doings. He came to know the bootleggers, thieves, love merchants, and rustlers. He came to know also the smalltime operators with the bigtime complex and their shallowness of human understanding. He came to know false friends that came to him and said, "We're throwing a dance. We've got a good crowd. The tickets are two dollars." And on feeling superior, once the two dollars had fattened their wallets and inflated their conceit, remarked upon seeing him at the dance, "Damn, even the barber came." But in time Garza has seen many of these grow fat. He has seen their women go unfaithful. He has seen them get spiritually lost in trying to keep up materially with the people next door. He has seen them go bankrupt buying gabardine to make up for their lack of style. Their hair had cooties but smelled of aqua-rosa. The edges of their underwear were frayed even though they wore new suits. They gave breakfasts for half of the city to prove that "they had" and only ended up with piles of dirty dishes. Garza watched, philosophized, cut more hair, and of this has more than once said in the course of a beer or idle conversation among friends, "Damned fools, when you go, how in the hell are you going to take it with you? You are buried in your socks. Your suit is slit in the back and laced on top of you."

So in time Garza became the owner of his own barber shop. Garza's Barber Shop with its three Koken barber chairs, its reception sofas, its shoeshine stand, wash bowls, glass kits, pictures, objects to be sold and raffled, and juke box. Second to none in its colorful array of true friends and false, of drunks, loafers, bullfighters, boxers, other barbers, moochers, and occasional customers. Perfumed with the poetry of the immortal Antonio Plaza, and seasoned with naughty jokes told at random.

Soon the night becomes old and empty beer bottles are collected and put in the little back room. Chonito, who has swept the floor while Garza and his friends have consumed beer, asks for a fifty-cent advance or swears with the power of his fourteen years that he will never sweep the shop again, and gets it. Lily-boy phones his wife again and tells her that he is about to start home and that he is sober. Rodríguez, if he worked that day, says he has a bad cold which he must go home to cure, but asks for an advance to buy his tonic at Tom's Liquor Store. Then the lights are switched off and Garza, his barbers, his friends, and Chonito, file out. Garza, not forgetting the words he heard while in the cradle, "To women neither all your love nor all your money," either goes up the street to the Royal Inn for a glass of beer or to the All States Pool Hall. Then he goes home. Garza, a philosopher. Owner of Garza's Barber Shop. But the shop will never own Garza.

The Hammon and the Beans

AMÉRICO PARÉDES

Once we lived in one of my grandfather's houses near Fort Jones. It was just a block from the parade grounds, a big frame house painted a dirty yellow. My mother hated it, especially because of the pigeons that cooed all day about the eaves. They had fleas, she said. But it was a quiet neighborhood at least, too far from the center of town for automobiles and too near for musical, night-roaming drunks.

At this time Jonesville-on-the-Grande was not the thriving little city that it is today. We told off our days by the routine on the post. At six sharp the flag was raised on the parade grounds to the cackling of the bugles, and a field piece thundered out a salute. The sound of the shot bounced away through the morning mist until its echoes worked their way into every corner of town. Jonesville-on-the-Grande woke to the cannon's roar, as if to battle, and the day began.

At eight the whistle from the post laundry sent us children off to school. The whole town stopped for lunch with the noon whistle, and after lunch everybody went back to work when the post laundry said that it was one o'clock, except for those who could afford to be old-fashioned and took the siesta. The post was the town's clock, you might have said, or like some insistent elder person who was always there to tell you it was time.

At six the flag came down, and we went to watch through the high wire fence that divided the post from the

town. Sometimes we joined in the ceremony, standing at
salute until the sound of the cannon made us jump. That
must have been when we had just studied about George
Washington in school, or recited "The Song of Marion's
Men" about Marion the Fox and the British cavalry that
chased him up and down the broad Santee. But at other
times we stuck out our tongues and jeered at the soldiers.
Perhaps the night before we had hung at the edges of a
group of old men and listened to tales about Aniceto
Pizaña and the "border troubles," as the local paper still
called them when it referred to them gingerly in passing.

It was because of the border troubles, ten years or so
before, that the soldiers had come back to old Fort Jones.
But we did not hate them for that; we admired them
even, at least sometimes. But when we were thinking
about the border troubles instead of Marion the Fox we
hooted them and the flag they were lowering, which for
the moment was theirs alone, just as we would have jeered
an opposing ball team, in a friendly sort of way. On these
occasions even Chonita would join in the mockery, though
she usually ran home at the stroke of six. But whether we
taunted or saluted, the distant men in khaki uniforms went
about their motions without noticing us at all.

The last word from the post came in the night when a
distant bugle blew. At nine it was all right because all the
lights were on. But sometimes I heard it at eleven when
everything was dark and still, and it made me feel that I
was all alone in the world. I would even doubt that I was
me, and that put me in such a fright that I felt like yelling
out just to make sure I was really there. But next morning
the sun shone and life began all over again, with its
whistles and cannon shots and bugles blowing. And so we
lived, we and the post, side by side with the wire fence in
between.

The wandering soldiers whom the bugle called home at
night did not wander in our neighborhood, and none of us
ever went into Fort Jones. None except Chonita. Every
evening when the flag came down she would leave off
playing and go down towards what was known as the
"lower" gate of the post, the one that opened not on Main
Street but against the poorest part of town. She went into
the grounds and to the mess halls and pressed her nose
against the screens and watched the soldiers eat. They sat

at long tables calling to each other through food-stuffed mouths.

"Hey bud, pass the coffee!"

"Give me the ham!"

"Yeah, give me the beans!"

After the soldiers were through the cooks came out and scolded Chonita, and then they gave her packages with things to eat.

Chonita's mother did our washing, in gratefulness—as my mother put it—for the use of a vacant lot of my grandfather's which was a couple of blocks down the street. On the lot was an old one-room shack which had been a shed long ago, and this Chonita's father had patched up with flattened-out pieces of tin. He was a laborer. Ever since the end of the border troubles there had been a development boom in the Valley, and Chonita's father was getting his share of the good times. Clearing brush and building irrigation ditches he sometimes pulled down as much as six dollars a week. He drank a good deal of it up, it was true. But corn was just a few cents a bushel in those days. He was the breadwinner, you might say, while Chonita furnished the luxuries.

Chonita was a poet too. I had just moved into the neighborhood when a boy came up to me and said, "Come on! Let's go hear Chonita make a speech."

She was already on top of the alley fence when we got there, a scrawny little girl of about nine, her bare dirty feet clinging to the fence almost like hands. A dozen other kids were there below her, waiting. Some were boys I knew at school; five or six were her younger brothers and sisters.

"Speech! Speech!" they all cried. "Let Chonita make a speech! Talk in English, Chonita!"

They were grinning and nudging each other except for her brothers and sisters, who looked up at her with proud serious faces. She gazed out beyond us all with a grand, distant air and then she spoke.

"Give me the hammon and the beans!" she yelled. "Give me the hammon and the beans!"

She leaped off the fence and everybody cheered and told her how good it was and how she could talk English better than the teachers at the grammar school.

I thought it was a pretty poor joke. Every evening almost, they would make her get up on the fence and yell, "Give me the hammon and the beans!" And everybody would cheer and make her think she was talking English. As for me, I would wait there until she got it over with so we could play at something else. I wondered how long it would be before they got tired of it all. I never did find out because just about that time I got the chills and fever, and when I got up and around Chonita wasn't there anymore.

In later years I thought of her a lot, especially during the thirties when I was growing up. Those years would have been just made for her. Many's the time I have seen her in my mind's eyes, in the picket lines demanding not bread, not cake, but the hammon and the beans. But it didn't work out that way.

One night Doctor Zapata came into our kitchen through the back door. He set his bag on table and said to my father, who had opened the door for him, "Well, she is dead."

My father flinched. "What was it?" he asked.

The doctor had gone to the window and he stood with his back to us, looking out toward the light of Fort Jones. "Pneumonia, flu, malnutrition, worms, the evil eye," he said without turning around. "What the hell difference does it make?"

"I wish I had known how sick she was," my father said in a very mild tone. "Not that it's really my affair, but I wish I had."

The doctor snorted and shook his head.

My mother came in and I asked her who was dead. She told me. It made me feel strange but I did not cry. My mother put her arm around my shoulders. "She is in Heaven now," she said. "She is happy."

I shrugged her arm away and sat down in one of the kitchen chairs.

"They're like animals," the doctor was saying. He turned round suddenly and his eyes glistened in the light. "Do you know what that brute of a father was doing when I left? He was laughing! Drinking and laughing with his friends."

"There's no telling what the poor man feels," my mother said.

My father made a deprecatory gesture. "It wasn't his daughter anyway."

"No?" the doctor said. He sounded interested.

"This is the woman's second husband," my father explained. "First one died before the girl was born, shot and hanged from a mesquite limb. He was working too close to the tracks the day the Olmito train was derailed."

"You know what?" the doctor said. "In classical times they did things better. Take Troy, for instance. After they stormed the city they grabbed the babies by the heels and dashed them against the wall. That was more humane."

My father smiled. "You sound very radical. You sound just like your relative down there in Morelos."

"No relative of mine," the doctor said. "I'm a conservative, the son of a conservative, and you know that I wouldn't be here except for that little detail."

"Habit," my father said. "Pure habit, pure tradition. You're a radical at heart."

"It depends on how you define radicalism," the doctor answered. "People tend to use words too loosely. A dentist could be called a radical, I suppose. He pulls up things by the roots."

My father chuckled.

"Any bandit in Mexico nowadays can give himself a political label," the doctor went on, "and that makes him respectable. He's a leader of the people."

"Take Villa, now—" my father began.

"Villa was a different type of man," the doctor broke in.

"I don't see any difference."

The doctor came over to the table and sat down. "Now look at it this way," he began, his finger in front of my father's face. My father threw back his head and laughed.

"You'd better go to bed and rest," my mother told me. "You're not completely well, you know."

So I went to bed, but I didn't go to sleep, not right away. I lay there for a long time while behind my darkened eyelids Emiliano Zapata's cavalry charged down to the broad Santee, where there were grave men with hoary hairs. I was still awake at eleven when the cold voice of the bugle went gliding in and out of the dark like something that couldn't find its way back to wherever it had been. I thought of Chonita in Heaven, and I saw her in her torn and dirty dress, with a pair of bright wings attached, flying round and round like a butterfly shouting, "Give me the hammon and the beans!"

Then I cried. And whether it was the bugle, or whether it was Chonita or what, to this day I do not know. But cry I did, and I felt much better after that.

Cecilia Rosas

AMADO MURO

When I was in the ninth grade at Bowie High School in
El Paso, I got a job hanging up women's coats at La Feria
Department Store on Saturdays. It wasn't the kind of a
job that had much appeal for a Mexican boy or for boys of
any other nationality either. But the work wasn't hard, only
boring. Wearing a smock, I stood around the Ladies' Wear
Department all day long waiting for women customers to
finish trying on coats so I could hang them up.

Having to wear a smock was worse than the work
itself. It was an agonizing ordeal. To me it was a loathsome stigma of unmanly toil that made an already degrad-
ing job even more so. The work itself I looked on as
onerous and effeminate for a boy from a family of miners,
shepherds, and ditchdiggers. But working in Ladies' Wear
had two compensations: earning three dollars every Saturday was one; being close to the Señorita Cecilia Rosas was
the other.

This alluring young woman, the most beautiful I had
ever seen, more than made up for my mollycoddle labor
and the smock that symbolized it. My chances of looking at
her were almost limitless. And like a good Mexican, I
made the most of them. But I was only too painfully
aware that I wasn't the only one who thought this
saleslady gorgeous.

La Feria had water fountains on every one of its eight
floors. But men liked best the one on the floor where Miss

279

Rosas worked. So they made special trips to Ladies' Wear all day long to drink water and look at her.

Since I was only fourteen and in love for the first time, I looked at her more chastely than most. The way her romantic lashes fringed her obsidian eyes was especially enthralling to me. Then, too, I never tired of admiring her shining raven hair, her Cupid's-bow lips, the warmth of her gleaming white smile. Her rich olive skin was almost as dark as mine. Sometimes she wore a San Juan rose in her hair. When she did, she looked so very lovely I forgot all about what La Feria was paying me to do and stood gaping at her instead. My admiration was decorous but complete. I admired her hourglass figure as well as her wonderfully radiant face.

Other men admired her too. They inspected her from the water fountain. Some stared at her boldly, watching her trimly rhythmic hips sway. Others, less frank and open, gazed furtively at her swelling bosom or her shapely calves. Their effrontery made me indignant. I, too, looked at these details of Miss Rosas. But I prided myself on doing so more romantically, far more poetically than they did, with much more love than desire.

Then, too, Miss Rosas was the friendliest as well as the most beautiful saleslady in Ladies' Wear. But the other salesladies, Mexican girls all, didn't like her. She was so nice to them all they were hard put to justify their dislike. They couldn't very well admit they disliked her because she was pretty. So they all said she was haughty and imperious. Their claim was partly true. Her beauty was Miss Rosas' only obvious vanity. But she had still another. She prided herself on being more American than Mexican because she was born in El Paso. And she did her best to act, dress, and talk the way Americans do. She hated to speak Spanish, disliked her Mexican name. She called herself Cecile Roses instead of Cecilia Rosas. This made the other salesladies smile derisively. They called her La Americana or the Gringa from Xochimilco every time they mentioned her name.

Looking at this beautiful girl was more important than money to me. It was my greatest compensation for doing work that I hated. She was so lovely that a glance at her sweetly expressive face was enough to make me forget my shame at wearing a smock and my dislike for my job with its eternal waiting around.

Miss Rosas was an exemplary saleslady. She could be

frivolous, serious or demure, primly efficient too, molding herself to each customer's personality. Her voice matched her exotically mysterious eyes. It was the richest, the softest I had ever heard. Her husky whisper, gentle as a rain breeze, was like a tender caress. Hearing it made me want to dream and I did. Romantic thoughts burgeoned up in my mind like rosy billows of hope scented with Miss Rosas' perfume. These thoughts made me so languid at my work that the floor manager, Joe Apple, warned me to show some enthusiasm for it or else suffer the consequences.

But my dreams sapped my will to struggle, making me oblivious to admonitions. I had neither the desire nor the energy to respond to Joe Apple's warnings. Looking at Miss Rosas used up so much of my energy that I had little left for my work. Miss Rosas was twenty, much too old for me, everyone said. But what everyone said didn't matter. So I soldiered on the job and watched her, entranced by her beauty, her grace. While I watched I dreamed of being a hero. It hurt me to have her see me doing such menial work. But there was no escape from it. I needed the job to stay in school. So more and more I took refuge in dreams.

When I had watched her as much, if not more, than I could safely do without attracting the attention of other alert Mexican salesladies, I slipped out of Ladies' Wear and walked up the stairs to the top floor. There I sat on a window ledge smoking Faro cigarettes, looking down at the city's canyons, and best of all, thinking about Miss Rosas and myself.

They say Chihuahua Mexicans are good at dreaming because the mountains are so gigantic and the horizons so vast in Mexico's biggest state that men don't think pygmy thoughts there. I was no exception. Lolling on the ledge, I became what I wanted to be. And what I wanted to be was a handsome American Miss Rosas could love and marry. The dreams I dreamed were imaginative master-pieces, or so I thought. They transcended the insipid realities of a casual relationship, making it vibrantly thrill-ing and infinitely more romantic. They transformed me from a colorless Mexican boy who put women's coats away into the debonair American, handsome, dashing and worldly, that I longed to be for her sake. For the first time in my life I revelled in the magic of fantasy. It brought happiness. Reality didn't.

But my window ledge reveries left me bewildered and shaken. They had a narcotic quality. The more thrillingly romantic fantasies I created, the more I needed to create. It got so I couldn't get enough dreaming time in Ladies' Wear. My kind of dreaming demanded disciplined concentration. And there was just too much hubbub, too much gossiping, too many coats to be put away there.

So I spent less time in Ladies' Wear. My flights to the window ledge became more recklessly frequent. Sometimes I got tired sitting there. When I did, I took the freight elevator down to the street floor and brazenly walked out of the store without so much as punching a time clock. Walking the streets quickened my imagination, gave form and color to my thoughts. It made my brain glow with impossible hopes that seemed incredibly easy to realize. So absorbed was I in thoughts of Miss Rosas and myself that I bumped into Americans, apologizing mechanically in Spanish instead of English, and wandered down South El Paso Street like a somnambulist, without really seeing its street vendors, cafes and arcades, tattoo shops, and shooting galleries at all.

But if there was confusion in these walks there was some serenity too. Something good did come from the dreams that prompted them. I found I could tramp the streets with a newly won tranquillity, no longer troubled by, or even aware of, girls in tight skirts, overflowing blouses, and drop-stitch stockings. My love for Miss Rosas was my shield against the furtive thoughts and indiscriminate desires that had made me so uneasy for a year or more before I met her.

Then, too, because of her, I no longer looked at the pictures of voluptuous women in the *Vea* and *Vodevil* magazines at Zamora's newsstand. The piquant thoughts Mexicans call *malos deseos* were gone from my mind. I no longer thought about women as I did before I fell in love with Miss Rosas. Instead, I thought about a woman, only one. This clear-cut objective and the serenity that went with it made me understand something of one of the nicest things about love.

I treasured the walks, the window-ledge sittings, and the dreams that I had then. I clung to them just as long as I could. Drab realities closed in on me chokingly just as soon as I gave them up. My future was a time clock with an American Mister telling me what to do and this I knew only too well. A career as an ice-dock laborer stretched ahead of me. Better said, it dangled over me like a Veracruz machete. My uncle, Rodolfo Avitia, a straw boss on the ice docks, was already training me for it. Every night he took me to the mile-long docks overhanging the Southern Pacific freight yards. There he handed me tongs and made me practice tripping three-hundred-pound ice blocks so I could learn how to unload an entire boxcar of ice blocks myself.

Thinking of this bleak future drove me back into my fantasies, made me want to prolong them forever. My imagination was taxed to the breaking point by the heavy strain I put on it.

I thought about every word Miss Rosas had ever said to me, making myself believe she looked at me with unmistakable tenderness when she said them. When she said: "Amado, please hang up this fur coat," I found special meaning in her tone. It was as though she had said: "Amadito, I love you."

When she gave these orders, I pushed into action like a man blazing with a desire to perform epically heroic feats. At such times I felt capable of putting away not one but a thousand fur coats, and would have done so joyously.

Sometimes on the street I caught myself murmuring: "Cecilia, *linda amorcita*, I love you." When these surges swept over me, I walked down empty streets so I could whisper: "Cecilia, *te quiero con toda mi alma*" as much as I wanted to and mumble everything else that I felt. And so I emptied my heart on the streets and window ledge while women's coats piled up in Ladies' Wear.

But my absences didn't go unnoticed. Once an executive-looking man, portly, gray, and efficiently brusque, confronted me while I sat on the window ledge with a Faro cigarette pasted to my lips, a cloud of tobacco smoke hanging over my head, and many perfumed dreams inside it. He had a no-nonsense approach that jibed with his austere mien. He asked me what my name was, jotted down my work number, and went off to make a report on what he called "sordid malingering."

Other reports followed this. Gruff warnings, stern admonitions, and blustery tirades developed from them. They came from both major and minor executives. These I was already inured to. They didn't matter anyway. My condition was far too advanced, already much too complex to be cleared up by mere lectures, fatherly or otherwise. All the threats and rebukes in the world couldn't have made me give up my window-ledge reveries or kept me from roaming city streets with Cecilia Rosas' name on my lips like a prayer.

The reports merely made me more cunning, more doggedly determined to city-slick La Feria out of work hours I owed it. The net result was that I timed my absences more precisely and contrived better lies to explain them. Sometimes I went to the men's room and looked at myself in the mirror for as long as ten minutes at a time. Such self-studies filled me with gloom. The mirror reflected an ordinary Mexican face, more homely than comely. Only my hair gave me hope. It was thick and wavy, deserving a better face to go with it. So I did the best I could with what I had, and combed it over my temples in ringlets just like the poets back in my hometown of Parral, Chihuahua, used to do.

My inefficiency, my dreams, my general lassitude could have gone on indefinitely, it seemed. My life at the store wavered between bright hope and leaden despair, unrelieved by Miss Rosas' acceptance or rejection of me. Then one day something happened that almost made my overstrained heart stop beating.

It happened on the day Miss Rosas stood behind me while I put a fur coat away. Her heady perfume, the fragrance of her warm healthy body, made me feel faint. She was so close to me I thought about putting my hands around her lissome waist and hugging her as hard as I could. But thoughts of subsequent disgrace deterred me, so instead of hugging her I smiled wanly and asked her in Spanish how she was feeling.

"Amado, speak English," she told me. "And pronounce the words slowly and carefully so you won't sound like a country Mexican."

Then she looked at me in a way that made me the happiest employee who ever punched La Feria's time clock.

"Amadito," she whispered the way I had always dreamed she would.

"Yes, Señorita Cecilia," I said expectantly.

Her smile was warmly intimate. "Amadito, when are you going to take me to the movies?" she asked.

Other salesladies watched us, all smiling. They made me so nervous I couldn't answer.

"Amadito, you haven't answered me," Miss Rosas said

teasingly. "Either you're bashful as a village sweetheart or else you don't like me at all."

In voluble Spanish, I quickly assured her the latter wasn't the case. I was just getting ready to say "Señorita Cecilia, I more than like you, I love you" when she frowned and told me to speak English. So I slowed down and tried to smooth out my ruffled thoughts.

"Señorita Cecilia," I said. "I'd love to take you to the movies any time."

Miss Rosas smiled and patted my cheek. "Will you buy me candy and popcorn?" she said.

I nodded, putting my hand against the imprint her warm palm had left on my face.

"And hold my hand?"

I said "yes" so enthusiastically it made her laugh. Other salesladies laughed too. Dazed and numb with happiness, I watched Miss Rosas walk away. How proud and confident she was, how wholesomely clean and feminine. Other salesladies were looking at me and laughing.

Miss Sandoval came over to me. *"Ay papacito,"* she said. "With women you're the divine tortilla."

Miss de la Rosa came over too. "When you take the Americana to the movies, remember not to speak Christian," she said. "And be sure you wear the pants that don't have any patches on them."

What they said made me blush and wonder how they knew what we had been talking about. Miss Arroyo came over to join them. So did Miss Torres.

"Amado, remember women are weak and men aren't made of sweet bread," Miss Arroyo said.

This embarrassed me but it wasn't altogether unpleasant. Miss Sandoval winked at Miss de la Rosa, then looked back at me.

"Don't go too fast with the Americana, Amado," she said. "Remember the procession is long and the candles are small."

They laughed and slapped me on the back. They all wanted to know when I was going to take Miss Rosas to the movies. "She didn't say," I blurted out without thinking.

This brought another burst of laughter. It drove me back up to the window ledge where I got out my package of Faros and thought about the wonderful thing that had happened. But I was too nervous to stay there. So I went to the men's room and looked at myself in the mirror again, wondering why Miss Rosas liked me so well. The mirror made it brutally clear that my looks hadn't influenced her. So it must have been something else, perhaps character. But that didn't seem likely either. Joe Apple had told me I didn't have much of that. And other store officials had bulwarked his opinion. Still, I had seen homely men walking the streets of El Paso's Little Chihuahua quarter with beautiful Mexican women and no one could explain that either. Anyway it was time for another walk. So I took one.

This time I trudged through Little Chihuahua, where both Miss Rosa and I lived. Little Chihuahua looked different to me that day. It was a broken-down Mexican quarter honeycombed with tenements, Mom and Pop groceries, herb shops, cafes, and spindly salt-cedar trees; with howling children running its streets and old Mexican revolutionaries sunning themselves on its curbs like iguanas. But on that clear frosty day it was the world's most romantic place because Cecilia Rosas lived there.

While walking, I reasoned that Miss Rosas might want to go dancing after the movies. So I went to Professor Toribio Ortega's dance studio and made arrangements to take my first lesson. Some neighborhood boys saw me when I came out. They bawled *"Mariquita"* and made flutteringly effeminate motions, all vulgar if not obscene. It didn't matter. On my lunch hour I went back and took my first lesson anyway. Professor Ortega danced with me. Softened by weeks of dreaming, I went limp in his arms imagining he was Miss Rosas.

The rest of the day was the same as many others before it. As usual I spent most of it stealing glances at Miss Rosas and slipping up to the window ledge. She looked busy, efficient, not like a woman in love. Her many other admirers trooped to the water fountain to look at the way her black silk dress fitted her curves. Their profane admiration made me scowl even more than I usually did at such times.

When the day's work was done, I plodded home from the store just as dreamily as I had gone to it. Since I had no one else to confide in, I invited my oldest sister, Dulce Nombre de María, to go to the movies with me. They were showing Jorge Negrete and María Felix in *El Rapto* at the Colon Theater. It was a romantic movie, just the kind I wanted to see.

After it was over, I bought Dulce Nombre *churros* and

hot *champurrado* at the Golden Taco Cafe. And I told my sister all about what had happened to me. She looked at me thoughtfully, then combed my hair back with her fingertips as though trying to soothe me. "Manito," she said, softly. "I wouldn't. ...." Then she looked away and shrugged her shoulders.

On Monday I borrowed three dollars from my Uncle Rodolfo without telling him what it was for. Miss Rosas hadn't told me what night she wanted me to take her to the movies. But the way she had looked at me made me think that almost any night would do. So I decided on Friday. Waiting for it to come was hard. But I had to keep my mind occupied. So I went to Zamora's newsstand to get the Alma Norteña songbook. Pouring through it for the most romantic song I could find, I decided on *La Ce- cilia.*

All week long I practiced singing it on my way to school and in the shower after basketball practice with the Little Chihuahua Tigers at the Sagrado Corazón gym. But, except for singing this song, I tried not to speak Spanish at all. At home I made my mother mad by saying in English. "Please pass the sugar."

My mother looked at me as though she couldn't believe what she had heard. Since my Uncle Rodolfo couldn't say anything more than "hello" and "goodbye" in English, he couldn't tell what I had said. So my sister Consuelo did.

"May the Dark Virgin with the benign look make this boy well enough to speak Christian again," my mother whispered.

This I refused to do. I went on speaking English even though my mother and uncle didn't understand it. This shocked my sisters as well. When they asked me to explain my behavior, I parroted Miss Rosas, saying, "We're living in the United States now."

My rebellion against being a Mexican created an uproar. Such conduct was unorthodox, if not scandalous, in a neighborhood where names like Burciaga, Rodríguez, and Castillo predominated. But it wasn't only the Spanish language that I lashed out against.

"Mother, why do we always have to eat *sopa, frijoles, refritos, mondongo,* and *pozole?*" I complained. "Can't we ever eat roast beef or ham and eggs like Americans do?"

My mother didn't speak to me for two days after that. My Uncle Rodolfo grimaced and mumbled something about renegade Mexicans who want to eat ham and eggs even though the Montes Packing Company turned out the best *chorizo* this side of Toluca. My sister Consuelo giggled and called me a Rio Grande Irishman, an American Mister, a gringo, and a *bolillo*. Dulce Nombre looked at me worriedly.

Life at home was almost intolerable. Cruel jokes and mocking laughter made it so. I moped around looking sad as a day without bread. My sister Consuelo suggested I go to the courthouse and change my name to Beloved Wall which is English for Amado Muro. My mother didn't agree. "If *Nuestro Señor* had meant for Amadito to be an American he would have given him a name like Smeeth or Jonesy," she said. My family was unsympathetic. With a family like mine, how could I ever hope to become an American and win Miss Rosas?

Friday came at last. I put on my only suit, slicked my hair down with liquid vaseline, and doused myself with Dulce Nombre's perfume.

"Amado's going to serenade that pretty girl everyone calls La Americana," my sister Consuelo told my mother and uncle when I sat down to eat. "Then he's going to take her to the movies."

This made my uncle laugh and my mother scowl.

"*Qué pantalones tiene* (what nerve that boy's got)," my uncle said, "to serenade a twenty-year-old woman."

"La Americana," my mother said derisively. "That one's Mexican as pulque cured with celery."

They made me so nervous I forgot to take off my cap when I sat down to eat.

"Amado, take off your cap," my mother said. "You're not in La Lagunilla Market."

My uncle frowned. "All this boy thinks about is kissing girls," he said gruffly.

"But my boy's never kissed one," my mother said proudly.

My sister Consuelo laughed. "That's because they won't let him," she said.

This wasn't true. But I couldn't say so in front of my mother. I had already kissed Emalina Uribe from Porfirio Díaz Street not once but twice. Both times I'd kissed her in a darkened doorway less than a block from her home. But the kisses were over so soon we hardly had time to enjoy them. This was because Ema was afraid of her big brother, the husky one nicknamed Toro, would see us. But if we'd had more time it would have been better, I knew.

Along about six o'clock the three musicians who called themselves the Mariachis of Tecalitlán came by and whistled for me, just as they had said they would do. They never looked better than they did on that night. They had on black and silver charro uniforms and big, black, Zapata sombreros.

My mother shook her head when she saw them. "Son, who ever heard of serenading a girl at six o'clock in the evening," she said. "When your father had the mariachis sing for me it was always at two o'clock in the morning— the only proper time for a six-song *gallo*."

But I got out my Ramírez guitar anyway. I put on my cap and rushed out to give the mariachis the money without even kissing my mother's hand or waiting for her to bless me. Then we headed for Miss Rosas' home. Some boys and girls I knew were out in the street. This made me uncomfortable. They looked at me wonderingly as I led the mariachi band to Miss Rosas' home.

A block away from Miss Rosas' home I could see her father, a grizzled veteran who fought for Pancho Villa, sitting on the curb reading the Juárez newspaper, *El Fronterizo*.

The sight of him made me slow down for a moment. But I got back in stride when I saw Miss Rosas herself.

She smiled and waved at me. "Hello, Amadito," she said.

"Hello, Señorita Cecilia," I said.

She looked at the mariachis, then back at me.

"Ay, Amado, you're going to serenade your girl," she said. I didn't reply right away. Then when I was getting ready to say "Señorita Cecilia, I came to serenade you," I saw the American man sitting in the sports roadster at the curb.

Miss Rosas turned to him. "I'll be right there, Johnny," she said.

She patted my cheek. "I've got to run now, Amado," she said. "Have a real nice time, darling."

I looked at her silken legs as she got into the car. Everything had happened so fast I was dazed. Broken dreams made my head spin. The contrast between myself and the poised American in the sports roadster was so cruel it made me wince.

She was happy with him. That was obvious. She was smiling and laughing, looking forward to a good time. Why had she asked me to take her to the movies if she already had a boyfriend? Then I remembered how the other salesladies had laughed, how I had wondered why they were laughing when they couldn't even hear what we were saying. And I realized it had all been a joke, everyone had known it but me. Neither Miss Rosas nor the other salesladies had ever dreamed I would think she was serious about wanting me to take her to the movies.

The American and Miss Rosas drove off. Gloomy thoughts oppressed me. They made me want to cry. To get rid of them I thought of going to one of the "bad death" cantinas in Juárez where tequila starts fights and knives finish them—to one of the cantinas where the panders, whom Mexicans call *burros*, stand outside shouting "It's just like Paris, only not so many people" was where I wanted to go. There I could forget her in Jalisco-state style with mariachis, tequila, and night-life women. Then I remembered I was so young that night-life women would shun me and *cantineros* wouldn't serve me tequila.

So I thought some more. Emalina Uribe was the only other alternative. If we went over to Porfirio Díaz Street and serenaded her I could go back to being a Mexican again. She was just as Mexican as I was, Mexican as *chicharrones*. I thought about smiling, freckle-faced Ema.

Ema wasn't like the Americana at all. She wore wash dresses that fitted loosely and even ate the *melcocha* candies Mexicans like so well on the street. On Sundays she wore a Zamora shawl to church and her mother wouldn't let her use lipstick or let her put on high heels.

But with a brother like Toro who didn't like me anyway, such a serenade might be more dangerous than romantic. Besides that, my faith in my looks, my character, or whatever it was that made women fall in love with men, was so undermined I could already picture her getting into a car with a handsome American just like Miss Rosas had done.

The Mariachis of Tecalitlán were getting impatient. They had been paid to sing six songs and they wanted to sing them. But they were all sympathetic. None of them laughed at me.

"Amado, don't look sad as I did the day I learned I'd never be a millionaire," the mariachi captain said, putting his arm around me. "If not that girl, then another."

But without Miss Rosas there was no one we could sing

La Cecilia to. The street seemed bleak and empty now that she was gone. And I didn't want to serenade Ema Uribe even though she hadn't been faithless as Miss Rosas had been. It was true she hadn't been faithless, but only lack of opportunity would keep her from getting into a car with an American, I reasoned cynically.

Just about then Miss Rosas' father looked up from his newspaper. He asked the mariachis if they knew how to sing *Cananea Jail*. They told him they did. Then they looked at me. I thought it over for a moment. Then I nodded and started strumming the bass strings of my guitar. What had happened made it only too plain I could never trust Miss Rosas again. So we serenaded her father instead.

The Coming of Zamora

PHILIP D. ORTEGO

Alarcón has been sitting on the ground, haunched, his back flat against the adobe wall of the building, scratching strange marks upon the earth between his feet. He is not conscious of what he is doing although the marks seem to form some kind of deliberately mysterious design, perhaps drawn up from somewhere deep in the consciousness of his race. Mute and silent like the stones he pecks away once in a while with the tip of his stick, he has been sitting there for several hours, waiting and watching the entrance of the heavy beamed adobe court-house where the trial of Zamora has been going on for a week.

He is simply waiting there like some dark Olympian runner, waiting for the pronouncement of the inevitable news. There is something almost prehistoric in his face. It is gaunt, and the cut of his jaw gives him an inhospitable, almost hostile, look. He knows it is too soon for the news, and so he waits, recollecting in his mind's eye the events that precipitated the trial. Remembering, he can see the great smiling face of Zamora as he spoke to them the first time.

¡Amigos! The time has come! We have waited and waited, and now we can wait no longer!

But Alarcón remembers that the people were fearful, for the truth of the matter was that they had been betrayed many times, even by their own kind. Neverthe-

292

less, they listened to Zamora, for there was something imperative in his gaze and in his speech.

Alarcón nods slightly as he remembers that Zamora is not a tall man as one measures men physically, but his presence creates the impression of strength and height. And out of that impression, Alarcón recalls, grew the alliance that was to forge the people into a unified political body. He concedes that there were those who scoffed at first and those who have been waiting silently as though listening for the footfalls of some approaching catastrophe. But the people, the forgotten people, came once more from the fields as they had before to listen to Zamora and his message of hope.

Alarcón's eyes are closed now; the lines on his dark and furrowed Indian face seem to have been etched there by inconsolable years of anxiety. He is not yet old, but here and there are strands of gray in his hair which is still very black and lissic like the other Indian members of his race. The edges of his lips appear sunken, sagging from the high cheekbones that give his face a primitive air. He knows that he comes from a proud and illustrious race, but the decades of conflict and subjugation have dampened his pride and aspirations.

It is true, he recalls, that there is something in Zamora's words that seems to straighten the spines of the forgotten people who listen to him. That day when he told them once more of their long and arduous struggle to regain their lands which were to have been guaranteed under the treaty of Guadalupe-Hidalgo, when he told them what they already knew about the gringo, his politics, his culture, his arrogance . . . that day they walked home with heads held high instead of bowed, for there was something in the way he spoke that gave them hope, a hope that in this man they would not be deceived.

Yes, it was true what Zamora told them, but the thought disturbs Alarcón. They have indeed become strangers in their own land. *They,* who had been here with the land, were now regarded as the foreigners, the immigrants.

Remembering, Alarcón purses his lips angrily. His forebears did not ask to become citizens, he mutters to himself. Nevertheless, he *is* a cititzen as his parents before him and their parents before them. That should count for something! But he knows that it counts for naught. The gringo law is based upon possession. The government is the possessor; and the government is the law. How does one fight the law and the government? Through the Veterans Administration, people said after the war. You're a veteran! The government will help you! But he found out that the government is a gringo government; and it helps only gringos or those who look enough like gringos. But for those of us like me, Alarcón thinks, brown-skinned and indio, unable to pass for either gringo or Spanish, no one helps.

¡Hijos de la chingada! He curses silently. They! They are the foreigners! the gringos! the poachers! But Zamora will show them!

He will show them how to get back their land, Zamora explained that day. What the hell does the country want with so much national forest anyway?

The earth is not yellow. The thought intrudes insistently into Alarcón's mind. *La tierra no es amarilla.* The earth is dark and rich and brown. It is rather like the color of many of the people who have scratched upon its surface for a score of generations. Alarcón regards the back of his sinuous hand as he thinks about the land. What *has* happened to the land grants? he wonders.

He goes over the explanation by rote, for it is an old story. He begins: La Raza came to this land over three-hundred years ago. They tilled the soil, and it bore fruit. This was our way of life for over two-hundred years. And then the gringos came. We fought them valiantly but were defeated. Our land was annexed, but guaranteed. Hah! Then for sixty-three years the gringos robbed and cheated us out of our birthright. Then the government came, and our lands dwindled to even less. False claims processed in gringo courts dispossessed us. Exorbitant taxes devoured our land as delinquent. And now we walk the earth as aliens in the land of our fathers.

Alarcón nods, assuring himself that Zamora had not told them what they did not already know. But it was more than this that drew the dispossessed to him. He had a plan! A plan no less significant than Zapata's plan of Ayala. There was a way, he told us, to regain the land. The law could be challenged. The government was not above the law. And though there was fear among the people, there was also newfound hope.

The alliance was struck! Remembering the episode once more, Alarcón begins to feel like a revolutionary again. No! Not the stereotype of the revolutionary with machete and mauser, but a revolutionary filled with the spirit of progress. This was how he felt that July 4th weekend when they walked to the capitol of the state to protest the injustice of the government. The walk had been beneficial in many ways. It gave them all a sense of purpose and accomplishment. They were really doing something now after all the years of waiting and doing nothing.

Then there was the fracas at the park. Alarcón sighs, remembering the incident. Everything was going along fine until the rangers became aggressive. It may have been a foolish act to arrest them for trespassing, but the news of the incident catapulted their cause into the national limelight. They were no longer the forgotten people. Alarcón is a philosopher; *he* sees the justice of his cause and he wonders why others don't. But Alarcón is a victim of the romantic fallacy: he believes that good eventually triumphs over evil. If he did not believe this, then he would not have joined so quixotic a cause. But he does not mistake a windmill for an adversary. No. He recognizes his adversaries well enough. He clenches his jaw, for he cannot help to feel betrayed, considering the outcome of the venture. He knows that many people have regarded it simply as an *ad*venture, headed by an upstart outsider. But he knows better, and so he suppresses his agitation.

Instead he focuses his gaze upon a mongrel dog that has cast itself upon the ground in the shade of an adjacent building. Alarcón knows that it will do no good to become angry, especially now. They have all become marked men, but Zamora is bearing the crushing weight of retaliation. If the governor had only heeded their plea, Alarcón thinks. Why did he fail to keep that appointment with them? Alarcón is cloaked in the garment of belief, and so he cannot understand the failings of others.

The dog is sleeping, but occasionally it opens one eye to survey the world. By some act of transmutation, Alarcón regards himself as Zamora's eye. All morning he has sat and waited, watching. He cannot define the nature of his devotion, except to say that he has committed himself to a course of action. But there has been a transformation of other sorts that he is only now aware of. According to the gringos, he has become an agitator, an advocate of violence, even a Communist.

The act of fury came at noon two days following a raid of one of their meetings. Alarcón remembers it vividly. The police swooped down upon them like a sinister and avenging bird of prey. In return, Zamora attempted a citizen's arrest of one of the officials, but the situation turned into an affray with shooting and hostages. They fled to the hills to escape the wrath of the government that had sent out the militia with armored tanks, for the government officials called it a state of siege.

For the next five days, Alarcón recalls, they lived like hunted animals, burdened by fear and frustration. There were few places to go. The people were afraid to give them refuge. Five days later they had all been rounded up, including Zamora.

Alarcón scratches his beard and meditates. The government kept Zamora in jail for two weeks before releasing him on bond. The charges were fantastic. But the law had been challenged. And soon they would know if the government was above the law.

Alarcón knows now that the law, like God, works in mysterious ways. It is an alchemy of signs and symbols and rituals which Alarcón mistrusts. A sharp glint comes into his metallic eyes as he thinks about the law.

In the shade, the dog yawns as if tired of the human spectacle. Some other time, Alarcón would have whistled for the mongrel. He would have scratched its head, sending it home with a pointed finger. But today he is dispassionate and his will dulled by the inexorable pain in his heart. He has kept his vigil like a spider waiting patiently in the center of its web, waiting for the slightest vibration from without.

For two days Alarcón has slept only off and on, but he has not succumbed to the sleep that is gnawing at the edges of his consciousness. He has grown accustomed to the sleeplessness of conflict. Zamora warned them there would be trying days. No more trying than the deprivations of war, Alarcón thinks. For he has come to look upon this conflict for the repossession of the land as a war, no less serious or intense than the war for the Pacific in which he fought. He shakes his head even before he asks himself the question. No. There is no gratitude. A plastron of medals is a meager compensation for the blood of one's own kind. Alarcón suddenly feels torpid and perplexed. The hope inside of him is turning to emptiness. He is numb now from sitting so long in one position. But he simply shifts his body as the mongrel watches him with a curious sense of tolerance and amusement. Alarcón picks up one of the pebbles near his feet and flings it at the dog who rises suddenly from the path of the projectile. It stands for a moment, looking puzzled at Alarcón who shoos it away with a quick nod of his head.

¡Vete! Go! he grunts at the animal, who seems undecided about the meaning of Alarcón's words. The dog finally trots away, and Alarcón resumes his watch.

When he looks at the clock in front of the bank, he notes that it is almost noon. The jury has been out for almost two hours now, deliberating the fate of Zamora and his accomplices. Alarcón tries to subdue a twinge of guilt, but he cannot, for he feels he is as culpable as the rest. Zamora is not the guilty one! he wants to scream. The government is at fault! That faceless and amorphous institution that exacts its pound of flesh at the expense of its victim. Alarcón wants to shout, for he feels as if the world is pressing in on him. Here! Take the rest of my blood and body! But he suppresses the panic ticking in his brain.

The nervous rush of people toward the entrance of the courthouse signals the return of the jury. Alarcón rests his head upon his knees as if in prayer, but he is simply fortifying himself for the announcement that will come as no surprise to anyone.

Right now Alarcón needs to feel the soft ground of his *tierra amarilla.* He needs to walk its gashed furrows, inhaling its fragrance. Though it is no longer his, the land is still there. And remembering this, his anger mounts, though he promised Zamora that he would be calm.

Into the bright sunlit day Zamora strides, and the forgotten people search his face for a sign. The news has preceded him. The government has found him guilty. But Zamora is appealing to a higher court.

Alarcón struggles to restrain his emotion. He looks at Zamora, questioningly, puzzled. Zamora smiles at the forgotten people. They cheer triumphantly. And Zamora tells them that they have not lost. This is but the first step in challenging the law. For the moment, the government has won. But it cannot win every battle. Every Goliath meets his David, he tells them.

¡Váyanse a sus casas! Zamora tells them. Go home! And he raises his hands in a Christian gesture of pacification. But the people know the meaning of the sign.

Alarcón turns and walks away slowly. Turning into the street where he had kept his vigil, he notices the mongrel sitting in the middle of the road as if waiting for him. He whistles, and the dog lopes toward him, wagging its tail and panting. Alarcón reaches down and scratches its head.

Qué vago eres, he says to the dog, who looks up at him as if understanding the words.

Alarcón sighs and continues up the street with the dog trailing at his heels. The dog is oblivious of the fact that Alarcón is going home to await the coming of Zamora.

The Week of the Life of Manuel Hernández

Diary

NICK C. VACA

Monday, March 9, 1943

This morning when I woke up, I felt dissatisfied. I've been waking up this way for sometime now. I don't know what it is or how to stop it. There are mornings when this ugliness is worse. Always I feel like vomiting, like an animal is inside of me tearing at my guts the moment I open my eyes. At night it sleeps with me to save its strength so that it can torment me while my mind is alive. At first I thought it was María, my girl, who was like an animal on my back. A vulture. Waiting for me to tire and fall so she could peck at my eyes. Love she called it. It wasn't María. That's for certain now. I gave her up. It was violent. I couldn't make her understand about this animal. "Its another woman, cabrón. Ni que nada con un pinche animal," she said. Stupid bitch. Getting rid of María didn't help. This morning when my mother yelled, "Levántate huevón, time for work!" the animal was waiting for me. Its eyes wide and bright. I can't escape it. It stays with me as if it were me, or a part of me. It can't be a part of me. It's too horrible. It has to be something outside of me.

"Buenos días, hijo," my mother tells me this morning as I stumble into the kitchen, yawning and buttoning my shirt. "Buenos pinche días," I answer. "Ya estas condenado," she informs me. "Qué bueno, pues ya no tengo apuros," I answer. My breakfast is laid out for me on the table. A round, yellow scrambled egg that looks like the jefita sat on it, beans, burned tortillas to keep the witches away, and a cup of canela. "No seas perdidizo, eat your

breakfast. Don't pick at it, its hard to come by," my
mother tells me. "Don't be wasteful," but how can I help
it, when this animal has my stomach tied up in knots. Pick
at the food, pick at my nose, sip the canela, yawn, rub my
face. Pinche food, pinche animal. "Estas empachado," my
mother tells me. "Empachado madre, I've got an animal
inside my stomach," I answer. "Qué animal, estas empachado te digo," my mother insists. Please help me with
this animal so that I can breathe good again. Pinche
animal. "Tómate una poca de yerba buena. Allí está en el
cajón junto de la llelera," she tells me. "Madre, por favor
listen, yerba buena doesn't kill this animal, nothing
does."

En un troque viejo a las four in the morning going to the
fils al trabajo. Un wino de skidrow en mi lado, with breath
of overnight wine and Salvation Army soup. Me repugna
el hombre and me dice, "Where you think we're headed,
friend?" With his hot, cheap breath me sopla en la cara.
"Chíngate, I'm no friend of yours, que no ves, I'm tired
and want to rest," le digo sin cariño.

Todavía es noche cuando el troque para y nos escupe
into the fils. Pasa el tiempo muy slow. A las five in the
morning con el sol apenas comenzando to rise en el cielo
del este con rayos azules, red, yellow y naranjados, y un
purple horizon to the west, El Mow, our foreman grita,
"Hoy muchachos tenemos que pisquear todo este fil. Si
acabamos pronto you can go get some birrias." El Dios
del fil ha dicho. Because in this field, like so many other
fields surrounded by tiny houses de palo and an occasional
lone oak tree that got lost from its brothers, Mow is Dios.
Tan feo y sangrón, but still he Dios. "Tú Hernández, take
this, this, and this row. Y no dejes nada behind. Ya, te
conozco, Hernández. First chansa you get you screw up the
whole row. Nada de eso," dice Dios.

Pero que sabe ese Mow. Está frío, y mis manos estan
heladas, con el frío y la fog of the morning. Chingado
animal, even in the cold of the morning you don't leave
me alone. Vete, antes que me mate, then you will have no
home at all. La mañana pasa tan despacio, como una
lágrima caminando en un rostro. "A hundred boxes by
noon, Manuel," I tell myself. My mind is caught in mis
pensamientos cuando suena el pito, and we stop and eat
lunch. Saco mis tacos, unos de frijoles con huevo, y otros
de papas con chorizo, and I start una lumbre de palitos. I
heat my tacos y como muy sabroso. El animal está quieto

and I'm content. I finish my lunch and I want to sleep. Cierro mis ojos muy slowly y mi mente starts to see vague formless things. Mow kicks my balls and I jump up to find him laughing hard and telling me to go play with myself if I don't like what he does. Pero where do I go? Con quién? Who will help me?

En la tarde el sol sale caliente and strong. El sudor en mis hombros fuses my skin to my clothes. Dirt under my fingernails, my knees are getting raw. My neck feels two feet wide as it sinks into my shoulders when I try to lift the box of tomatoes, to take it to the end of the curco to stack it up with the rest of the cajas. Mow trips me in the middle of the fil. The tomatoes spill on the brown earth and I fall on my face. Toda la gente se ríe and the animal with them. I pick myself up y corro hacia las montañas del oeste y juro jamás volver.

Tuesday, March 10, 1947

I thought it was the wine I drank last night. That cheap rosé that said it was from Bordeaux. It wasn't. I just don't want to get up. I open my eyes and see that the fog from the ocean is beginning to melt under the gaze of the morning sun, but still I stay in bed, half asleep, half awake hoping that the morning will become night again. Earlier I tried to get up, but it was like my body weighed too much for my legs to support. I fell back into bed. Yesterday morning as I was sitting on the edge of my bed, clicking my tongue, tasting the phlegm in my mouth and rubbing my face, I had a great urge to vomit. I held it back. It took all my strength, gulping mouthfuls of air. But I did it. This morning I'm afraid that all I have to do is get up and yesterday's nausea will overtake me and I will vomit the whole day.

I stuck my nose out from under the covers just a while ago. It's cold this morning. Must be the fog. It was thick last night. The last thing I remember before falling asleep is looking over the house tops and seeing the fog creeping in from the ocean and hearing the fog horns bellowing to each other in anticipation. It must be the fog that's making the morning cold. I have to get up. Final examinations are beginning at the university and I haven't begun to review the books. Maybe if I stay in bed until the examinations are over I'll be safe. I can always tell my professors that my mother died, and that the shock was too much for me to take. They're sure to fall for that. After all, I'm not really lying. She did die, but that was some five or was it seven years ago? I don't really remember now and its too much trouble to try and recall the date. Even the date doesn't really matter because she's dead, and that's pretty final no matter when it happened. She's buried deep in the cold earth, her soul safely in purgatory where it shall rest until I have the time and desire to do penance for its release.

Perhaps it wouldn't be so much to get up and go to class and face my pale-faced professors with their narrow, sloping shoulders and balding heads, if I could convince myself that these warm blankets are not as reassuring as what they will say to me. It seems quite clear to me that instead of soothing my fears and anxieties about my own existence they do quite the opposite. They inflame those dormant creatures of doubt and insecurity feeding fire to my imagination and crumbling those things that I hold sacred and inviolable. With what do they replace my sacred beliefs? With nothing but tentative conclusions based on questionable research, unproved theoretical schemes and a benign smile to those questions that have no answers.

Last week when I walked into my seminar class professor what's his name, from the history department, the one that looks like a bird, greeted me with a tight smile and told me that he was looking forward to hearing my presentation on the relationship between the works of Vico and contemporary theories of history. "Right," I say. He tells me about his wife and kids and how they had a good time at the zoo and the playland the Sunday before. All the while he has that tight smile on his parakeet face. Then he tells me a joke about an Irishman and an Englishman. The Irishman loses. A most typical joke. Then I begin my presentation and he promptly falls asleep, being careful not to snore, waking up at the last part of my presentation to comment on the cogency of my statements and the lucidity of my presentation. All around the seminar table heads nod in agreement like stalks of wheat in a strong breeze. I smile and let a fart, hoping that he would catch the subtlety of my meaning.

I've never noticed it before, but this bed is indeed the most comfortable bed I've ever slept in during my entire life. Now, if only there were a girl. . . . No, girls do sicken me so. Ever since María . . . Maybe, if I jump out of bed,

put on my pants real fast and run out into the street I can
escape the nausea. That way I can leave it in the bed. At
night I'll come back and burn the bed and that damn
animal with it. It's so depressingly futile. I cannot escape
my animal. My whole being is slowly becoming dismem-
bered. I have no control over my body anymore, it seems
as if the animal has gained in strength over the years.

I read Ovid's description of Pan while I eat olives,
cheese, sour bread and drink that cheap rosé. I want
to escape. I'm suffocating.

Wednesday, March 11, 1950

> There are occasions when it gives one a sense of in-
> finite sadness to see a human being standing all alone
> in the world. Thus the other day I saw a poor girl
> walk all alone to church to be confirmed.
> —Sören Kierkegaard

> In addition to the rest of the numerous circles of my
> acquaintances, I still have one intimate confidante—
> my melancholy. In the midst of my joy, in the midst
> of my work, she beckons to me and calls me aside,
> even though physically I do not budge. My melan-
> choly is the most faithful mistress I have known;
> what wonder, then, that I love in return.
> —Sören Kierkegaard

> Life has become a bitter drink to me, and yet I
> must take it like medicine, slowly, drop by drop.
> —Sören Kierkegaard

> Oh mother, yourself a child, when giving birth
> As my playmate, why did you not stay,
> How could I grow up, with whom?
> And hence a child I remained to my old age.
> —Paul de La Garde

> The worst in life
> Is silent loneliness
> In which the soul forgets all speech
> And neither speaks nor hears,
> But as a petrifaction of days by gone
> Is left like rubble on the road.
> —Paul de La Garde

Among pillars
       Fallen,
Among temples
       Desecrated,
Among people
       Cultivated,
Among girls
       Corrupted,
I walk and find no rest.

                    —Langbehn

The question is, then, not so much how to attain the greatest result with the most limited amount of civil war, the least number of victims, and a minimum of mutual embattlement. For that end there is only one means; namely that the oppressed part of society should obtain the clearest possible conception of what they intend to achieve and how. . . .

                    —Prince Peter Kropotkin

. . . in human development when a conflict is un-avoidable, and civil war breaks out quite indepen-dently of the will of particular individuals, let, at least, these conflicts take place, not on the ground of vague aspirations but upon definite issues; not upon secondary points, the insignificance of which does not diminish the violence of conflict, but upon broad ideas which inspire men by the grandness of the horizon which they bring into view.

                    —Prince Peter Kropotkin

I am an alien in all places.

                    —Paul de La Garde

Thursday, March 11, 1952

Six months have transpired since my arrival in England and I have accomplished very little. I've read sporadically and spent nearly all my time sleeping and reading maga-zines of limited value. I definitely feel like Gonchorov's Oblomov. I think it's the terrible, bone shattering cold of England. I never awaken before ten and then only at the insistence of my landlady's bitch who keeps barking at the mailman. When I do awaken my head always aches from the intense cold in my bedroom. I get out of bed only long enough to start the coal fire in the living room, then I jump back into bed again. Really there is no reason to get up. A hundred years could pass and England would be the same. When I finally manage to get up I feel as if I am in some nightmare. The days and the people are so predictable. I really don't need eyes to know that the day is gray, the sky merging with the horizon. It's as if someone thought up and completed a devilish plot against England and painted the sky an indelible grey. I used to feel a little like opening the curtains in the kitchen every morning, in anticipation of a sunny day, but now even that urge has disappeared. Whether I open them or not is insignificant. The weather is still cold and the skies grim.

As these dreary days go by I become more and more dissatisfied with my existence here. At first everything was novel. The food, the money, the accents, even the countryside fascinated me. I was kept from thinking. I was so excited with this new life that I ignored most everything else. Now everything is commonplace, and quite dull. I find the money cumbersome, the food bland, the accents irritable and the countryside polluted by people and rubbish. My only respite from this flat in Leicester is an occasional trip to London that only satisfies me for the length of time that I am there. Even that is becoming very boring.

Handel is playing on the BBC. I went for a walk this afternoon in spite of the cold. When I returned I built a glorious fire and read Turgenev.

I am despondent. I'm tired of England. God, I'm tired. I want to get out so desperately. I'm so very unhappy.

Friday, March 12, 1956

Today is election day and it shows. Everyone in the graduate commons room wants to discuss politics but doesn't. There seems to be even less desire to talk than ever before. It's as if all has been said before and repeating it is such a boring and tedious task. Not a yawning boring, just a listless boring. An "I don't even care to think about it," boring. Yes, that type of boring. Even the most politically active students seem to have exhausted their constant stream of rhetoric: Tired I guess. They've probably concluded that talking is of little value and have resigned themselves to that discovery.

Today I got the feeling that being in this university is a little bit like being at the pinnacle of things. There's really no place else to go. And being here we find that we are now the gods on the distant Mount Olympus. It is to us, the holders of knowledge, that the peasants look to for enlightenment and guidance. Then, to our amazement, we find that we too are mortal, and that is a very despairing discovery. We cannot accept the fact that we are gods. We know only too well that we too are mortals. We find the same anxieties and confusions that plague the poor and blind mortals also plague us. Most of us hide these anxieties behind facades of rhetoric and purported scientific answers, but some can't.

I enjoy walking in the plaza because no matter how many people are milling around it is still like being in a cemetery. Cold, quiet, distant and frightful. Everyone, I am convinced, is dead, stone, cold dead. When I first came to this fine place, I thought perhaps here people knew the significance of man. His great gulf of insecurity, his sensitivity, his fragileness, but like everywhere else I found that there lies a vast schism between the analysis of man and the interaction with man. For all of the rhetoric about the concern with humanity and the individual, my peers do little to rectify the situation. They find it necessary to restructure the university so that they go up to a pleasant person and say a simple "hello." But always there is a structure that keeps people apart. So my peers say.

I like to come to the plaza at dusk, when the sun is shining its last rays, and the buildings and trees take on long shadows, while dogs play in the fountain and the wind begins to blow cold off the bay. Then my loneliness is real and I know that I am ultimately alone.

Saturday, March 13, 1964

At the meeting with my colleagues yesterday I felt a great desire to leave. Just to get up from the seminar table and walk out into the street and inhale the air. "However, Dr. Hernández, it is the feeling of the board that your publications are not really very relevant to the field of your specialty. Perhaps within the next few months you will be able to float a few more articles that have more of a sociological nature. Your works that deal with social commentary and social problems are both good and well, but they do nothing for you when it comes to enhancing you in the eyes of your academic peers. So, within the next few months?" Yes, my dear God, you will have some articles floated, and they will be relevant. Dr. Jones is his name. The Chairman. He looks a lot like Mow, except that of course Mow was a Chicano and this guy is gringo. But if it were not for the difference in color of skin, Dr. Jones could pass for Mow. I wonder? He probably would make a very good field foreman. Yes, indeed, he would.

I walked out of the conference room wound so tightly that I felt I would burst. It is times like this when I come to the sea to speak to the waves, to blind my eyes by looking at the sun reflecting off the waves before they crash into the sea. I am afraid there is no escape from this animal that plagues me. It has many masks. Nausea, boredom, depression.

Sunday, March 14, 1968

This morning when I opened my right eye and both my ears I heard the doctor say, "He won't last long now. His heartbeat is getting weaker. Maybe tonight, but definitely by tomorrow. The steering wheel punctured both his lungs." The nausea is rising . . .

Un Hijo del Sol

GENARO GONZÁLEZ

Nacer: al amanecer

Adán as a child had an ability to remain unnoticed. Not
withdrawn: He merely accommodated himself to the campesino environment to become a part of it. While his jefitos
harvested a stranger's crops, Adán milled thru the fields,
scroungy, chocolate. A misplaced Mexican mirage in the
backroads of Michigan, a boy-creature shimmering in
heat. He picked the harvest only when it betrayed a strain
of overabundance, a cow whose swollen teats *must* be
milked. He spent his nights in el Norte smearing firefly
glow on his body or sometimes in an abandoned car feeling
up a little girl his own age whose name he never knew or
later forgot. When playing las escondidas behind tents and
trucks someone inevitably glimpsed a woman in white or
heard a whistling lechuza, and that was enough to break up
the games for the night. Bedding on the floor, veiled by a
surplus store mosquito net, Adán often pretended to be a
spider waiting behind its web for insects, although he
wouldn't have known what to do after actually catching
one, being that spiders were very mysterious about this.
Adán did not consciously regard his life as free and
happy; he lived it out of a continuous necessity. Today his
only real appreciation of that life comes from remembering that he used to lie on a cotton-filled truck bed and
gaze at an imposing sky while his parents drove thru a
temperatureless night. Adán hoisted himself up the side of
a wooden panel, to be thrust back by the wind onto a
sinking sea of silent cotton, impossible to walk on. Just

308

stretch out and breathe in the smells, covered up snugly by a huge cotton bodymuff. Not warm, just unable to conceive of differences such as heat or cold.

Adán went back to McAllen to begin the process of growing up, of growing old. He discovered freedom (natural, not the castrate freedom of societies) by having it taken away. Attendance in kindergarten forced and sporadic, fiasco. Assignment: Acculturation Process, Lesson 1. Stand up in front of the class and deliver a mutilated version of simple songs in English. Adán swaggers thru "Aquí está el águila negra." Someone missed the boat! No, no, Adán. You must sing in English now. So he just stopped attending kindergarten.

Circos y selvas

Adán could recall only once having seen a robin in el Valle during his entire childhood. Robins and other northern birds supposedly migrated southward in search of warmth, but to Adán's knowledge only shriveled snowbirds roosted here in winter. The snowbirds, or turistas, were valued more than whooping cranes for the golden eggs they laid unto other capitalist birds of prey; they were protected under the auspices of the local Chamber of Commerce. (In spite of the traffic problems their cumbersome vehicles caused in winter, the turistas were repaid in kind: The summer months saw families of Valle migrants in el Norte, temporarily invading the land—an appropriate cultural exchange program to rival the best of colleges.)

The South is known for its whitewashed "Southern hospitality." But the hospitality-handout is a phenomenon peculiar to el Valle, wherein wintering snowbirds strew crumbs among the natives. Apparently the tourist trade, regarded as a sacred sort of foreign aid to the el Valle poor, cannot be stressed strongly enough. In school Adán would be led to believe it was a symbiotic ass-kiss-ass process (i.e.: "they buy more oranges, thus creating more jobs for orange pickers"), but for him their lives crossed only when the turistas slummed thru the barrios ("here, but for the grace of God, live I") or lost their way, in the utmost arrogance honking to break up and glide thru interrupted street games. Their bewildered stares at the surounding motley bandidos only broadened the vacuum between the simple sweltering streets and their elaborate world. The car/tomb. Antiseptic. Shielding. Plush in its doctor's office chill. One day Prieto had enough and hurled a stone at a black Cadillac (to him they all drove Cadillacs). Not as an act of chosen insurrection but as the natural way to destroy an antithesis. The glass screams, a gust of cold, sterile air escapes from within, giving Adán a pee-chill. Too lifeless, too unlike the surrounding heat he knew. The withered mummies inside startle from their death, the opened tomb vomits a cold, foreign air unto the torrid barrio streets. Las viejitas—the caked putrid faces, sexless, haunted at themselves. No life: anti-sensual. They come here to die. El Valle: an elephant graveyard hidden from the outside world. An empty nightmare that recurs.

Labores

That school vacations were during summer seemed no accident: *How else* could the cotton be gleaned and the ripe tomatoes raped from the vines, if not for the jefitas with their miniature children-hordes marching across the jungle fields of el Valle? A few of the more fortunate families would leave for el Norte and return with tales of a campesino Cibola, where one merely rustled the cherry-laden limbs for the fruit to fall heavily onto his hands. Best of all, they said, the patrones are considerate and "understand us." Adán could not figure out how it was possible for a patrón to "understand" his workers and remain their patrón. Adán tried to recall his life, his *other* life in el Norte but could only remember having known *things*—air, trees, soil, streams—not people (maybe people as *objects* that blended into the soil).

Instead Adán would find himself in el Valle, transported at odd intervals to a new "campo," there to spend his time, keep out of trouble and even make some money. Besides, no vatos stayed on the streets during the day, they all put in *their* time somewhere. Cover up, "no te vayas a poner prieto." Decked out in faded shirt and jeans (the cotton picker jumpsuit), the shirt several sizes too small and belonging to another era, sleeves thru vanity rolled up 2½ times, but otherwise ideal for la pisca.

Sunrise. Vamos a piscar. Cool morning with cotton moisture-heavy. Straddled over plants—jean legs wet with dew—alarm clock for rabbits and snakes. Showdowns of cotton boll battles trusting no one within 50 feet, old

women ducking stray shots screaming some philosophy
about might-as-well-throw-away-money. "La cagan, rucas,"
Adán philosophized back. Eventually don Ernesto, the
sweat-patched truck driver, came to squelch the free-
for-all, warning the "bastardos huevones" that he had but
to contact some border patrolmen on his truck telephone
(an old disintestined radio). These officers, he explained,
were his intimate friends and had agreed to deport any
troublemakers from his camp; then an old man who flirted
with girls replied that don Ernesto did indeed attract
special attention from la migra: Whenever patrolmen
checked the camp for wetbacks they always corralled don
Ernesto first due to his suspicious, outlaw looks. Finally
don Ernesto flatly threatened to leave the chavalos in the
field to walk back home if they kept fighting. His peculiar
diplomacy won.

Adán moves on, dragging his sack like a huge, stuffed
albino serpent. He inspects his hands, smudged with leaf
stains and squashed caterpillars, perfumed with pesticide.
He stands up, sees his shadow almost gone. Hora de
comer, or just about ... Adán hammocks his sack under
the trailer; he reclines roman-style, feasting on tacos de
frijoles y papas, lukewarm pale-red Kool-Aid, and sometimes a soft splotchy banana almost turned pudding. Over
such cuisine he discusses the day's work with an elite
group of young goldbrickers who have retired for brunch.
The patrón drops by in his pickup, a pained, crowsfeet
expression around the eyes a snarl around the mouth a
bulge around his belt. He climbs up the trailer. Taking a
sample of picked cotton in one hand, he stares at the
piscadores, scans the field in utter disgust, as if seeking
whoever picked *that* particular handful of shitty cotton.
And liquid, bedroom eyes lazily looked out from the
pickup: The patrón's teenaged daughter smiles in cleopatra lust from her nileriver pickup-barge. Los vatos, their
theories on gavacha promiscuity rekindled, mutter back
and huddle around the pickup. What his friends saw in the
plump, slackmouth girl—necklaced in prickly heat rash—
was beyond Adán; it seemed not so much lust as a method
to hit the patrón thru his daughter. (Christ, those chicanitos
calientes would proposition any girl outside of their immediate family!; los bordos, levees outside of McAllen
notorious as makeout places for their older brothers, were
already legendary in their conversations.)

Again the drag of pisca . pisca . . pisca ... Daydreams

border on sunfed hallucinations, eyes and hands automatically discriminate whiteness of cotton from field of vision.
Pisca, pisca. A girl removes her picking sack and walks off
to a deserted patch in the field. Her head bobs down, body
bends, she squats, disappears. Macho heads young and old
bob up, bodies unbend, they stretch, dissimulate silence of
mutual hards-on. Then back to . . . pisca . pisca. Sweat
and pesticide—nostril nausea. Sweat salt burns his eyes.
(For some time Adán thought the sickening odor was a
natural by-product of the plants. Only much later did he
correlate the airplane dusters with the nausea, that being
when a duster once sprayed a field where Adán had wandered chasing a rabbit.) . . . Goddamn, not *one* cloud to
cool things off.

   TIRED. DEAD. Stand fixedly on a burning dying afternoon. Feel not just a dull backache but *being tired* with:
the motionless soil, the meaningless horizons, the lightyear-
distant truck—all suffocated and weak in this french-fried
heat. Having scorned all movement and murdered all
time. Staring achingly at the penitents in the plastic Pur-
gatorio, bent upon their work, eyes and minds as one, only
the dangling carrot/mirage of the American cornucopia
(Let them eat cotton.); expecting in his favor to see them
all stand up, gaze contentedly at the bullfight passes of a
far-off airplane duster; then agonized, remove the heavy
yoke of the albatross picking sack from their necks and
. . . as One . . . walk away proud. (Adán yanks off a
yet-green cotton boll, an act tabooed by the pinche
patrón. He fingers the boll-juicy flesh inside, unnatural in
its pallor. Because of me, Adán reasons, it will never serve
its purpose. Adán then shreds the compact fibers and
throws the ravaged, undeveloped cotton boll away. He
turns in the lazy heat to look at Sylvia, her bent body
straining her tight full ass. Nude Woman Picking Cotton,
1959 . . . Then (Lubbock, Tejas . . . A crude sign: white
cotton boll. The sentence: "No niggers, dogs or meskins
allowed."))

La raíz

   As man reversing to child to seed to ancestors. And
then beyond. Querétaro, México. Dawn thru greenglass
of bus, past primitive nonyears. Adán, unable to sleep all
night, now sees the soft countryside with somnambulist
eyes, with slowmotion mind where images bisect and burst

in time-war explosions; images breathe in dull luster of
confrontation with senses where artificial levels—time,
maps—dissolve to yield unique experience. Marineblue
sky he never would have thought possible. Land and low
clouds in serape color and design. Transparent beauty.
Coupled with invisible indio presence hangs in revolution
atmosphere leaps in galvanic-genetic stimulus within Adán.
Lucio, seated in the next row, likewise hypnotized by some
kinetic kinship with the peopled land.

Adán continues to stare out. A hunched, burdened
figure streaks by in the opposite direction and Adán looks
back. Outside of the detached bubble of the bus a man
dressed in black—his age undetermined—carries a small
coffin upon his back. The coffin of a child, deceptively
simple—brown and smooth—as the simplicity of a child's
life. His gaze downcast, he strides carefully over rough,
plowed ground. Clouds mountains valleys fields provide a
sharp immobile background to the plodding man; they
seem at once respectfully silent and aloofly indifferent.
The man walks slowly, whether because of the coffin's
weight or the terrain or perhaps his sorrow Adán doesn't
know. He watches until the man and the coffin fuse into a
single blur . . .

Then walking thru downtown México, D.F. Trying to
merge yet always separate, as oil film on water. Prodigal
son transfigured thru time and travel, now unrecognized
by his family. As Adán seeks a country's life-source he is
blitzed by props of lopsided miniskirts, effeminate super
heroes, "clases de inglés." People en masse running
crawling in the opposite direction, the lost look of lemings
toward cliffs of u. s. a.-emulation.

Further down into barrios with street soccer games
religiously played on every block. Chavalas bien chulas
walk by, baptized by the sprinkling of rain. Children's
voices in rhythmic mimicry of barrio slang. Los locos
under the shelter of awnings, red dreaming eyes enter-
tained by crazy raindrops shooting down like crystal b.b.'s
on non-hips. Other locos drift with extrovert smile out onto
the street among chavalitos. Ojos grifos, mostly slits in
sunlight, now bloom with the cool fascination of single
raindrops tapping on their person, wide-eyed that something falling from So High doesn't hurt at all; each rain-
drop comes as a surprise, like suddenly "crashing" thru
chunks of fog in the night. They lift their faces to the sky,
perhaps to lingering Aztec spirits of rain and yerba; they

offer their minds in sweet sacrifice to herbs. Eyes become rain magnets become the very rain . . .

El sol. An old woman wrinkled within the folds of her shawl sells religious tokens in the name of Christ. Passers-by give her looks of disgust for her unchristian hunger. She seems somewhat grateful for the patrons and shade of a cathedral which hangs huge in its background irony. In partial balance a young man of indio features pores with brown eyes over something simply entitled *El Che*. Adán notes that the indio sits on a bench in the sunlight, away from the shadow of the church. He seems not at all to shy from the steeple's shadow in vampire fright, but is perhaps annoyed that the church is itself a shadow.

It begins to rain again. Lucio walks alone. Adán walks alone. Alone in the company of outsiders and other outlaws. For the moment there is nothing more in his head worth saying aloud. Adán walks in silence thru gauze curtains of rain, his face very much Alive as cool raindrops burst upon animal warmth then evaporate into*** (He remembers fadedly feels vibrantly as multiple episodes superimpose on his mind. Stained snapshots: A dark boy running from the nowhere heat of smoldered afternoons, slapped softly by wet sheets flapping on laundry lines, hot chocolate chest licked cool by moisture of dampsmelling towels. Simultaneously, he hurries across a scorching street—asphalt brands urgent tingles on bare feet, shock runs up behind his neck and cascades in warm pools of liquid eyes; a whiff of nostril blood, body trembles in heat shivers, he leaps under the neutral shade of a mesquite, his feet become concrete cool become dry-ice cold for an instant; the hot rush from his face sinks to his lungs to his legs out from his toes in total release, as warm shudders of a bursting pee on powder dirt; he stands quietly alone in his triumph over pain, ready to conquer the streets.) He stands quietly alone—

El mestizo y su misterio: sin fin

A feeling of abysses, of canyons, of losing someone to the hungers of time and the universe. Houses—their windows x'd with boards—hung out in el Valle, paralyzed in iron lungs. This feeling within Adán, as of losing someone and finding his own sense of self that much more. Eternity of ghost town streets, emptiness sweeps a vacuum. Something part air part fire and part death surrounds him.

Adán breathes the air to live; the fire—burning in his mind —to act; the other stagnates into history and afterthought.

Yet the heat in the fields and barrios of el Valle had fused. A fire had sparked. For Adán, his life proved more demanding, more insistent: It forced him to live with this fire or burn out. A harsher sun enveloped el Valle. Before, it had drowsed Adán, had drained his commitment and his raza's life thru centuries of evaporation. Today the sun can not wither Adán; it exposes, it reveals. He can no longer ignore that the sun feeds him fire. El sol. Burning timepiece of a burning mestizo. The sun being time. The time being Now.

"Sale a dar la vuelta," suggests 'Milio. "Cirol, 'ta bien agüitado." Roaming the town with the magnetism of Mexico's bordertowns clutching their minds harder. They decide to give McAllen one last look. El drive-in. Muerto. El parque. El centro. Muerto. Walking by a store something catches Adán's attention.

A large wall mirror faces him. He tries to look at the mirror with detached inspection, but his gaze immediately locks him *into* the mirror. His eyes seem fascinated with themselves, with their mad prophet reflection, at seeing themselves thru themselves. In doing so, his eyes alternately become beholder and beheld, beheld and beholder. As if they can only see and know themselves by being *other* eyes, ouside eyes which likewise must be seen by what they see. Adán stared . . . Stared back . . . Stared . . . Stared back. Two pairs of eyes—those of himself and of his reflection— mesmerized each other and met at some *distance between* the mirror and Adán. He felt himself as being some place *outside* of his body. Where am *I?* he thought. Space. Spaced out. Estoy afuera. Yo soy . . . Adán nadA. Adán nadA. adán nada . . .

His mind had no recourse but to accept this rebellion, this extreme awareness taking place. Adán realizes that he is paradoxically *more* than himself, that something *within* him is also beyond him. He is beyond his own understanding.

Later, they decide to go to a rock dance. They enter the building. The heavy bass thumps deep inside their chests like a second heartbeat. Sauntering with almost staged ease toward the musicians' platform, they slip thru crevices of crushed teenagers. Adán notices a group of Chicanas. Next to them, a large cluster of gavachas with characteristic plump-ass-pants/tiny-chiches-shirt had at-

tracted the attention of a few older, foppishly dressed
Chicanos, who in turn had attracted the attention of some
heavy-set gavachos. 'Milio was noticeably pissed at the
reglaje behavior of the older Chicanos, adding that they
probably called themselves Spanish-American to boot.

Slowly at first, then steadily, the gavachos trickle
toward the mismatched crowd of gringas and Chicanos,
prepared to defend the already torn-down bastion of white
female virginity. A scuffle—one of the well-dressed Chicanos falls, bleeding. Adán and several others rush to the
small circle. More people, fighting, pushing, running away.
Adán looks at the Chicano on the floor; a hard fist is
thumped onto his kidneys. Adán moves away, reaches for
his knife, turns back to see a shock of blond hair and eyes
crying . . . Adán suspends the knife in final decision, weigh-
ing the victim versus the act . . . An obsidian blade traces
a quick arc of instinct—somewhere in time an angry
comet flares, a sleeping mountain erupts, an Aztec sun
explodes in birth***

GLOSSARY

(In order of appearance)

Un hijo del sol, a son of the Sun
Nacer: al amanecer, Birth: at dawn
Adán, Adam
jefitos, parents
las escondidas, hide-and-go-seek
lechuza, a witch in the form of a nightowl who torments an
   individual who has been cursed.
"Aquí está el águila negra," "Here is the black eagle."
   The title of a Mexican folksong about a hero who
   avenges the injustices against the poor
Circos y selvas, Circuses and jungles
el Valle, the Rio Grande Valley at the Southern tip of
   Texas
barrio, a Chicano community, usually low-income
las viejitas, shriveled, old women
Labores, fields. Generally, the Spanish word for "fields" is
   campo. But the *campesino*, or farm worker, calls his
   field *labor* to emphasize the sweat and agony that accompany his labor.
vatos, barrio slang word meaning "Guys"
"no-te vayas a poner prieto," don't get too dark skinned
Vamos a piscar, Let's go pick cotton
"La cagan, rucas," "You're full of shit, you old
   whores."
"bastardos huevones," "Lazy bastards"
la migra, immigration officer
chavalos, young men
gavacha, gringa
pinche patrón, someone who is excessively stingy
La raíz, the root or origin

317

Chavalas bien chulas, exceptionally beautiful young women

loco, a "head"

Ojos grifos, pothead eyes

yerba, weed

El mestizo y su misterio: sin fin, The mestizo and his mystery: endless

"Sale a dar la vuelta," "Let's go riding around"

"Cirol, 'ta bien agüitado," "Yeah, it's really dull"

Estoy afuera, I am outside

gavacho, gringo

reglaje, supply, obedient, conforming

℗ ℗ ℗ ℗ ℗

___Z5010 BREAKTHROUGHS IN MATHEMATICS,
Wolff $2.75

___Z5011 HISTORY OF POSTWAR RUSSIA,
Pethybridge $2.45

___Z5012 THE LIVING CITY, Wright $2.95

___Z5013 NATURAL HOUSE, Wright $2.95

___Z5014 FUTURE OF ARCHITECTURE, Wright $2.95

___Z5019 THE SCOTCH, Galbraith $2.95

___Z5020 EPIGRAMS OF MARTIAL, Bovie $3.95

___Z5021 MARTHA QUEST, Lessing $2.95

___Z5022 PRICKSONGS & DESCANTS, Coover $2.45

___Z5024 ROOTS OF APPEASEMENT, Gilbert $3.50

___Z5025 HERO ON A DONKEY, Bulatovic $2.75

___Z5027 EUROPEAN POWERS 1900-1945, Gilbert . . $3.50

___Z5029 CLIMAX OF ROME, Grant $3.95

___Z5030 HARD TRAVELLIN', Allsop $3.75

___Z5031 GARIBALDI & HIS ENEMIES, Hibbert $3.95

___Z5046 DEATH KIT, Sontag $2.95

___Z5047 OCTOBER FERRY TO GABRIOLA, Lowry . . $3.50

___Z5048 THE BECKER WIVES, Lavin $3.50

THE NEW AMERICAN LIBRARY, INC.,
P.O. Box 999, Bergenfield, New Jersey 07621

Please send me the PLUME BOOKS I have checked above. I am
enclosing $_____(check or money order—no currency
or C.O.D.'s). Please include the list price plus 25¢ a copy to cover
handling and mailing costs. (Prices and numbers are subject to
change without notice.)

Name_____

Address_____

City_____State_____Zip Code_____
Allow at least 3 weeks for delivery